W9-ASV-841

Ostsee

RUßLAND

Königsberg
(Kaliningrad)

OSTPREUßEN

Danzig
(Gdansk)

MMERN

Stettin
(Szczecin)

Part of Germany until 1945
(Now under Polish adm.)

POLEN

Warschau

Weichsel
(Vistula)

Oder

Neiße

Breslau (Wroclaw)

SCHLESIEN

Elbe

Prag

Krakau

RUßLAND

TSCHECHO-SLOVAKEI

Donau

Wien

EICH

Graz

DIE DEUTSCHEN LÄNDER

-------- Ländergrenzen

I SCHLESWIG - HOLSTEIN
II HAMBURG
III BREMEN
IV NIEDERSACHSEN
V NORDRHEIN - WESTFALEN
VI HESSEN
VII RHEINLAND - PFALZ
VIII SAARLAND
IX BADEN-WÜRTTEMBERG
X BAYERN

V. Gray - '58

$ 4.00

Curtis C. D. Vail was Professor of Germanic Languages and Literature at the University of Washington. He received his A.B. from Hamilton College and his Ph.D. from Columbia University. Dr. Vail taught German at Hunter College and Columbia and was President of the American Association of Teachers of German and Editor of its publication, the *German Quarterly*.

Dieter Cunz is Chairman of the Department of German at The Ohio State University. He received his Ph.D. from the University of Frankfurt-am-Main. Dr. Cunz formerly taught at the University of Maryland.

GERMAN for Beginners

CURTIS C. D. VAIL
University of Washington

DIETER CUNZ
The Ohio State University

THE RONALD PRESS COMPANY › NEW YORK

Copyright, ©, 1958, by
THE RONALD PRESS COMPANY

All Rights Reserved

The text of this publication or any part thereof may not be reproduced in any manner whatsoever without permission in writing from the publisher

15-VR

Library of Congress Catalog Card Number: 58-6656

PRINTED IN THE UNITED STATES OF AMERICA

Preface

This book is due largely, if not entirely, to the convictions of the authors as to what ends a beginning German grammar should achieve and how it should attempt to attain them.

In line with the goals of the pioneers in German word lists, we have tried to use as many frequent words as possible, but did not feel restricted to the AATG *Minimum Standard German Vocabulary*. By dividing the lesson vocabularies into active and passive words * and by restricting the Translation Exercises almost entirely to active words, we hope that the student will acquire a manageable active vocabulary while he is building a far larger passive one.

In the preparation of the Reading Selections we soon realized that here two principles seem to militate against each other. One is the principle that a word, once it has been added to the active vocabulary, should be repeated as often as possible. A book that goes too far in this practice will become dull and repetitious. The other principle is to provide interesting and stimulating readings and to enlarge the vocabulary of the student. A book that goes too far in this direction will violate the sound pedagogical principle of "step by step" and "little by little." We tried to find a happy medium. We followed the proverb *repetitio est mater studiorum* as much as possible, but we have felt that too limited a vocabulary would fail adequately to prepare the student for the more advanced courses to follow.

The lesson vocabularies, especially the supplementary vocabularies, may at first sight seem rather long, since inactive

* Active words, starred in the lesson vocabularies, should be learned backward and forward, i.e., the student should not only recognize *das Buch* on sight or by hearing; he should also be able to reproduce it when the German equivalent of *the book* is called for.

Passive words, on the other hand, are merely to be recognized by the student when encountered in a German text or conversation.

words have been repeated in these vocabularies as they recur. Once a word is listed as active, it is not repeated in subsequent vocabularies. We have used the concept "idiom" very loosely —the purpose was to gather under this heading phrases which might cause the student difficulty in vocabulary or grammar.

In Section III we have tried to describe the grammar used in the Reading Selections in simple terms which the student can comprehend readily, and to avoid a maze of exceptions and rare usages. The Grammatical Exercises, insofar as these are in German, use even passive vocabulary with fair freedom, since this involves only the same sort of recognition that is expected in the Reading Selections. The Questions, to be used particularly by those who favor oral-aural emphasis, make full use of the vocabulary and are to be answered in complete sentences in order to practice the variety of syntactical forms used in them. The Translation Exercise, on the other hand, is restricted almost entirely to the active vocabulary. The Supplementary Readings were written with the intent to give the beginner, even in a grammar book, a glimpse into some of the facets of German folklore, history, geography, and culture.

The authors are indebted for patient help and advice to their friends and colleagues Professor Annemarie M. Sauerlander, Professor Wolfgang Fleischhauer, and Professor Oskar Seidlin.

We dedicate this grammar to the beginning German student in the hope that it may smooth his path to the acquisition of the German language, which has given to the world so much in so many fields.

Curtis C. D. Vail
Dieter Cunz

September, 1957

CONTENTS

Appendix

GERMAN for Beginners

INTRODUCTION

It must be noted that 1) German is pronounced with more stress and energy than English; and that 2) German vowels are pure, i.e., they preserve the same sound from beginning to end and do not "glide" as do English vowels.

In print we can only approximate the German pronunciation by giving the closest English equivalents. Correct pronunciation must be learned through oral practice from your instructor or in the language laboratory.

I. Pronunciation of German Vowels

A German vowel is long when

1. doubled, e.g., **Haar, See, Boot;**
2. followed by the silent letter *h*, e.g., **nehmen, Bahn, ihn;**
3. followed by a single consonant (except in uninflected one-syllable words where there is no fixed rule as to length), e.g., **Gabe, oben, Hut;**
4. followed by inflectional or suffix consonants, if the vowel was long in its simple, dictionary form—*cf.* **fragen, frage, fragst, fragt** (all of which have the same vowel length).

German vowels are usually short when unaccented or followed by two consonants (not counting inflectional endings).

A. Simple Vowels

long a is like *a* in *father* (but the vowel is held longer than is usual in English): **Bahn, sagen, Haar, fragen**

short a is the same as long *a* but much shorter in length, e.g., as in *artistic*: **Mann, Stadt, kann, lang**

long e is like *a* in *gate*: **Regen, gehen, legen, See**
short e is like *e* in *met*: **Bett, retten, Ecke, setzen** [Note that final or unaccented **e** is like *a* in *comma,* e.g., in the second syllable in **sagen, Regen, Lampe, Ecke.**]

long i is like *i* in *machine*: **Lid, ihn, Silo**
[**long i** is usually spelled **ie** in German: **liegen, Marie, viel, die.**]

short i is like *i* in *hit*: **mit, Mitte, finden, hinter**

long o is like *o* in *joke*: **so, Boot, holen, wohnen**
short o is like *o* in *hot*: **kosten, Sommer, Wort, Gott**

long u is like *oo* in *shoot*: **du, gut, Hut, Blume**
short u is like *u* in *put*: **Mutter, Butter, Suppe, und**

B. Umlaut-vowels. The vowels **a, o, u** may be modified by "*Umlaut.*" Visually this means two dots are printed or written over the vowel; orally or aurally it means they have an entirely different sound:

long ä is like *a* in *share*: **Schläge, sähe, Mädchen, Väter**
short ä is like *e* in *met* (i.e., like German **short e**): **Städte, Männer, hält, Hände**

long ö is similar to *ur* in British *burn* (when the British drop this *r*): **schön, Söhne, mögen, höflich** [To produce this sound, round your lips for *oh* and then, holding the mouth in that position, say *a* as in *gate.* Note the difference between **schon** and **schön.**]

short ö To produce this sound, round your lips for *au* as in *automobile* and then, holding the mouth in that position, say *e* as in *met*: **Götter, können, gösse, öffnen** [Note the difference between **kennen** and **können.**]

long ü To produce this sound, round your lips for *oo* as in *shoot* and then, holding the mouth in that position, say *i* as in *machine*: **grün, Hüte, Tür, über** [Note the difference between **gute** and **Güte.**]

short ü To produce this sound, round your lips for *u* as in *put* and then, holding the mouth in that position, say *i* as in *hit*: **Hütte, Mütter, fünf, müssen** [Note the difference between **Kissen** and **küssen.**]

C. Diphthongs. Diphthongs are, almost without exception, considered to be long vowel combinations:

au is like *ou* in *house*: **Haus, auf, laut, kaufen**

ei, **ai** are like *i* in *bike*: **ein, mein, Fleisch, Main**

eu, **äu** are like *oi* in *oil*: **heute, Europa, läuft, Häuser**

II. Pronunciation of German Consonants

A. Similar German Consonants

b **Boot, Baum, aber, Abend**

d **dann, danken, finden, Lied**

g is normally like *g* in *good*: **gut, geben, sagen, Berg** [Note that final **–ig** is always pronounced like German **ich.**]

f **fallen, rufen, auf, Fenster**

h at the beginning of words is like English *h*: **haben, Herr, hinter, Haus** [Otherwise it is usually silent and merely shows that the preceding vowel is long: **ihn, Sohn, geht.**]

k **kalt, denken, Kaiser, Physik** (pronounce the **y** like **ü**)

l is formed with the tongue broadened and far forward, touching the back of the upper teeth: **will, Wille, sollen, liegen, laut**

m **mein, Mutter, Dame, kam**

n **nun, Nuß, nehmen, nennen**

p **Park, Oper, April, Pumpernickel**

s 1) is normally pronounced like *s* in *sit*, e.g., **es, best, Haus, uns;** 2) before a vowel is usually pronounced like *s* in *was*, e.g., **sie, sehen, Häuser, Hase;** 3) before **p** or **t** at the beginning of syllables is pronounced like *sh* in *shape*, e.g., **stehen, Stunde, Stein, Bleistift, still, sprechen, spät, spielen, Beispiel**

ss
ß } are always like *s* in *sit*: **Klasse, Straße, Flusses, Fußes** [Note that **ß** is always used after a long vowel; it is also used after short vowels at the end of syllables or before another consonant, e.g., **ich esse** but **ihr eßt; des Flusses** but **der Fluß.** When you write, **double–s** usually replaces **ß.**]

t **Teil, tun, beten, Hut**

x is rare, but is usually like *x* in *fix*: **Max, Axt**

y mostly in diphthong combinations such as **Bayern, Meyer** and is then pronounced like *i* in *bite*; seldom alone—if so, then usually in words of foreign origin and then pronounced as **ü**: **Physik, Lyrik, typisch**

B. Differing German Consonants

c is rarely used alone, except in foreign words where it may be like **k** as in **Café** before **a, o, u**), or like **ts** as in **Cäsar** (before **e, i, y, ä**). [It is most commonly found in the combination **ck** which is pronounced like English *k*: **backen, Stück.**]

j is like *y* in *yes*: **ja, jeder, jung, Jahr**

q is always followed by **u,** and this **qu** is pronounced like English *kv* as in *Nookville*: **Quelle, Qualität, Quantität**

r is very difficult for Americans to imitate at the beginning of syllables or before vowels. It may be produced 1) by vibrating the tip of the tongue against the upper gums for the **trilled r**, or 2) by vibrating the uvula against the back of the tongue for the **uvular r.** Try to imitate your instructor: **sprechen, Sprache, brauchen, treffen, rufen, rot, Radio, rein**

is similar to the American *r* when final or after an unaccented vowel: **Mutter, Vater, Schwester, jeder**

v is like *f* in *father*: **Vater, von, viel, vor, verstehen** (except in words of foreign origin, where it is like English *v*).

w is like *v* in *villain*: **was, Wasser, Winter, Wilhelm**

z, **tz** } are like *ts* in *hats off* (practice saying *ha—tsoff* to get used to starting a word with *ts*!): **kurz, setzen, Katze, Herz; zehn, Zug, Zimmer, zahlen, zwei**

C. Clusters of Consonants

ch is formed at the back of the mouth after **a, o, u, au** by letting air escape between the arched tongue and the palate: **ach, doch, hoch, Buch, auch**
is formed in the front of the mouth after **e, i, ä, ö, ü, ei, eu (äu)** as above (one way to say **ich** is to try to say **isch** with the tip of the tongue pressed against the back of the lower front teeth): **echt, mich, Bäche, Köche, Bücher, reich, euch**
is like *k* at the beginning of some words of foreign origin: **Christ, Chor, Charakter**

chs is like *ks* when it is part of the stem of a word: **sechs, wachsen** (otherwise like **ch** plus **s**)

ck is like *k*: **backen, Stück**

dt is like *t*: **sandte, Stadt**

gn Pronounce both letters, e.g., **Gnade**

kn Pronounce both letters, e.g., **Knabe**

ng is always like *ng* in *singer* (never as in *finger*!): **singen, bringen, sang, gesungen**

nk as in *bank*: **trinken, Bank**

pf Pronounce both letters, e.g., **Pfund, pflanzen, Pfennig**

ph is like *f*: **Philosophie, Physik**

ps Pronounce both letters, e.g., **Psychologie, psychologisch**

qu like English *kv* in *Nookville*: **Quelle, Qualität, Quantität**

sch like *sh* in *shape*: **schicken, Schiff, schmecken, geschehen**

sp as in English—except at the beginning of syllables, where **s** before **p** is pronounced like *sh* in *shape*, yielding a **schp** sound: **spät, sprechen, spielen, Sprache**

st as in English—except at the beginning of syllables, where **st** is pronounced **scht**: **Stadt, stark, stehen, stellen**
th is pronounced like *t*: **Theater, Theodor**
tz is like *ts* in *hats*: **jetzt, sitzen, setzen, Platz.**

III. The Glottal Stop

English, like French, tends to carry over a final consonant from one word to the initial vowel of the next word, e.g., to pronounce *roses are* as *rozizar,* i.e., all run together. German does not do this, and uses the glottal stop, or glottal catch, to prevent it.

For example, if you say *a apple* very clearly and distinctly, you will notice that your breath comes forth explosively just before each *a*—that is the glottal stop. Try this on the following examples: **ein Apfel, der Apfel, das Essen, erinnern.**

English also palatalizes between vowels, e.g., we often pronounce (and especially sing) *the Alps* in such a way that the result is *the yalps.* German never does this either, but uses the glottal stop to prevent running vowels together, e.g., **beobachten, beachten, eine Ehre.**

IV. Capitalization

All German nouns, or words used as nouns, are capitalized: **das Zimmer, die Schule, der Alte** (*the old man*).

German adjectives (when not used as nouns or part of an official title) are regularly spelled without a capital, e.g., **die deutsche Sprache.** [Names of places plus **–er** are not really adjectives and are capitalized, e.g., **die Schweizer Landschaft,** *the Swiss landscape,* or **Münchener Bier,** *Munich beer.*]

The polite personal pronoun **Sie** and its adjective **Ihr** are always capitalized. [In correspondence all German words for *you* and *your* are capitalized.]

V. Syllabification and Vowel Length

A single consonant goes with the following syllable; and a vowel at the end of a syllable is long: **schla-fen, re-den, lo-ben, Ha-fen.**

[The clusters **ch, chs, st** also normally go with the following syllable, but they tell us nothing about the length of the preceding vowel.]

Of more than one consonant, only the last one usually goes with the following syllable, and the preceding vowel is short.

Our rule for vowel length, after syllabification, is this: If the syllable ends in a vowel, the vowel is long **(Me-ter, Schu-le, Stra-ße, Bo-den);** if the syllable ends in a consonant, the vowel is short **(Mes-ser, Mut-ter, Klas-se, Som-mer).**

Compounds are broken down into their components: **Schul-zeit, Frei-heit, Blei-stift.**

VI. Accent

In general, the accent is on the first, or root syllable of German words and stays there: **Mäd′chen, Win′ter, Schu′le, stell′en, stell′te, gestellt′.**

The prefixes **be–, ge–, emp–, ent–, er–, ver–, zer–** are never accented.

Compound nouns are regularly accented more heavily on the first element, e.g., **Son″nenschein′**, *sun″shi′ne.*

Foreign words are usually accented on the last syllable: **Student′, interessant′, Philosoph′, Kultur′, Natur′.**

VII. Punctuation

A comma is always used: 1) to separate main clauses from each other, if each is complete (having a verb and subject of its own); 2) to separate main clauses from subordinate clauses; 3) before an infinitive phrase when it has modifiers.

Aufgabe Eins

ARTICLES AND CASES
PRESENT OF HABEN AND SEIN
PREDICATE ADJECTIVES

I. Reading Selection

Mein Freund Herbert und ich sind Studenten aus Amerika. Aber wir sind jetzt nicht in Amerika, denn wir wohnen jetzt in Deutschland. Wir haben ein Zimmer bei einer deutschen Familie. Das Zimmer hat zwei Fenster. In dem Zimmer sind ein Tisch, ein Sessel, eine Lampe und zwei Betten. Hier wohnen Herbert und ich. Herbert sitzt auf dem Stuhl und schreibt die Aufgabe. Er braucht viel Zeit, denn die Aufgabe ist sehr schwer.

Herbert fragt: „Conrad, schreibst du deine Aufgabe?“

Ich sage: „Nein, ich bin krank.“

Er sagt: „Du bist nicht krank, du bist faul.“

Ich sage: „Ich sehe ein Schulbuch, und ich bin sofort krank. So ist es.“

Er sagt: „Ja, ja, Conrad, die Schule ist nicht gut für deine Gesundheit.“

. . .

Herbert und ich haben einen Lehrer. Er lehrt Deutsch. Er ist alt, denn sein Haar ist weiß. Der Lehrer fragt: „Seid ihr fertig? Habt ihr die Aufgabe?“ Herbert schreibt die Aufgabe an die Tafel. Der Lehrer sagt: „Herbert, das ist sehr gut. Conrad, wo ist deine Aufgabe?"

Aber es klingelt in diesem Augenblick, und der Lehrer sagt: „Du hast Glück. Du schreibst deine Aufgabe morgen an die Tafel."

II. Vocabulary

Starred items (*) are *active vocabulary,* i.e., the student is expected to be able to give the German word in response to its English equivalent, or to use it in sentences independently. The other items are *passive vocabulary,* i.e., the student is expected only to be able to recognize the meaning of such words when he sees or hears them.

aber but, however
***alt** old
***Amerika** (*neut.*) America
an alongside of, on, onto
auf upon, on, onto, up
***die Aufgabe** the lesson
der Augenblick the moment
aus out of, from
bei with, at the house of
***das Bett, die Betten** the bed, beds
brauchen, er braucht (to) need, he needs
***das** that
deine your (*singular familiar*)
***denn** for, because
***der, die, das** (*definite article*) the
***deutsch, Deutsch** German
***Deutschland** (*neut.*) Germany
diesem this (*dative* of dieser)
***du** you (*singular familiar*)
***ein, eine, ein** (*indefinite article*) a, an
***eins** one
***er** he, it
***es** it
die Familie the family
faul lazy
***das Fenster** the window
fertig ready, done, finished
fragen, er fragt (to) ask, he asks
***der Freund** the friend
für for
die Gesundheit the health
das Glück luck, good fortune
***gut** good, well
***das Haar** the hair
***haben** (to) have
***hier** here
***ich** I
***ihr** you (*plural familiar*)
***in** in, into
***ja** yes
jetzt now
klingeln, es klingelt (to) ring, it (the bell) rings
***krank** sick, ill
die Lampe the lamp
***lehren, er lehrt** (to) teach, he teaches
***der Lehrer** the teacher
mein my

***morgen** tomorrow
***nein** no
***nicht** not
***sagen, ich sage** (to) say, I say
***schreiben, du schreibst, er schreibt** (to) write, you write, he writes
das Schulbuch the school book
***die Schule** the school
***schwer** heavy, hard, difficult
sehen, ich sehe (to) see, I see
***sehr** very
***sein** (to) be
***der Sessel** the armchair, easy chair
***sie** they
***Sie** you (*formal form, singular or plural*)
***sitzen, er sitzt** (to) sit, he sits
***so** so, thus, this way
***sofort** at once, immediately
***der Student, die Studenten** the student, students
***der Stuhl** the chair
***die Tafel** the blackboard
***der Tisch** the table
***und** and
***viel** much, a lot (of)
***wann** when
***was** what
***weiß** white
***wie** how
***wir** we
***wo** where
***wohnen** (to) live
die Zeit the time
***das Zimmer** the room
zwei two

IDIOM

Glück haben to be lucky

III. Grammar

A. THE ARTICLES

German has three genders: masculine, feminine, and neuter. These genders are indicated by the three different forms of the definite article: **der** for the masculine, **die** for the feminine, **das** for the neuter. There is no logical way of determining the gender of a German noun, except for living beings, although we will be able to give you a few helpful hints later on. Naturally, **der Mann** (*man*) will be masculine, and **die Frau** (*woman*) will be feminine. However, when we come to nouns referring to things and ideas, the gender cannot be predicted. For instance, **der Tisch** (*table*) is masculine, **die Tafel** (*blackboard*) is feminine, and **das Fenster** (*window*) is neuter.

German, like English, has a definite article (**der, die, das**—*the*) and an indefinite article (**ein, eine, ein**—*a* or *an*).

B. THE CASES

Every noun can appear in four different cases, according to the grammatical function which the noun has in the sentence. These cases are called 1) the nominative, 2) the genitive, 3) the dative, 4) the accusative. Unlike English, the form of the article does not remain unchanged throughout the different cases, so that in German you can usually (although not always) recognize the case by looking at the article. We say in English: 1) *The* man is here; 2) *The* man's hat is here; 3) I give *the* man the hat; 4) I see *the* man. You see that the article (*the*) remains unchanged although in these four sentences the noun (*man*) appears in the four different cases. In German, these sentences would read: 1) D e r Mann ist hier; 2) D e s Mannes Hut ist hier; 3) Ich gebe d e m Mann den Hut; 4) Ich sehe d e n Mann. So in German the four different cases are distinguished by four different forms of the article.

The Nominative Case. The nominative is the "naming" case and is usually the subject of the sentence. (The subject is the noun or pronoun the sentence primarily talks about.) In our four sentences the subjects are: 1) *the man;* 2) *hat;* 3) *I;* 4) *I.*

The Genitive Case. The genitive relates two nouns (or a pronoun and a noun) to each other in a sense which indicates possession (therefore in English this case is called the possessive case) or belonging to each other. To give a few examples: The house of my father = the house which my father possesses. The roof of the house = the roof which belongs to the house. A student of this university = a student who is part of (belongs to) this university. The price of the book = the price which "goes with" the book. As you notice, in English the genitive is expressed by the preposition *of* entering between the two related nouns. However, when referring to a human being the genitive can also be expressed by placing the "owner" in front of the other noun and adding an *'s* (the house of my father = my father's house). This can likewise be done in German. So in sentence 2) of our samples you could have Der Hut des Mannes instead of Des Mannes Hut.

The Accusative Case. The accusative is used for the direct object, i.e., the "something" (or "someone") to which the action (or state), expressed by the verb, refers. So in sentence 4) of our sample "I see *the man*," *the man* is the object of my seeing and therefore in the accusative case. (For this reason this case is in English often called the objective case.)

The Dative Case. The dative is used for the so-called indirect object, i.e., the person (or thing) that gets the direct object. In English this case is often expressed by the preposition *to* or sometimes *for*. It is possible in English to omit the *to*, but in this case the order of words is changed. So in sentence 3) of our sample instead of "I give *the man* the hat" you may say "I give the hat *to the man*." In German we use the dative case without any preposition in both instances.

All cases, except the nominative, may also be used with prepositions requiring one case or the other, and also in certain adverbial phrases; that will be explained later on.

Below you find a table showing the declension of one noun of each gender in the singular with both the definite and the indefinite articles. Note that all nouns in German are capitalized; also that in the feminine and neuter the accusative for articles and nouns is always identical with its nominative. Study especially the articles in this lesson.

NOUNS WITH DEFINITE ARTICLE IN THE SINGULAR

	MASC.	FEM.	NEUT.
NOM.	**der** Freund	**die** Aufgabe	**das** Fenster
GEN.	**des** Freundes (*)	**der** Aufgabe	**des** Fensters (*)
DAT.	**dem** Freund(e) (*)	**der** Aufgabe	**dem** Fenster
ACC.	**den** Freund	**die** Aufgabe	**das** Fenster

NOUNS WITH INDEFINITE ARTICLE IN THE SINGULAR

NOM.	**ein** Lehrer	**eine** Tafel	**ein** Bett
GEN.	**eines** Lehrers (*)	**einer** Tafel	**eines** Bettes (*)
DAT.	**einem** Lehrer	**einer** Tafel	**einem** Bett(e)
ACC.	**einen** Lehrer	**eine** Tafel	**ein** Bett

Note that **ein** has no ending in the singular nominative masculine, and in the singular nominative and accusative neuter. Also note that in the starred forms (*) not only the article but the noun itself changes; this will be explained in the next lesson.

C. Haben AND Sein IN THE PRESENT TENSE

Nouns and articles aren't much good alone—we need verbs to put them together into sentences. The most basic verbs in English and German are *to be* **(sein)** and *to have* **(haben).** Here is what they look like in the present tense:

PRESENT TENSE

SINGULAR				
1.	**ich habe**	I have	**ich bin**	I am
2.	**du hast**	you have	**du bist**	you are
3.	**er / sie / es hat**	he / she / it has	**er / sie / es ist**	he / she / it is
PLURAL				
1.	**wir haben**	we have	**wir sind**	we are
2.	**ihr habt**	you have	**ihr seid**	you are
3.	**sie (Sie) haben**	they (you) have	**sie (Sie) sind**	they (you) are

The pattern of the conjugation of a verb is, of course, the same in English and German. However, for the word *you* (the person addressed) the German has three different forms: **du, ihr, Sie.**

The pronoun **du** is the singular, the pronoun **ihr** the plural of the so-called "familiar form" of address. In general we can say that this familiar form is used among members of the family, in talking to people whom we call by their first names, and in addressing children and lower-teen-age youngsters.

In all other instances the so-called "polite form" of address **Sie** (always capitalized) is used. It is both singular and plural, i.e., applicable no matter whether one person or two or more persons are being addressed. The verb form that goes with the capitalized pronoun **Sie** is the third person plural. Thus: **Herr Schmidt, sind Sie krank?** (Mr. Schmidt, are you sick?) **Herr und Frau Schmidt, sind Sie krank?** (Mr. and Mrs. Schmidt, are you sick?)

D. PREDICATE ADJECTIVES

Predicate adjectives, as in English, do not have any endings. A predicate adjective is normally used after the verb to be **(sein)** and is not followed by a noun. Some examples from our reading selection are: **ich bin krank; du bist faul; er ist alt.**

IV. Grammatical Exercises

A. Fill in the missing form of **haben** or **sein**:

1. Ich ____ krank. 2. ____ ihr fertig? 3. Ich ____ die Aufgabe. 4. Wir ____ Studenten. 5. Wir ____ ein Zimmer bei einer deutschen Familie. 6. ____ Sie faul? 7. Das ____ sehr gut. 8. ____ du deine Aufgabe? 9. ____ ihr die Aufgabe? 10. Du ____ nicht alt. 11. Der Lehrer ____ weißes Haar. 12. Sie ____ ein Schulbuch.

B. Supply the proper form of the definite article:

1. Was sagt ____ Lehrer? 2. Ist das ____ Schule? 3. Wo ist ____ Stuhl? 4. ____ Student schreibt ____ Aufgabe an ____ Tafel. 5. Wo wohnt ____ Freund? 6. ____ Stuhl und ____ Tisch sind alt. 7. ____ Haar ist nicht schwer. 8. ____ Zimmer hat zwei Fenster. 9. ____ Bett ist weiß. 10. Das ist ____ Sessel.

C. Do Exercise B using the indefinite article.

V. Translation Exercise

1. I am not sick. 2. We have a room. 3. Are you (*three forms*) German? 4. The hair is white. 5. The chair and the table are old. 6. The lesson is very difficult. 7. They have a bed. 8. We are from America. 9. Have you (*three forms*) the lesson? 10. The teacher teaches German. 11. They are students. 12. We have a room. 13. It has a window. 14. He sits here. 15. He writes the lesson. 16. Is he old? 17. The teacher is old. 18. Herbert has a lesson. 19. Your (*sing.*) lesson is good. 20. You write very much.

VI. Fragen

(Always answer in complete sentences!)

1. Was sind Herbert und Conrad? 2. Sind Conrad und Herbert in Amerika? 3. Wo wohnen sie? 4. Ist Herbert krank? 5. Was lehrt der Lehrer? 6. Wie ist sein Haar? 7. Was schreibt Herbert an die Tafel? 8. Was sagt der Lehrer? 9. Wann schreibt Conrad die Aufgabe an die Tafel?

VII. Lesestück

Vier Tage, zweihundert Dollar, dreitausend Meilen

Amerika ist ein Kontinent. Deutschland ist ein Land. Zwischen Amerika und Deutschland liegt der Atlantische Ozean. Er ist 3 000 (dreitausend) Meilen breit. Im Jahre 1620 (sechzehnhundertzwanzig) fuhr ein Schiff, die Mayflower, über den Atlantischen Ozean. Die Reise dauerte 9 (neun) Wochen. Ein großes, modernes Schiff in unserer Zeit macht die Reise in 4 (vier) oder 5 (fünf) Tagen, ein Flugzeug in einem Tag. Amerika und Deutschland sind getrennt durch 3 000 (dreitausend) Meilen Entfernung, 4 (vier) Tage Fahrzeit und 200 (zweihundert) Dollar Fahrpreis in der Touristenklasse.

Viele Schiffe fahren von Europa nach Amerika über den Atlantischen Ozean. Die meisten Schiffe landen in New York. New York ist die größte Stadt und der größte Hafen auf dem amerikanischen Kontinent. Die Schiffe fahren dann wieder zurück nach Europa, d.h. nach England, Deutschland, Frankreich, Holland, Italien oder Schweden. Sie landen in Southampton, Hamburg, Le Havre, Genua oder Göteborg.

Die Reise über den Atlantischen Ozean ist im Sommer oft sehr schön. Das Wasser ist dann glatt, ruhig und blau. Im Winter ist der Ozean oft sehr bewegt, unruhig und grau. Doch ein modernes Schiff fährt ruhig und sicher durch den größten Sturm.

VIII. Wörterverzeichnis

The vocabulary of the Reading Selections was chosen primarily for everyday use of the language, for conversational purposes. Our main idea in including Supplementary Readings (*Lesestücke*) was to present certain material and to familiarize you—on a modest scale—with the folklore, the geographical background, and the cultural history of the country whose language you are beginning to learn. We also hope that they will help you to acquire a certain efficiency in reading a simple German text.

Words with an asterisk, given in the Reading Selections of previous lessons, are of course not repeated here. Even some new words are not listed. We did not want to insult your intelligence by telling you the English equivalents of some words, such as "England, Holland, Rotterdam, Hamburg," etc. We have used such words as "Pastor, Tradition, Uniform, Symbol, Theater, Museum" without translating them in the supplementary vocabularies. We even did not list words which are not completely identical, but so close that everyone will know their meanings at first sight, such as "Manuskript, Charakter, Oktober, Medizin." Of course, these omissions will deprive you of the pleasure of knowing the gender of these words, but this slight mist of uncertainty will not prevent you from translating the Supplementary Readings.

amerikanisch American
der Atlantische Ozean the Atlantic Ocean
auf on
bewegt rough
blau blue
breit wide
dann then
d.h. abbr. for **das heißt** i.e., that is
dauerte lasted
doch however, but, yet
durch through, by
die Entfernung the distance
fahren; fährt; fuhr (to) go; goes; went
der Fahrpreis the fare
die Fahrzeit the travel time
das Flugzeug the airplane
Frankreich France
getrennt separated
glatt smooth
grau gray
groß; der größte big; the biggest
der Hafen the harbor
heute today
Italien Italy
im Jahre in the year
der Kontinent the continent
das Land the land, country
landen (to) land
liegt lies
macht makes
die Meilen the miles
die meisten the most
modern modern
nach to
oder or
oft often
die Reise the trip
ruhig calm, quiet
das Schiff the ship
schön nice, beautiful
Schweden Sweden
sicher safe
im Sommer in the summer
die Stadt the city
der Sturm the storm
der Tag; in einem Tag the day; in a day
die Touristenklasse the tourist class
über over
unruhig restless
unser our
viele many
von from
das Wasser the water
wieder again
im Winter in the winter
die Woche the week
die Zeit the time
zurück back
zwischen between

Aufgabe Zwei

DECLENSION OF SINGULAR NOUNS
DATIVE PREPOSITIONS

I. Reading Selection

Das Fenster des Zimmers ist offen. Die Luft kommt durch das Fenster in das Zimmer. Der Lehrer sagt: „Die Farbe des Bleistifts ist rot." Mein Freund Herbert sagt: „Die Farbe des Buches ist grün." Der Lehrer fragt: „Haben wir auch die Farbe weiß in dem Zimmer?" „Ja", sagt Herbert, „das Heft ist weiß, die Wand und die Kreide sind weiß."

Der Lehrer fragt: „Haben wir auch die Farbe schwarz in dem Zimmer?" Ich sage sofort: „Ja, die Tafel ist schwarz, mein Haar ist schwarz, die Schuhe sind schwarz." Der Lehrer lacht und sagt: „Auch dein Gewissen ist schwarz, denn du hast deine Aufgabe nicht in dem Heft."

Der Lehrer sagt: „Wir üben jetzt den Genitiv: Conrads Aufgabe ist schwer. Das Glück des Schülers ist groß. Die Geduld des Lehrers ist sehr groß."

Herbert sagt: „Ich übe den Dativ: Ich bin in dem Zimmer. Ich zeige dem Freund das Buch. Ich schreibe der Mutter den Brief. Ich schreibe mit dem Bleistift."

„Gut", sagt der Lehrer, „Conrad, schreibst du jetzt einen Satz mit dem Accusativ an die Tafel?"

„Nein", sage ich, „es ist zu schwer, und ich bin zu dumm."

„Ja", sagt der Lehrer, „Mark Twain schreibt: I would rather decline a good drink than decline a German noun."

II. Vocabulary

*auch also
*aus from, out of
*bei near, with, at the place of
*der Bleistift the pencil
*der Brief the letter
*das Buch the book
*dumm stupid, dumb
*durch through
*die Farbe the color
*fragen to ask
die Geduld the patience
das Gewissen the conscience
*groß big, large, great
*grün green
*das Heft the notebook
*jetzt now
*kommen, er kommt (to) come, he comes
*die Kreide the chalk
*lachen, er lacht (to) laugh, he laughs
*die Luft the air
*mein my
*mit with
die Mutter the mother
*nach to, toward (*usually with places*), after
*offen open
*rot red
*der Satz the sentence
*der Schuh, die Schuhe the shoe, shoes
*schwarz black
*seit (*preposition*) since
*üben; er übt (to) practice; he practices
*von of, from
*die Wand the wall
*warum why
werden, ich werde (to) get, become; I get, I become
*zeigen, ich zeige, er zeigt (to) show, I show, he shows
*zu too
*zu (*preposition*) to
*zwei two

III. Grammar

A. The Noun in the Singular

By now you have learned the forms of the definite and the indefinite articles in the singular. For this lesson you should refer back to Section III B of Lesson I. Read it with care, and then study the reading selection to this lesson to see how the cases of the nouns are used.

We saw in Lesson I that the articles had a variety of endings to indicate the different cases of the noun: four for the masculine, two for the feminine, and three for the neuter.

The noun is fortunately less complicated. A few rules should describe its changes and prove helpful to you: 1) There is no change in the singular of any feminine noun; thus.

once we know the word **Frau**, we know that only this form will be used throughout the singular. 2) All neuter and most masculine nouns form their genitive by adding **–s**, e.g., **Fensters** and **Lehrers** in the table in Lesson I. However, if the masculine or neuter noun is a monosyllable (e.g., **Freund** or **Bett**) or ends in an s-sound (e.g., **Tisch** or **Satz**), we add **–es** to form its genitive singular (e.g., **Freundes, Bettes, Tisches, Satzes**). 3) Those same monosyllabic nouns may take an **–e** in the dative singular (e.g., **Manne, Bette, Tische, Satze**), but this is by no means necessary. 4) Proper names normally add **–s** for the genitive singular, e.g., **Conrads, Herberts, Maries.**

A few nouns, almost all of them masculine, do not follow the above pattern, but add in all cases (except in nominative, of course) an **–n** or **–en**. Most of these nouns end in an **–e** (in which case only **–n** is added) or they are words (mostly of foreign origin) accented on the last syllable. For example: **der Knabe, des Knaben, dem Knaben, den Knaben** (*the boy*, etc.); or **der Student, des Studenten, dem Studenten, den Studenten.**

B. PREPOSITIONS

There are four different groups of prepositions. The feature that distinguishes these four groups is the fact that they are followed by different cases of the noun or pronoun. So that your memory will not be unduly burdened, we shall introduce these groups one at a time. So let us take first:

PREPOSITIONS WITH THE DATIVE. We have already encountered all those prepositions which are *always* followed by the dative case. They are: **aus, bei, mit, nach, seit, von, zu.**

IV. Grammatical Exercises

A. List in order all of the nominative cases in the Reading Selections of Lessons I and II and explain why the case is used.

B. Do the same for all genitive cases.

C. Do the same for all dative cases.

D. Do the same for all accusative cases.

E. Fill in the proper endings where needed:

1. Was ist d____ Farbe d____ Luft? 2. D____ Haar ein____ Lehrer____ ist weiß. 3. D____ Farbe d____ Kreide und d____ Wand ist auch weiß. 4. D____ Farbe d____ Tafel ist schwarz. 5. D____ Aufgabe d____ Student____ ist schwer. 6. D____ Fenster ein____ Zimmer____ ist offen. 7. D____ Farbe d____ Bleistift____ ist grün. 8. D____ Farbe d____ Buch____ ist rot. 9. Was ist d____ Farbe d____ Fenster____? 10. Ist d____ Zimmer d____ Schüler____ groß?

F. Fill in the proper endings where needed:

1. Wir haben ein____ Lehrer. 2. Ich habe ein____ Zimmer. 3. D____ Student schreibt d____ Aufgabe. 4. Ich sehe d____ Schulbuch. 5. Hast du d____ Aufgabe? 6. Schreibt er d____ Satz? 7. Wir üben jetzt d____ Accusativ. 8. Hat d____ Schüler ein____ Heft? 9. Er hat ein____ gute Mutter. 10. Schreibst du ein____ Brief?

G. Fill in the proper endings:

1. Wie ist es nun mit d____ Dativ? 2. Er kommt aus d____ Zimmer. 3. Er geht (*goes*) zu d____ Schule. 4. Sie geht sofort zu d____ Mutter. 5. Wir haben d____ Kreide von d____ Student____. 6. D____ Schüler schreibt d____ Freund d____ Brief. 7. Er sitzt mit d____ Buch bei d____ Tisch. 8. Schreiben Sie mit d____ Bleistift?

H. Re-do Exercise G using the indefinite article instead of the definite article, wherever it makes sense.

V. Translation Exercise

1. I have the book. 2. He practices the sentence. 3. He has the pencil. 4. The color of the book is black. 5. The

color of the wall is green. 6. The teacher's hair is white. 7. I show the book to the teacher. 8. You write the letter to the friend. 9. The teacher shows the student a sentence from (*aus*) the book. 10. He writes with the pencil. 11. I live with the friend. 12. Is the exercise from the book? 13. The hair of the friend is not white. 14. Conrad comes with the friend from America.

Re-do the above sentences replacing the definite article with the indefinite article.

VI. Fragen

1. Wie ist das Fenster des Zimmers? 2. Was kommt durch das Fenster? 3. Wie ist die Farbe des Buches? 4. Wie ist das Heft? 5. Was fragt der Lehrer? 6. Warum ist Conrads Gewissen schwarz? 7. Wie ist die Geduld des Lehrers? 8. Warum schreibt Conrad den Satz nicht?

VII. Lesestück

Amerika und Deutschland

Ein Mann in Deutschland sagt: „Ich habe ein amerikanisches Auto." Er meint damit, er hat ein Auto aus den Vereinigten Staaten, einen Ford, einen Pontiac oder einen Chrysler. Ein anderer Mann sagt: „Die Amerikaner haben zu viel Geld." Er sagt „Die Amerikaner" und er meint „Die Leute aus den Vereinigten Staaten." Für viele Leute in Europa sind die Worte Amerika und Vereinigte Staaten fast Synonyme.

Ein Mann in Amerika sagt: „Ich war im Sommer in Deutschland." Finden wir auf der Karte von Europa ein Land mit dem Namen Deutschland? Nein. Es gibt heute zwei deutsche Staaten, aber keiner heißt Deutschland. Der eine Staat im Westen heißt „Bundesrepublik Deutschland", der andere im Osten „Deutsche Demokratische Republik."

Von 1871 (achtzehnhunderteinundsiebzig) bis 1945 (neunzehnhundertfünfundvierzig) hieß das Land im Herzen Europas „Deutsches Reich." In den tausend Jahren vor 1806 (achtzehnhundertsechs) war Deutschland ein Teil des „Heiligen Römischen Reiches."

Für die Bundesrepublik Deutschland gebrauchen wir heute oft den Namen Westdeutschland. In Amerika gibt es 48 (achtundvierzig) „Vereinigte Staaten." In Westdeutschland gibt es 10 (zehn) Länder. Sie heißen Schleswig-Holstein, Niedersachsen, Nordrhein-Westfalen, Hessen, Rheinland-Pfalz, Baden-Württemberg, Bayern, Saarland, Hamburg und Bremen. Hamburg und Bremen sind Stadtstaaten.

Die Verfassung der Bundesrepublik Deutschland hat viele Ähnlichkeiten mit der amerikanischen Verfassung. Es gibt aber auch Verschiedenheiten. An der Spitze der amerikanischen Regierung steht ein Mann, der Präsident. An der Spitze der deutschen Bundesrepublik stehen zwei Männer, der Bundespräsident und der Bundeskanzler. Der eine repräsentiert, der andere regiert.

VIII. Wörterverzeichnis

aber but
Ähnlichkeiten similarities
der Amerikaner the American
amerikanisch American
der andere the other
bis until
der Bundeskanzler the Federal Chancellor
der Bundespräsident the Federal President
die Bundesrepublik Deutschland the Federal Republic of Germany
damit by that
die Deutsche Demokratische Republik the German Democratic Republic
das Deutsche Reich the German Empire
der eine the one
Europa Europe
fast almost
finden wir? do we find?
für for
gebrauchen (to) use
das Geld the money
es gibt there is, there are
das Heilige Römische Reich the Holy Roman Empire
heißt, hieß; sie heißen is called; was called; they are called
das Herz the heart
heute today
auf der Karte on the map

keiner none, neither
das Land; die Länder the land, country; the lands, countries. (Technical constitutional term for "The States" of the Federal Republic of Germany)
die Leute the people
der Mann; die Männer the man; the men
meint means
der Name the name
der Osten the east
der Präsident the president
regiert rules
die Regierung the government
repräsentiert represents
im Sommer in the summer
an der Spitze at the head
die Staaten the states
die Stadtstaaten the city states
steht stands
Synonyme synonyms
tausend Jahre a thousand years
der Teil the part
die Vereinigten Staaten the United States
die Verfassung the constitution
die Verschiedenheiten the differences
viele many
vor before
war was
Westdeutschland West Germany
der Westen the west
wie like
das Wort the word

Aufgabe Drei

PRESENT TENSE CONJUGATION ACCUSATIVE PREPOSITIONS

I. Reading Selection

Herbert und ich wohnen in dem Hause der Familie Löwenzahn. Wir wohnen und essen mit der Familie. Es wird jetzt spät, und ich werde hungrig. Ich gehe in die Küche und frage Frau Löwenzahn: „Essen wir bald?"

Sie sagt: „Wir essen in einer halben Stunde. Warum bist du so hungrig?"

Ich antworte: „Die Arbeit in der Schule macht mich so hungrig. Wir arbeiten zu viel."

„Nein", sagt Frau Löwenzahn, „du wächst zu schnell. Du wirst zu groß."

Ich gehe nun in das Wohnzimmer. Hier sitzt Herr Löwenzahn. Er sitzt in einem Sessel und liest die Zeitung. Er trägt eine Brille auf der Nase, denn er sieht nicht gut. Er hört auch nicht gut. Wir sprechen, aber er versteht uns nicht immer.

Herbert spricht zu Herrn Löwenzahn: „Was lesen Sie in der Zeitung?"

Herr Löwenzahn sieht durch die Brille und sagt: „Wasserleitung? Warum Wasserleitung?"

Ich sage zu Herbert: „Warum sprichst du nicht lauter?"

Herbert sagt noch einmal sehr laut: „Was lesen Sie in der Zeitung?"

Herr Löwenzahn antwortet: „Ich lese den Wetterbericht. Er sagt für morgen: sonnig, warm und trocken. Das ist gut für den Garten."

Frau Löwenzahn kommt in das Wohnzimmer und sagt: „Conrad, holst du Blumen für mich aus dem Garten? Ich brauche Blumen für das Eßzimmer."

Ich sage: „Blumen? Vielleicht Löwenzahn? Oder Löwenmaul?"

Sie lächelt und sagt: „Nein, nein, wir haben Tulpen und Vergißmeinnicht im Garten. Wir haben schon genug Löwen im Haus, nicht wahr, Papa?"

Herr Löwenzahn fragt: „Möwen? Möwen? So weit vom Ozean?"

II. Vocabulary

*__aber__ but, however
*__antworten__ (to) answer, reply
*__die Arbeit__ the work
*__arbeiten__ (to) work
*__auf__ on, upon, onto
*__bald__ soon
*__die Blume, die Blumen__ the flower, flowers
*__brauchen__ (to) need
die Brille the glasses
*__drei__ three
einmal once, one time
*__essen (i)__ (to) eat
*__das Eßzimmer__ the dining room
*__die Familie__ the family
*__die Frau__ the woman, Mrs.
*__für__ for
*__der Garten__ the garden
*__gegen__ against, towards
*__gehen__ (to) go, walk
genug enough
halb half
*__das Haus__ the house
der Herr the gentleman, Mr., sir
holen (to) get, fetch
*__hören__ (to) hear
hungrig hungry
ihn (*accusative*) him
im = in dem
*__immer__ always
*__die Küche__ the kitchen
*__lächeln__ (to) smile
laut, lauter loud, louder
*__lesen (ie)__ (to) read
der Löwe the lion
das Löwenmaul the snapdragon
der Löwenzahn the dandelion
*__machen__ (to) make, do
mich (*accusative*) me
die Möwe, die Möwen the sea gull, sea gulls
die Nase the nose
*__nun__ now; well
*__ohne__ without
der Ozean the ocean
schnell quick, fast
*__sehen (ie)__ (to) see
sonnig sunny
*__spät__ late
*__sprechen (i)__ (to) speak

*die Stunde the hour
*tragen (ä) (to) carry; wear
trocken dry
die Tulpe, die Tulpen the tulip, tulips
*um around
uns (*dative* or *accusative*) us
das Vergißmeinnicht the forget-me-not
verstehen (to) understand
vielleicht perhaps
vom = von dem
*wachsen (ä) (to) grow
wahr true
*warm warm
die Wasserleitung the plumbing
weit far
*werden (i) (to) get, become
der Wetterbericht the weather report
*das Wohnzimmer the living room
*die Zeitung the newspaper

IDIOMS

***in einer halben Stunde** in half an hour
***nicht wahr** is used at the end of questions and means literally "isn't it true?" To accomplish the same purpose, English repeats the main verb and the noun (or pronoun in place of the noun). Thus in each of the following questions, **nicht wahr** would translate the italicized portion: We live with the Löwenzahns, *don't we?* We are going to school, *aren't we*? He does study, *doesn't he*? etc.
noch einmal again, once more

III. Grammar

A. THE PRESENT TENSE OF VERBS

English verbs are really more complicated in one way than German, because we regularly use three different forms. For example: aside from the normal form *I come*, we also have a so-called progressive form *I am coming,* and a so-called emphatic form *I do come* (used in English also for the negated and interrogative form of the verb). For all three of these, German has only the one conjugational form **ich komme.** Thus **ich komme** may mean *I come, I am coming,* or *I do come;* **du kommst nicht** may mean *you do not come, you are not coming;* **kommt er?** *does he come? is he coming?*

The form of the verb you will find in all dictionaries or vocabularies is called the *infinitive,* and the *present tense* is formed from it. In German the infinitive always ends in **–en** or **–n.** We remove this **–en** or **–n** ending to get the *stem* which is really the part we work with.

The vast majority of German verbs will form the *present tense* by adding to the stem the endings shown below in boldface type:

SINGULAR		PLURAL	
1. ich komm**e**	*I come*	wir komm**en**	*we come*
2. du komm**st**	*you come*	ihr komm**t**	*you come*
3. er / sie / es } komm**t**	*he / she / it* } *comes*	sie / (Sie) } komm**en**	{ *they* / *(you)* } *come*

Note that the infinitive is always identical with the first and third person plural forms (except for the verb **sein** which specializes in being an exception).

There are a few minor deviations from the norm in the present tense:

1) Verbs whose stem ends in **–t** or **–d** add the vowel **e** between the stem and the endings **–st** and **–t,** for instance **du arbeitest, er arbeitet, ihr arbeitet.**

2) Verbs whose stem ends in an **s**-sound **(s, ss, ß, z, tz)** add only **–t** (instead of **–st**) in the second person singular, for instance **du sitzt, du ißt.**

3) There is a group of verbs which change the stem vowel in (and *only* in) the second and third persons singular. The vowels affected are:

a) **a** changing to **ä**
b) **e** (short) changing to **i** (short)
e (long) changing to **ie, i** (long)

In the vocabulary this change of vowel is given in parentheses following the infinitive, such as **wachsen (ä), essen (i),** or **lesen (ie).** The table on page 31 shows the present tense conjugation of three verbs with vowel changes.

	tragen	sprechen	sehen
1.	ich trage	spreche	sehe
2	du trägst	sprichst	siehst
3.	er / sie / es } trägt	spricht	sieht
1.	wir tragen	sprechen	sehen
2.	ihr tragt	sprecht	seht
3.	sie / (Sie) } tragen	sprechen	sehen

One very important verb of this group, **werden,** *to get* or *become*, is slightly irregular in the singular present tense:

ich werde	wir werden
du **wirst**	ihr werdet
er / sie / es } **wird**	sie / (Sie) } werden

B. USE OF THE PERSONAL PRONOUNS: **er, sie, es**

Because gender in German is grammatical, the personal pronoun **er** will always be used to refer to a masculine noun (e.g., der Stuhl ist hier; **er** ist braun), and **sie** will always be used to refer to a feminine noun (e.g., ich sehe die Kreide; **sie** ist weiß). Thus **er** really corresponds both to English *he* or *it*; **sie** to English *she* or *it*; and **es** (except in a few rare cases) corresponds to English *it*.

C. WORD ORDER

Normally the verb is the second unit in a German sentence. You may start a German declarative sentence with any part you please (for instance: adverb, direct object, indirect object), but the verb must be the second grammatical unit. Examples: **Ich schreibe dem Lehrer jetzt einen Brief. Jetzt schreibe ich dem Lehrer einen Brief. Dem Lehrer schreibe ich jetzt einen Brief. Einen Brief schreibe ich jetzt dem Lehrer.**

D. PREPOSITIONS WITH THE ACCUSATIVE

Prepositions which are always followed by the accusative case are: **durch, für, gegen, ohne, um.**

(Note that **in**, which we use in this lesson, takes the dative unless it means *into* when it takes the accusative. For example: ich wohne **in dem Haus;** ich gehe **in das Haus.** The complete list of prepositions which may take either the accusative or the dative will be given in the next lesson.)

IV. Grammatical Exercises

A. Fill in the proper verb endings:

1. Ich komm____ in das Haus. 2. Du schreib____ an die Tafel. 3. Der Lehrer lach____. 4. Herbert und ich lern____ die Aufgabe. 5. Geh____ ihr in die Küche? 6. Die Studenten wohn____ bei der Familie Löwenzahn. 7. Herr Löwenzahn hör____ nicht gut.

B. Fill in the proper form of the verb indicated:

1. (Werden) ____ du hungrig? 2. Warum (tragen) ____ Herr Löwenzahn eine Brille? 3. Das Wetter (werden) ____ sonnig. 4. Herbert (wachsen) ____ zu schnell. 5. Er (essen) ____ zu viel. 6. (Arbeiten) ____ er auch zu viel? 7. Der Herr (lesen) ____ in der Zeitung. 8. Herbert (gehen) ____ in die Küche. 9. Frau Löwenzahn (kommen) ____ aus der Küche. 10. Conrad (sprechen) ____ nicht laut. 11. (Sprechen) ____ du lauter? 12. Was (lesen) ____ du in der Schule? 13. (Tragen) ____ du auch eine Brille? 14. Du (wachsen) ____ auch zu schnell. 15. Was (sehen) ____ du in der Zeitung?

C. Re-do sentences 1, 2, 3, 4, 6, and 7 of IV, A, and sentences 3, 4, 5, 7, 8, 9, 10, and 14 of IV, B, beginning each sentence with *Jetzt.*

V. Translation Exercise

1. Herbert is growing, isn't he? 2. You are speaking (*three forms*) to Mrs. Löwenzahn. 3. What is she reading in the newspaper? 4. You carry (*three forms*) the flowers, don't you? 5. Do you see (*three forms*) my notebook? 6. Herbert answers: you do work (*three forms*) very hard. 7. Conrad eats too much. 8. He goes into the kitchen, and that makes him (*ihn*) hungry (*hungrig*). 9. Mrs. Löwenzahn sits and smiles, for he is getting too big. 10. She needs flowers from the garden for the table. 11. The teacher does not see and does not hear well.

VI. Fragen

1. Wo wohnen Herbert und Conrad? 2. Warum wird Conrad jetzt hungrig? 3. Was fragt er Frau Löwenzahn? 4. Arbeitet er zu viel? 5. Was macht Herr Löwenzahn? 6. Was trägt er auf der Nase? 7. Versteht er Herberts Frage? 8. Wie wird das Wetter morgen? 9. Was holt Conrad aus dem Garten? 10. Wo braucht Frau Löwenzahn Blumen?

VII. Lesestück

Zwei deutsche Humoristen

In Amerika lachen die Leute über die Geschichten von Mark Twain. Auch die Deutschen haben Humoristen, z.B. Wilhelm Busch und Fritz Reuter. Wilhelm Busch schrieb seine Geschichten in Versen. Sehr berühmt wurde seine Geschichte von Max und Moritz. Max und Moritz, zwei Schuljungen, begehen viele böse Streiche. Sie töten die Hühner einer alten Frau. Sie ärgern einen alten Schneider und lassen ihn in einen Bach fallen. Schließlich bekommen sie die Strafe für ihre bösen Streiche. Max und Moritz wurden später auch in Amerika berühmt unter dem Namen Katzenjammerkids.

Fritz Reuter schrieb seine Geschichten in dem Dialekt der norddeutschen Ebene. Dieser norddeutsche Dialekt heißt „Plattdeutsch." Wir lernen in der Schule „Hochdeutsch." Alle Bücher und Zeitungen gebrauchen Hochdeutsch. Die Leute außerhalb der norddeutschen Ebene können Fritz Reuters Plattdeutsch kaum verstehen.

Hier erzählen wir eine Geschichte von Fritz Reuter, aber wir erzählen sie auf Hochdeutsch.

Fritz Reuter kommt an einem Sonntag in ein kleines norddeutsches Dorf und geht in die Kirche. Nach der Predigt geht er zu dem Pastor und sagt: „Es war eine schöne Predigt, aber ich habe zu Hause ein Buch, und in dem Buch steht diese Predigt, Wort für Wort."

Der Pastor wird rot und sagt: „Es war meine Predigt. Ich habe sie geschrieben. Könnten Sie mir das Buch schicken?"

„Ich schicke es Ihnen morgen", sagt Fritz Reuter.

Am nächsten Tag bekam der Pastor mit der Post ein Wörterbuch.

VIII. Wörterverzeichnis

ärgern (to) annoy
außerhalb outside of
der Bach the brook, creek
begehen (to) do, commit
bekommen; bekam (to) receive, get; received, got
böse bad
die Bücher the books
die Deutschen the Germans
der Dialekt the dialect
dieser, diese this
das Dorf the village
die Ebene the plain
erzählen (to) tell
fallen (to) fall
flach level
gebrauchen (to) use
die Geschichte; die Geschichten the story; stories
geschrieben written
zu Hause at home
heißt is called
Hochdeutsch High German
die Hühner the chickens
der Humorist; Humoristen the humorist; humorists
ihn him
Ihnen to you
kaum hardly
die Kirche the church
klein small
können; könnten Sie? can; could you?
lassen (to) let
lernen (to) learn
die Leute the people
mir to me
am nächsten Tag the next day

der Name the name
norddeutsch North-German
mit der Post by mail
die Predigt the sermon
sagte said
schicken (to) send
schließlich finally
der Schneider the tailor
schön beautiful
schrieb wrote
die Schuljungen the schoolboys
seine his
der Sonntag Sunday
später later
steht is, stands
die Strafe the punishment
die Streiche (*plu.*) the tricks, pranks
töten (to) kill
unter under
in Versen in verse
verstehen (to) understand
viele many
von of, by
war was
das Wort the word
das Wörterbuch the dictionary
wurde, wurden got, became
z.B. *abb. for* **zum Beispiel** e.g., for example

Aufgabe Vier

DER-WORDS AND EIN-WORDS
TWO-WAY PREPOSITIONS

I. Reading Selection

Frau Löwenzahn ruft aus ihrer Küche: „Euer Essen ist fertig."

Jetzt gehen wir in unser Eßzimmer. Wir sitzen an unserem Tisch und warten auf Frau Löwenzahn. Sie trägt die Schüsseln, und Herbert hilft. Dann falten wir alle die Hände und beten

> Danket dem Herrn, denn er ist freundlich
> und seine Güte währet ewiglich.[1]

Auf dem Tisch steht mein Teller. Neben meinem Teller liegen mein Löffel, meine Gabel und mein Messer.

Zuerst essen wir unsere Suppe. In der Mitte des Tisches steht ein Teller mit Brot. Das Brot ist sehr dunkel. Man nennt es Pumpernickel.

Frau Löwenzahn sagt: „Dieses Brot ist sehr gut. Es kommt vom Lande. Ich bekomme es jeden Dienstag von einer Bauernfrau."

Herr Löwenzahn fragt: „Sauerkraut?"

„Bauernfrau", ruft Frau Löwenzahn laut.

Mein Freund Herbert fragt: „Was essen wir heute?"

Frau Löwenzahn antwortet: „Heute essen wir Schweinebraten, Kartoffeln, Sauerkraut und Tomatensalat."

[1] Give thanks unto the Lord, for He is gracious, and His mercy endures forever.

Herr Löwenzahn schüttelt den Kopf und sagt zu seiner Frau: „Ich verstehe wieder Sauerkraut."

Frau Löwenzahn sagt: „Richtig. Wir essen Sauerkraut, keine Bauernfrau. Die Deutschen essen immer Sauerkraut—das denken viele Amerikaner."

Nach dem Essen sagt Frau Löwenzahn: „Conrad und Herbert, tragt eure Teller in die Küche."

Wir tragen unsere Teller in die Küche und gehen in unser Zimmer. Jetzt ist es sehr ruhig im Haus, denn Herr Löwenzahn schläft. Jeden Nachmittag schläft er auf seinem Sofa. Sein Kopf liegt auf einem Kissen. Auf diesem Kissen lesen wir ein Sprichwort:

Ein gutes Gewissen
Ist ein sanftes Ruhekissen.[2]

II. Vocabulary

*__alle__ (*plural*) all
*__der Amerikaner, die Amerikaner__ the American, Americans
*__an__ at, to
__die Bauernfrau__ the peasant woman
__bekommen__ (to) get, receive
*__beten__ (to) pray
__das Brot__ the bread
*__dann__ then
*__dein__ your
__denken__ (to) think
*__die Deutschen__ the Germans
__der Dienstag__ Tuesday
*__dieser__ this; *plu.* these
__dunkel__ dark
*__das Essen__ the meal, food
*__euer__ your
__falten__ (to) fold
__fertig__ ready
__die Gabel__ the fork
*__die Hand, die Hände__ the hand, hands
*__helfen (i)__ (to) help (takes the dative in German)
*__heute__ today
*__hinter__ behind
*__ihr__ her, their
*__Ihr__ your
*__jeder__ each, every
*__die Kartoffel, die Kartoffeln__ the potato, potatoes
*__kein__ (*adj.*) no, not any
__das Kissen__ the pillow
*__der Kopf__ the head
*__das Land__ the country, land
*__liegen__ (to) lie, be situated
__der Löffel__ the spoon
*__mancher__ many a
__das Messer__ the knife
__die Mitte__ the middle
*__der Nachmittag__ the afternoon

[2] A good conscience is a soft pillow.

*__neben__ alongside of, by
__nennen__ (to) call, name
__der Pumpernickel__ pumpernickel
__richtig__ correct, right
*__rufen__ (to) call, shout
__ruhig__ quiet, calm
__das Sauerkraut__ sauerkraut
*__schlafen (ä)__ (to) sleep
__die Schüssel, die Schüsseln__ the platter, dish
__schütteln__ (to) shake
__der Schweinebraten__ the pork roast
*__sein__ his, its
__das Sofa__ the sofa
*__solcher__ such (a)
__das Sprichwort__ the proverb
*__stehen__ (to) stand, be
__die Suppe__ the soup
*__der Teller__ the plate
__der Tomatensalat__ the tomato salad
*__über__ over, above
*__unser__ our
*__unter__ under, beneath
*__viele__ many
*__vier__ four
*__vor__ in front of, before
*__warten auf__ (*with acc.*) (to) wait for
*__welcher__ which, what
*__wieder__ again
__zuerst__ first, at first
*__zwischen__ between

IDIOMS

*__jeden Nachmittag__ every afternoon
*__vom Lande__ from the country

III. Grammar

A. Der WORDS IN THE SINGULAR

We have already learned how to decline **der** in the singular in all three genders (Lesson I, Section III, B). The following is a list of other words which belong to the same group: **dieser, jeder, mancher, solcher, welcher,** and **all** (when it has an ending); **jener** (that) is also a **der word** but it is not used too frequently in present-day speech. All these words are called **der words** because they are declined like the definite articles **der, die, das:**

	MASCULINE	FEMININE	NEUTER
NOM.	dieser Mann	diese Frau	dieses Buch
GEN.	dieses Mannes	dieser Frau	dieses Buches
DAT.	diesem Mann(e)	dieser Frau	diesem Buch(e)
ACC.	diesen Mann	diese Frau	dieses Buch

In addition to mastering these endings, the **der words** should be remembered as a group since they affect the declension of adjectives, as we shall see later.

B. Ein WORDS IN THE SINGULAR

In Section III, B of Lesson I we also learned how to decline **ein** in the singular. The group of **ein words** is as follows: **ein, kein,** and the possessive adjectives (which are **mein, dein, sein, ihr, sein; unser, euer, ihr,** and **Ihr**). They are declined exactly like **ein,** except that **unser** and **euer** may drop their **e** before an ending (e.g., **unserem, unsrem,** and **unserm** are equally correct; **eure** and **unsre** are frequently used in place of the longer forms **euere** and **unsere**).

Do not be confused because **ihr, unser, euer,** and **Ihr** happen to end in **–r**; they are still **ein words** and therefore take no ending in the following three cases: a) the nominative masculine, b) the nominative neuter, c) the accusative neuter.

The following endings are typical for all **ein words**:

	MASCULINE	FEMININE	NEUTER
NOM.	mein Kopf	seine Hand	Ihr Haus
GEN.	mein**es** Kopf**es**	sein**er** Hand	Ihr**es** Haus**es**
DAT.	mein**em** Kopf(e)	sein**er** Hand	Ihr**em** Haus(e)
ACC.	mein**en** Kopf	sein**e** Hand	Ihr Haus

Each possessive adjective corresponds to a certain personal pronoun; it will be helpful to remember the following sequence:

ich habe mein Buch	wir haben unser Buch
du hast dein Buch	ihr habt euer Buch
er hat sein Buch	sie haben ihr Buch
sie hat ihr Buch	(Sie haben Ihr Buch)
es hat sein Buch	

(Needless to say, there are numerous combinations possible, such as **ich habe sein Buch, sie hat unser Buch, wir haben ihr Buch,** etc.)

The possessive adjective **dein** can only refer to the personal pronoun **du; euer** only to **ihr;** and **Ihr** only to **Sie.**

German prefers to use the definite article (instead of the possessive adjective, as in English) to refer to parts of the body or clothing (usually in other than the subject position). Examples: Herr Löwenzahn hat eine Brille auf **der** Nase. Er schüttelt **den** Kopf.

C. VERB FIRST POSITION

You learned in the preceding lesson that the verb is *normally* the second grammatical unit in a German sentence. However, there are two instances when the verb is placed first, as in English:

a) in a question without an interrogative (**Lerne** ich Deutsch? **Wächst** er zu schnell? **Gehst** du in den Garten?);

b) in a command or imperative (**Tragt** eure Teller in die Küche. *Carry* your dishes into the kitchen!).

It should be noted that **ja** and **nein,** interjections, or calling someone by name, do not count in determining word order, e.g., Ja, ich **lerne** Deutsch. Nein, er **wächst** nicht zu schnell. O, was **mache** ich nun? Conrad, **gehst** du in den Garten? The verb is in the same position it would have occupied, if we had not used the words **ja, nein, O,** or **Conrad.**

D. TWO-WAY PREPOSITIONS

There are some "two-way prepositions" which may require either the accusative or the dative. They are: **an, auf, hinter, in, neben, über, unter, vor, zwischen.** They take the *accusative* when *motion or direction toward or into* a certain place is implied. They take the *dative* when *position or location within* a certain place is expressed.

(Some idiomatic usages will vary: **über** meaning *concerning* will always take the accusative; **warten auf,** *to wait for,* likewise is always followed by the accusative.)

IV. Grammatical Exercises

A. Supply the proper endings where needed:

1. D____ Buch dies____ Schüler____ liegt auf mein____ Tisch. 2. Jed____ Frau arbeitet in ihr____ Küche. 3. Welch____ Blume holt Conrad aus unser____ Garten? 4. Herr Löwenzahn geht nicht in sein____ Küche. 5. Er trägt sein____ Zeitung in unser____ Wohnzimmer. 6. Er liest eine halbe Stunde in sein____ Zeitung. 7. Dann schläft er auf dies____ Sofa. 8. Er kommt in unser____ Zimmer ohne sein____ Bleistift. 9. Hinter unser____ Haus liegt ein____ Garten. 10. Wir gehen hinter euer____ Haus. 11. Ich gehe an dies____ Tisch. 12. Ich sitze an dies____ Tisch. 13. Neben unser____ Eßzimmer ist unser____ Wohnzimmer. 14. Über mein____ Tisch ist ein____ Lampe. 15. Steht ihr____ Freund vor Ihr____ Haus? 16. Zwischen mein ____ Messer und mein____ Gabel steht mein____ Teller.

B. Practice the **ein word** endings:

1. Mein____ Bleistift ist rot. 2. Die Farbe unser____ Hauses ist weiß. 3. Sein____ Buch liegt auf ihr____ Tisch. 4. Unser____ Lampe ist grün. 5. Die Farbe euer____ Lampe ist auch grün. 6. Liegt ihr____ Zeitung neben Ihr____ Lampe? 7. Ich sehe mein____ Lampe. 8. Dein____ Buch ist schwarz. 9. Die Farbe sein____ Buches ist nicht schwarz. 10. Ihr____ Heft liegt auf unser____ Buch. 11. Euer____ Buch ist groß.

C. Re-do Exercise B using **dieser** in place of the **ein words.**

V. Translation Exercise

1. Is Mrs. Löwenzahn calling from her kitchen? 2. Do you go into your dining room? 3. I go to my table. 4. We are

sitting at our table. 5. Now you (*Sie*) are in your dining room. 6. This table stands in the middle (*in der Mitte*) of this room. 7. I go into my room. 8. Our dining room is situated between our living room and our kitchen. 9. They have no garden in front of their house. 10. What does Mr. Löwenzahn say to his wife? 11. What does he do every afternoon after the meal? 12. He carries his plate into the kitchen. 13. Is Mrs. Löwenzahn in our kitchen? 14. The teacher helps his wife.

VI. Fragen

1. Was ruft Frau Löwenzahn? 2. Wohin (*where to*) gehen wir dann? 3. Was macht Herbert? 4. Was machen wir alle vor dem Essen? 5. Was steht auf dem Tisch? 6. Was liegt neben meinem Teller? 7. Was essen wir zuerst? 8. Wie ist das Brot? 9. Wie nennt man dieses Brot? 10. Warum spricht Frau Löwenzahn so laut? 11. Was essen wir heute? 12. Was denken viele Amerikaner? 13. Wohin gehen die Studenten nach dem Essen? 14. Was macht Herr Löwenzahn jeden Nachmittag? 15. Warum ist es jetzt so ruhig im Hause?

VII. Lesestück

Grenzen und Nachbarn

Deutschland liegt im Herzen Europas. Es hat nur im Norden und Süden natürliche Grenzen, im Norden die See und im Süden ein Gebirge. Der Nachbar im Norden ist Dänemark. Deutschland und Dänemark haben fast immer in Frieden gelebt; nur einmal, im Jahr 1864 (achtzehnhundertvierundsechzig), waren sie in einem Krieg. Im Norden von Deutschland sind die Nordsee, ein Teil des Atlantischen Ozeans, und die Ostsee. Nordsee und Ostsee sind durch den Nord-Ostsee-Kanal verbunden. Der Kanal beginnt bie der Stadt Kiel, so sprechen wir oft vom Kiel Kanal.

Die Nachbarn im Süden sind die Schweiz und Österreich. Beide Länder waren früher ein Teil des Deutschen Reiches. In Österreich und im größten Teil der Schweiz sprechen die Leute deutsch. Es gab nie einen Krieg zwischen Deutschland und der Schweiz, aber es gab im Jahre 1866 (achtzehnhundertsechsundsechzig) einen Krieg zwischen den norddeutschen Staaten und Österreich. Nach dem Krieg wurde Österreich ein selbständiger Staat.

Die Nachbarn Deutschlands im Westen sind die Niederlande, Belgien, Luxemburg und Frankreich. Die Grenze im Westen hat oft gewechselt. Wir lesen in der deutschen Geschichte von vielen Kriegen wegen dieser Grenze. Frankreich und Deutschland haben viele Kriege geführt. Elsaß-Lothringen und das Saarland waren manchmal in deutschen, manchmal in französischen Händen, und die größte Stadt im Elsaß hieß manchmal Straßburg, manchmal Strasbourg.

Die Nachbarn im Osten sind Polen und die Tschecho-Slowakei. Hier war keine natürliche Grenze, kein Gebirge, kein Ozean. Die Grenze im Osten war noch problematischer als die Grenze im Westen. Polen und Deutschland, Rußland und Deutschland haben Kriege geführt wegen des Landes an der Oder und Weichsel. Noch in unserer Zeit ist das Problem der deutschen Grenze im Osten eins der größten Probleme der europäischen Politik.

VIII. Wörterverzeichnis

als than
der Atlantische Ozean the Atlantic Ocean
beginnen (to) start, begin
beide both
Belgien Belgium
Dänemark Denmark
das Deutsche Reich the German Empire
einmal once
Elsaß-Lothringen Alsace-Lorraine
Europa Europe
europäisch European
fast almost
Frankreich France
französisch French
der Friede; im Frieden the peace; in peace
es gab there was
das Gebirge the mountain range

gelebt lived
die Geschichte history
gewechselt changed
die Grenze; Grenzen the boundary; boundaries
der größte the greatest
das Herz the heart
hieß was called
das Jahr the year
der Kanal the canal
der Krieg the war
Krieg führen (to) wage war
die Leute the people
manchmal sometimes
der Nachbar the neighbor
natürlich natural
nie never
die Niederlande Holland
noch still
norddeutsch North-German
der Norden the north
die Nordsee the North Sea
nur only
die Oder the Oder (River)
oft often
der Osten the east
Österreich Austria
die Ostsee the Baltic Sea
Polen Poland
die Politik politics
das Problem; Probleme the problem; problems
problematischer more problematic
Rußland Russia
das Saarland the Saarland (*before 1957 the "Saar District"*)
die Schweiz Switzerland
die See the sea
selbständig independent
der Staat the state
die Stadt the city
der Süden the south
der Teil the part
die Tschecho-Slowakei Czechoslovakia
verbunden connected
war, waren was, were
wegen on account of
die Weichsel the Vistula (River)
weil because
der Westen the west
wurde became
die Zeit the time

Aufgabe Fünf

PERSONAL PRONOUNS
TIME BEFORE PLACE

I. Reading Selection

Herbert und ich haben eine Verabredung mit zwei Mädchen auf dem Tennisplatz. Der Tennisplatz liegt auf einem Berg über der Stadt. Neben unserm Tennisplatz ist ein Wald.

Um drei Uhr sind wir am Tennisplatz. Die Mädchen sind noch nicht da. Wir warten auf sie. Mädchen kommen immer zu spät.

Hinter dem Tennisplatz steht ein Häuschen. Darin verkauft ein Mann Limonade, Coca Cola, Schokolade und Zigaretten. Wir gehen zu dem Häuschen und sprechen mit dem Mann.

„Eine Limonade für mich", sage ich zu ihm. Er gibt mir eine Flasche Limonade mit einem Glas. Ich nehme das Glas und trinke daraus.

„Ein Coca Cola für mich", sagt Herbert. Der Mann gibt ihm die Flasche. Sie ist noch nicht offen.

Plötzlich sagt Herbert: „Ich habe kein Geld bei mir."

Sofort nimmt der Mann seine Flasche zurück und sagt: „Ohne Geld keine Flasche."

Ich nehme mein Geld aus der Tasche und sage: „Ich habe Geld. Ich zahle für ihn und mich."

Ich gebe dem Mann eine Mark. Damit zahle ich für uns beide. Der Mann gibt mir zehn Pfennig zurück. Ich gebe sie ihm zurück. „Das ist ein Trinkgeld für Sie", sage ich.

Jetzt sehen wir auf dem Weg zwischen dem Wald und dem Tennisplatz die Mädchen. Wir treffen sie vor dem Tennisplatz.

Monika gibt Herbert und mir die Hand und sagt: „Es tut mir leid, wir kommen zu spät, und wir haben keine Entschuldigung. Sie kennen meine Freundin Vera Sütterlin noch nicht. Vera und ich spielen heute Tennis gegen Sie."

Sie sagt zu ihrer Freundin: „Vera, dies sind meine Freunde Herbert Craig und Conrad Hofer aus den Vereinigten Staaten. Sie leben ein Jahr in Deutschland und lernen Deutsch. Ich hoffe, wir schlagen sie im Tennis."

Ich sage: „Sie hoffen zu viel. Unser Tennis ist nicht so schlecht wie unser Deutsch."

II. Vocabulary

beide both
***der Berg** the mountain
***da** there, here
die Entschuldigung the excuse
***die Flasche** the bottle
***die Freundin** the friend (*female*), girl friend
***fünf** five
***geben (i)** (to) give
***das Geld** the money
***das Glas** the glass
das Häuschen the little house
***hoffen (auf)** (to) hope (for)
das Jahr the year
kennen (to) be acquainted with, know
***leben** (to) live
die Limonade the lemonade
***das Mädchen, die Mädchen** the girl, girls
***der Mann** the man, husband
***die Mark** the mark (*German coin = 23.8 cents*)
***nehmen (nimmst, nimmt)** (to) take
***der Pfennig** the pfennig (*100 pfennig make one mark*)
***plötzlich** suddenly
schlagen (ä) (to) beat, hit, strike
schlecht bad
die Schokolade the chocolate
spielen (to) play
die Stadt the city
***die Tasche** the pocket
***der Tennisplatz** the tennis court
***treffen (i)** (to) meet
***trinken** (to) drink
das Trinkgeld the tip
die Uhr the clock
die Verabredung the appointment, date
***die Vereinigten Staaten** the United States
***verkaufen** (to) sell
***der Wald** the forest, woods
der Weg the way, road
***zahlen** (to) pay
zehn ten
die Zigarette, die Zigaretten the cigaret, cigarets
***zurück** back

IDIOMS

*(einem) **die Hand geben** to shake hands with (one)
***es tut mir leid** I am sorry
***noch nicht** not yet
***so . . . wie** as . . . as
***um drei Uhr** at three o'clock

III. Grammar

A. DECLENSION OF PERSONAL PRONOUNS

The personal pronouns, like the nouns, may appear in the four different cases. However, the genitive of the pronouns is so rarely used that we will not bother with it. The dative and accusative, however, are used and needed frequently.

SINGULAR

	1st	*2nd*		*3rd*	
			masc.	*fem.*	*neut.*
NOM.	**ich**	**du**	**er**	**sie**	**es**
DAT.	**mir**	**dir**	**ihm**	**ihr**	**ihm**
ACC.	**mich**	**dich**	**ihn**	**sie**	**es**

PLURAL

	1st	*2nd*	*3rd*	*(polite)*
NOM.	**wir**	**ihr**	**sie**	**(Sie)**
DAT.	**uns**	**euch**	**ihnen**	**(Ihnen)**
ACC.	**uns**	**euch**	**sie**	**(Sie)**

Remember (and look up again Lesson III, Section III, B): the personal pronoun of the third person singular (in English almost always *it* when referring to an inanimate object) must take in German the gender of the noun which it replaces. Examples: **Der Bleistift** ist grün = **er** ist grün; **die Blume** ist rot = **sie** ist rot; **das Buch** ist schwarz = **es** ist schwarz.

B. Da-Combinations

English for the most part makes very little use of such combinations as *therewith, therefrom, thereto, thereby,* etc., as substitutes for *with it, from it, to it, by it,* etc.

German still uses such combinations frequently. *When a pronoun in conjunction with a preposition refers to a thing (rather than a person), German is apt to make a* **da-combination** instead of using the personal pronoun. Such possibilities include **dabei, damit, danach, davon, dazu; dadurch, dafür, dagegen; dahinter, daneben, davor, dazwischen.** If the preposition begins with a vowel, an **–r–** is inserted between **da–** and the respective preposition. Thus we get forms such as **daraus, darum, daran, darauf, darin, darüber, darunter.**

Looked at from the English viewpoint, we have an equation: **German da + preposition = English preposition + it** (or **them**). From English to German, of course, the equation can simply be reversed.

C. Prepositional Contractions

We have already seen that **in dem** can be contracted to **im,** or **von dem** to **vom.** Such contractions are frequent, but not necessary. The more common ones are: **am** (an dem), **ans** (an das), **aufs** (auf das), **im** (in dem), **ins** (in das), **beim** (bei dem), **vom** (von dem), **zum** (zu dem), and **zur** (zu der).

D. Word Order

1. *No separation of noun and verb by adverb.* In a simple declarative sentence the adverb never enters between subject and verb. He suddenly takes the money: **er nimmt plötzlich** das Geld. He also sells his house: **er verkauft auch** sein Haus.

2. *Position of direct and indirect objects.* In German the indirect object precedes the direct object, unless the latter is a personal pronoun. Some examples: Ich gebe **dem Mann das**

Buch. Ich gebe **es dem Mann.** Ich gebe **es ihm.** Ich gebe **ihm das Buch.**

3. *Time before place.* In German, time expressions precede place expressions. Note the following examples: Wir sind **um drei Uhr auf dem Tennisplatz.** Sie gehen **morgen in die Schule.** Er ißt **heute in der Küche.**

If an expression of manner (answering to the question *how?*) joins expressions of time and place, it will enter between time and place. Examples: Er schläft heute **sehr gut** auf seinem Sofa. Sie schreibt jetzt **mit der Kreide** an die Tafel.

E. **Dies** AND **Das**

When **dies** and **das** come first in a clause, thus anticipating a noun (singular or plural) to follow, they take no endings. Examples: **Dies** (or **das**) **ist mein Buch,** *This* (or *that*) *is my book;* **Dies** (or **das**) **ist ihr Mann,** *This* (or *that*) *is her husband;* **Dies** (or **das**) **sind Amerikaner,** *These* (or *those*) *are Americans.*

IV. Grammatical Exercises

A. Rearrange the German sentences in III D 3) above, beginning each sentence with the expression of time.

B. Replace the nouns in parentheses with personal pronouns:

1. (Die Studenten) sind aus den Vereinigten Staaten. 2. (Das Zimmer) hat zwei Fenster. 3. Ich sehe (den Stuhl). 4. Sehen Sie (die Amerikaner)? 5. Was denken Sie von (den Amerikanern)? 6. (Der Tennisplatz) liegt auf einem Berg. 7. (Die Flasche) kostet eine Mark. 8. Hat Conrad (eine Flasche)? 9. Ich sehe (ein Häuschen). 10. Er gibt (der Frau) eine Flasche Coca Cola. 11. Der Schüler gibt (dem Mann) die Hand.

C. Supply the proper form of the personal pronoun for the English:

1. Der Mann gibt *me* eine Mark. 2. Ist diese Flasche für *you* (*use three forms*). 3. Dieses Mädchen gibt *you* (*use three forms*) die Hand. 4. Kommt ihr mit *us*? 5. Sie sehen *us*. 6. Herr Löwenzahn ruft *me*.

D. Replace the prepositional phrases with a **da-combination:**

1. Die Studenten sind in ihrem Zimmer. 2. Herbert sitzt auf seinem Stuhl. 3. Die Schule ist nicht gut für seine Gesundheit. 4. Ich schreibe die Aufgabe an die Tafel. 5. Plötzlich kommt die Luft durch das Fenster 6. Ich schreibe mit einem Bleistift. 7. Er lebt von seinem Geld. 8. Du holst ein paar Blumen aus dem Garten. 9. Mein Buch liegt neben der Lampe. 10. Was sagen Sie zu diesem Buch? 11. Ein Häuschen liegt hinter dem Tennisplatz. 12. Nach der Schule essen wir. 13. Der Tennisplatz liegt über der Stadt. 14. Die Stadt liegt unter dem Berg. 15. Vor dem Haus ist kein Garten.

E. Replace all nouns in bold-face with personal pronouns:

1. Ich schreibe einen Brief an **meine Mutter.** 2. Wir wohnen bei **einer deutschen Familie.** 3. Wir warten auf **Frau Löwenzahn.** 4. Sie bekommt **das Brot** von **einer Bauernfrau.** 5. Was sagt **Herr Löwenzahn** zu **seiner Frau?** 6. **Die Studenten** haben eine Verabredung mit **zwei Mädchen.** 7. **Die Flasche Coca Cola** ist für **meinen Freund.** 8. Wir spielen gegen **die Mädchen.** 9. **Herbert** steht neben dem Mädchen. 10. **Herbert und Conrad** stehen zwischen **den beiden Mädchen.**

F. In the following sentences replace 1) the indirect object with a personal pronoun, 2) the direct object with a pronoun, and 3) both objects with pronouns.

1. Der Mann gibt meinem Freund eine Flasche. 2. Ich gebe dem Mann eine Mark. 3. Herbert gibt dem Mädchen die Hand. 4. Ich zeige dem Freund das Buch. 5. Ich schreibe der Mutter einen Brief.

V. Translation Exercise

1. I am waiting for money; I am waiting for it. 2. I am waiting for my friend; I am waiting for him. 3. The man in the house takes my Mark and gives me five Pfennig back. 4. We hope they do not come too late. 5. Is this your book? 6. We do not pay for the flowers from the garden. 7. Is that your friend? 8. Those are Americans. 9. My friend (*fem.*) writes me a letter, and I write her also one (*einen*). 10. The girls shake hands with him. 11. They are near the forest at four o'clock. 12. He sells much in his house and lives on that (from it).

VI. Fragen

1. Wo treffen die Studenten die Mädchen? 2. Wo liegt der Tennisplatz? 3. Was liegt daneben? 4. Was steht dahinter? 5. Was bekomme ich von dem Mann? 6. Was kostet sie? 7. Was gebe ich dem Mann? 8. Wen (*whom*) sehen wir auf dem Weg zum Tennisplatz? 9. Warum kommen die Mädchen zu spät? 10. Wie ist das Tennis der Studenten aus Amerika?

VII. Lesestück

Hauptstädte

Jedes Land hat eine Hauptstadt. Die Hauptstadt der Vereinigten Staaten ist Washington. Auch die 48 (achtundvierzig) amerikanischen Staaten haben Hauptstädte. Oft ist es die größte Stadt im Staat, wie Boston in Massachusetts oder Richmond in Virginia, oft ist es eine kleine Stadt, wie Annapolis in Maryland oder Dover in Delaware.

Deutschland hatte viele Jahrhunderte keine Hauptstadt. Der König hatte Burgen. Er wohnte zwei oder drei Monate auf einer Burg, dann auf einer anderen und so weiter. In Frankfurt wurden die deutschen Könige gewählt, in Aachen wurden sie gekrönt, aber weder Frankfurt noch Aachen waren Hauptstädte wie Paris in Frankreich oder London in England. Die deutschen Staaten hatten Hauptstädte: München war die Hauptstadt von Bayern, Stuttgart die Hauptstadt von Württemberg, Dresden die Hauptstadt von Sachsen. Im Jahre 1871 (achtzehnhunderteinundsiebzig) hatte das Deutsche Reich zum ersten Mal eine Hauptstadt: Berlin. Berlin war die deutsche Hauptstadt von 1871 bis zum Ende des zweiten Weltkriegs.

Heute ist die Hauptstadt von Westdeutschland die Stadt Bonn am Rhein. Früher war es eine kleine Universitätsstadt, aber seit 1949 (neunzehnhundertneunundvierzig) wächst die Stadt sehr schnell. Bonn ist der Sitz des Bundespräsidenten, des Bundeskanzlers und des Bundestags. Auf dem Haus des Bundestags sieht man die schwarz-rot-goldene Fahne der Bundesrepublik.

Auch jedes deutsche Land hat eine Hauptstadt. Es ist nicht immer die größte Stadt des Landes. Frankfurt ist die größte Stadt im Lande Hessen, aber die Hauptstadt ist Wiesbaden. Sehr oft ist die größte Stadt auch die Hauptstadt: München in Bayern, Hannover in Niedersachsen, Kiel in Schleswig-Holstein. Die Hauptstadt von Nordrhein-Westfalen ist Düsseldorf. „Dorf“ ist das deutsche Wort für *village,* aber Düsseldorf ist kein Dorf, es ist eine große Stadt mit mehr als 500 000 (fünfhunderttausend) Einwohnern.

VIII. Wörterverzeichnis

eine andere another
Bayern Bavaria
der Bundeskanzler the Federal Chancellor
der Bundespräsident the Federal President
die Bundesrepublik the Federal Republic

der Bundestag the Federal Legislature
die Burg; Burgen the castle; castles
das Dorf the village
der Einwohner the inhabitant
bis zum Ende until the end
die Fahne the flag
Frankreich France
früher formerly, earlier
gekrönt crowned
gewählt chosen
der größte the largest
hatte, hatten had
die Hauptstadt; Hauptstädte the capital; capitals
im Jahre in the year
das Jahrhundert the century
klein little
der König the king
mehr als more than
der Monat the month
München Munich
oft often
am Rhein on the Rhine
Sachsen Saxony
der Sitz the seat
der Staat the state
die Stadt the city
und so weiter; usw. and so on; etc.
die Universitätsstadt the university city
viele Jahrhunderte for many centuries
von of; from
war, waren was, were
weder . . . noch neither . . . nor
der Weltkrieg the World War
wohnte lived
das Wort the word
wurden were
Württemberg Wurttemberg
der zweite the second

Aufgabe Sechs

PLURALS

I. Reading Selection

Frau Löwenzahn sagt: „Ich gehe heute in die Stadt. Conrad, kommst du mit mir?“

Ich antworte: „Gern. Wohin gehen Sie in der Stadt?“

Sie sagt: „Ich gehe in ein Warenhaus. Ich kaufe ein Geschenk für den Geburtstag meines Mannes.“

Wir fahren mit der Straßenbahn in die Stadt. Auf den Straßen sind viele Leute, Straßenbahnen und Autos.

„Wo ist das Warenhaus?“ frage ich.

„Es liegt hinter dem Marktplatz“, antwortet Frau Löwenzahn, „zwischen der Kirche und dem Park.“

Auf den Tischen im Warenhaus liegen viele Dinge. Hier auf diesem Tisch liegen Kleider für Frauen. Zwei Frauen vor dem Tisch haben einen Streit.

„Dies ist mein Kleid“, sagt die eine.

„Nein, es ist mein Kleid“, sagt die andere. „Ich kaufe es.“

Ein Verkäufer kommt und sagt: „Keinen Streit, meine Damen. Wir haben zwei Kleider in diesen Farben und mit diesem Kragen.“

Beide Frauen werden still.

„Was sagen Sie?“ ruft die eine, „zwei Kleider in diesen Farben und mit diesem Kragen? Dann kaufe ich dieses Kleid nicht.“

„Ich auch nicht“, sagt die andere und geht schnell weg.

„Auf welchem Stock haben Sie Schreibtischlampen?" fragt Frau Löwenzahn eine Verkäuferin.

„In der Abteilung für Möbel", antwortet die Verkäuferin. „Stock Nummer sechs."

In der Abteilung für Möbel stehen viele Tische, Schreibtische, Stühle, Sessel und Lampen. An den Wänden stehen Bücherbretter ohne Bücher.

Wir kaufen eine Schreibtischlampe für Herrn Löwenzahn. Sie ist gelb, sehr schön und kostet vierzig Mark zwanzig.

Ich kaufe zwei Hemden für mich und eine Krawatte für Herrn Löwenzahn. Dann fahren wir mit der Straßenbahn zurück.

II. Vocabulary

die Abteilung the department
*__das Auto__ the auto, car
das Bücherbrett the bookshelf, bookcase
*__die Dame__ the lady
*__das Ding__ the thing
die eine, die andere the one, the other
*__fahren (ä) mit__ (to) ride, travel, go by *or* with
*__der Geburtstag__ the birthday
*__gelb__ yellow
*__gern(e)__ gladly
*__das Geschenk__ the present
*__das Hemd__ the shirt
*__kaufen__ (to) buy
*__die Kirche__ the church
*__das Kleid__ the dress
*__kosten__ (to) cost
der Kragen the collar
die Krawatte the necktie
*__die Lampe__ the lamp
*__die Leute__ (*plu.*) people
*__manche__ some
der Marktplatz the market place
die Möbel the furniture
*__die Nummer__ the number
*__der Park__ the park
*__schnell__ quick, fast
schön beautiful, nice
der Schreibtisch the desk
die Schreibtischlampe the desk lamp
*__sechs__ six
*__die Stadt__ the city
*__still__ still, quiet
der Stock, *plu.*: **die Stockwerke** the floor, story
*__die Straße__ the street
*__die Straßenbahn__ the trolley, street car
der Streit the quarrel
*__der Verkäufer__ the salesman, seller, vendor
*__die Verkäuferin__ the salesgirl, seller, vendor
vierzig forty
das Warenhaus the department store
*__weg__ away, off
*__wohin__ where (to)
*__zwanzig__ twenty

IDIOMS

***ich auch nicht** nor I either
***in der Stadt** in the city, in town, downtown
***in die Stadt** to the city, to town, downtown

III. Grammar

A. NOMINATIVE PLURALS OF NOUNS

There are four ways in which German nouns normally form their plurals: 1) no ending, sometimes umlaut; 2) add **–e,** sometimes umlaut; 3) add **–er** and umlaut whenever possible; and 4) add **–n** or **–en,** never umlaut. We shall consider these four groups in order and list the plurals of the nouns we had so far as active vocabulary.

Group 1. Add no ending, sometimes umlaut the stem vowel. The following hints in regard to the membership of this group may be helpful: neuter nouns ending in the diminutives **–chen** and **–lein;** almost all masculines and neuters ending in **–el, –en, –er;** only two feminines, **die Mutter** (*the mother*) and **die Tochter** (*the daughter*).

With regard to the umlaut of plurals: 1) Remember that only **a, o, u, au** can change to an umlaut; 2) For the plurals of group 1, umlaut both feminines, no neuters, most masculines.

The plurals of Group 1-nouns which we have had so far as active vocabulary are:

MASCULINE	NEUTER
die Amerikaner	die Fenster
die Gärten	die Mädchen
die Lehrer	die Zimmer
die Sessel	
die Teller	
die Verkäufer	

Group 2. Add –e, sometimes umlaut the stem vowel. Umlaut all feminines, most masculines, and no neuters.

Courtesy of the German Tourist Information Office, New York

Berlin: Das Brandenburger Tor

Berlin: Das neue Schillertheater

Courtesy of the German Tourist Information Office, New York

Courtesy of the German Tourist Information Office, New York

Above—Das Charlottenburger Schloß in Berlin *Below*—Basel: die Fähre am Münster

Courtesy of Basel Tourist Office, Basel

Perhaps the most helpful hint for membership in this group is that it is composed mainly of masculine nouns of one syllable; there are relatively few neuters and feminines, and in fact no feminines of more than one syllable.

The plurals of Group 2-nouns we have had so far as active vocabulary are:

MASCULINE	FEMININE	NEUTER
die Berge	die Hände	die Dinge
die Bleistifte	die Lüfte	die Geschenke
die Briefe	die Städte	die Haare
die Freunde	die Wände	die Hefte
die Geburtstage		
die Köpfe		
die Nachmittage		
die Parke		
die Sätze		
die Schuhe		
die Stühle		
die Tische		

(Actually all of the above nouns, except **Geschenk,** are monosyllables—**Geburtstag** und **Nachmittag** are derived from **der Tag,** *the day,* and **Bleistift** is also a compound noun, meaning *lead pin.*)

Group 3. Add –er, and umlaut whenever possible.

There are no feminines, and only very few masculines in this group. It is composed mainly of neuter nouns of one syllable.

The plurals of Group 3-nouns we have had so far as active vocabulary are:

MASCULINE	NEUTER
die Männer	die Bücher
die Wälder	die Gelder (*not very frequent*)
	die Gläser
	die Häuser
	die Kleider
	die Länder

Group 4. Add –n or –en, never umlaut.

Here belong *all* feminine nouns, except **Mutter** and **Tochter,** and some one-syllable nouns which belong to Group 2; here also belong a few masculine nouns ending in **–e,** and masculine nouns of foreign origin accented on the last syllable, e.g., **der Student**; likewise some nouns ending in **–or** and taken over from Latin, e.g., **der Professor, der Doktor, der Autor, der Motor.**

The plural ending for this group is usually **–en.** Nouns ending in **–e, –el, –er** add only **–n.** Most nouns ending in **–e** are feminine.

Note that we can often turn masculine nouns into corresponding feminine nouns by adding the suffix **–in,** e.g., **der Freund—die Freundin; der Verkäufer—die Verkäuferin; der Lehrer—die Lehrerin; der Amerikaner—die Amerikanerin.** Such feminines add **–nen** to form their plurals.

The plurals of Group 4 feminine nouns we have had so far as active vocabulary are:

die Aufgaben	die Freundinnen	die Straßen
die Arbeiten	die Kartoffeln	die Straßenbahnen
die Blumen	die Kirchen	die Stunden
die Damen	die Kreiden	die Tafeln
die Familien	die Küchen	die Taschen
die Farben	die Lampen	die Verkäuferinnen
die Flaschen	die Nummern	die Zeitungen
die Frauen	die Schulen	

We have in our active vocabulary only two neuters of Group 4, **das Bett** and **das Hemd;** their plurals are **die Betten** and **die Hemden.** (One frequently used neuter is very irregular in the singular: NOM. **das Herz** (*the heart*), GEN. **des Herzens,** DAT. **dem Herzen,** ACC. **das Herz;** its plural is **die Herzen.**)

Many masculines of this group (especially those ending in **–e,** or accented on the last syllable) form all cases other than the nominative by adding **–n** or **–en,** e.g., **der Student** is in every case (other than the nominative singular) **Studenten;**

der Knabe (*boy*) other than in the nominative singular is always **Knaben.** This will be noted in future vocabularies by the genitive singular form of such nouns.

Belonging to Group 4, but also irregular is **der Herr** (*the gentleman*): NOM. **der Herr,** GEN. **des Herrn,** DAT. **dem Herrn,** ACC. **den Herrn;** all plural forms are **Herren.**

B. PLURAL FORMATIONS OF COMPOUND NOUNS

When we have a compound noun in German, the gender and the plural form is determined by the last element of the compound. Thus, since **Zimmer** is neuter and has the plural form **die Zimmer,** we also have **das Eßzimmer** and **das Wohnzimmer** with the plural forms **die Eßzimmer** and **die Wohnzimmer.** This is true of any compound noun in any group. **Das Mädchen** plus **die Schule** gives **die Mädchenschule** (*the girls' school*), with the plural **die Mädchenschulen.**

C. PLURAL DECLENSION OF NOUNS, **Der** WORDS AND **Ein** WORDS

As in the singular, there are four cases in the plural, but there is no differentiation of genders. Below we use the plural of **der-die-das** with one noun, of **dieser** with another, and of **mein** with a third to show the proper endings for the articles, the nouns, the **der** and **ein words.** [As a sample of the **ein words** we take the possessive adjective **mein,** since the indefinite article has, of course, no plural. Obviously the plural of **ein Buch** (*a book*) is **Bücher** (*books*).]

		PLURAL	
NOM.	die Fenster	diese Tische	meine Lampen
GEN.	der Fenster	dieser Tische	meiner Lampen
DAT.	den Fenstern	diesen Tischen	meinen Lampen
ACC.	die Fenster	diese Tische	meine Lampen

Notice and remember: the dative plural of every German noun ends in an **–n.** If the nominative plural does not already show an **–n,** you have to add it in the dative.

D. Infrequent –s Plurals

A very few nouns of foreign origin form **–s** plurals, e.g., **die Autos, die Radios, die Restaurants.** Family names likewise form **–s** plurals: **die Löwenzahns, die Meyers,** etc. Such nouns do not add **–n** to the dative plural.

E. Some Idiomatic Irregularities

With expressions of weight and measure the singular is used where logically the plural would be required. Thus, **DM 5,20** is **fünf Mark zwanzig,** or **DM 0,20** is **zwanzig Pfennig.** (German regularly uses a comma as a decimal mark.) This corresponds to the English "he is six *foot* two."

IV. Grammatical Exercises

A. Put the following sentences into the plural:

1. Der Student schreibt seine Aufgabe. 2. In dem Zimmer ist ein Tisch, ein Sessel und eine Lampe. 3. Ich schlafe in diesem Bett. 4. Du siehst durch das Fenster. 5. Der Amerikaner ist jetzt in Deutschland und wohnt bei dieser Familie. 6. Das Haar des Lehrers ist weiß. 7. Der Stuhl ist nicht grün. 8. Mein Schuh ist auch nicht grün. 9. Ich sitze an einem Tisch und schreibe die Aufgabe in mein Heft. 10. Ich schreibe sie auch in mein Buch und an die Tafel. 11. Du schreibst den Brief mit deinem Bleistift. 12. Der Freund geht aus dem Haus in den Garten. 13. Der Mann gibt mir dieses Geschenk. 14. Trinkt das Mädchen Coca Cola aus der Flasche oder aus einem Glas? 15. Die Dame trägt eine Blume.

B. Put the following sentences into the singular:

1. Die Freundinnen tragen die Kleider in ihre Häuser. 2. Die Blumen wachsen in den Wäldern. 3. Die Frauen

haben Stühle in ihren Küchen. 4. Sie haben keine Teller für die Kartoffeln. 5. Die Schulen liegen zwischen den Parken und den Kirchen. 6. Die Männer lesen die Zeitungen. 7. Ihr fahrt mit zwei Autos. 8. Sie geben uns Hemden zu unseren Geburtstagen. 9. Die Farbe der Wände ist gelb. 10. Treffen die Studenten die Mädchen in den Städten oder auf den Bergen? 11. Sprechen die Mädchen mit den Verkäuferinnen?

V. Translation Exercise

1. Mr. Löwenzahn speaks of his autos. 2. They sleep every afternoon in their beds. 3. The friends are going downtown now. 4. The ladies ride on the street cars. 5. The salesladies show us clothes. 6. The colors of the lamps are green and red. 7. They cost five marks twenty. 8. The students go to school with their books. 9. Their pencils only cost twenty pfennigs. 10. They have tables, chairs, and easy chairs in their rooms. 11. Some people in the cities in Germany go to their parks every afternoon. 12. How many rooms are in your school? 13. Mrs. Löwenzahn is buying presents for her husband's birthday. 14. Many churches are in these cities. 15. Where is he going (to)? 16. Now he is going away. 17. They are soon coming back into their houses.

VI. Fragen

1. Wohin geht Frau Löwenzahn heute? 2. Wer geht mit ihr? 3. Wie fahren sie in die Stadt? 4. Wo liegt das Warenhaus? 5. Warum geht Frau Löwenzahn in das Warenhaus? 6. Was liegt auf den Tischen des Warenhauses? 7. Was verkaufen die Verkäufer in einem Warenhaus? 8. Was für Möbel stehen in der Abteilung? 9. Was kaufen sie für Herrn Löwenzahn? 10. Wie ist diese Lampe? 11. Was kostet sie? 12. Was kauft Conrad?

VII. Lesestück

Berlin

Berlin war nicht nur viele Jahre die deutsche Hauptstadt, es war auch seit Jahrhunderten die Hauptstadt von Preußen. In der Mitte des 17. (siebzehnten) Jahrhunderts war Berlin eine kleine Stadt mit nur 8 000 (achttausend) Menschen. Berlin ist groß geworden als Hauptstadt von Preußen. Die Könige von Preußen, die Hohenzollern, hatten hier ihr Schloß. Der berühmteste der Hohenzollernkönige, Friedrich der Große, hatte Berlin nicht gern. Er baute ein neues Schloß, das Schloß Sanssouci, außerhalb von Berlin.

Im 18. (achtzehnten) und 19. (neunzehnten) Jahrhundert wuchs die Stadt mehr und mehr, aber erst nach der Gründung des Deutschen Reiches wurde sie eine Millionenstadt. Seit 1930 (neunzehnhundertdreißig) leben zwischen drei und vier Millionen Menschen in Berlin. Es war nicht nur die Hauptstadt des Deutschen Reiches und die Hauptstadt von Preußen, es war auch eine der größten Industrie- und Handelsstädte des Landes. Der Fluß, der durch Berlin fließt, die Spree, ist nur sehr klein, aber durch Kanäle ist die Stadt mit zwei großen Flüssen (Elbe und Oder) und mit den Industriestädten im Westen verbunden.

In den 50 (fünfzig) Jahren vor dem zweiten Weltkrieg wurde Berlin berühmt durch seine kulturellen Institutionen, seine Theater, Konzerte, Museen und eine große Universität. In der Mitte der Stadt läuft von Osten nach Westen eine breite Straße. Sie heißt „Unter den Linden." An einem Ende der Straße ist die Universität, die Oper und das Rathaus, am anderen Ende das berühmte Brandenburger Tor, das Reichstagsgebäude und ein großer Park.

Nach dem Weltkrieg wurde Berlin von amerikanischen, britischen, französischen und russischen Soldaten besetzt. Bald war die Stadt in einen Westsektor und einen Ostsektor geteilt.

Dadurch wurde das Leben der Berliner sehr schwierig. Aber die Berliner sind in Deutschland berühmt durch ihren Witz und Humor. Sie haben gelernt, das Leben leicht zu nehmen.

VIII. Wörterverzeichnis

amerikanisch American
das andere the other
außerhalb von outside of
baute built
die Berliner the Berliners
berühmt; berühmtest famous; most famous
besetzt occupied
das Brandenburger Tor the Brandenburg Gate
breit broad
britisch British
der; in der which; in which
das Deutsche Reich the German Empire
das Ende the end
erst only, not until
fließen (to) flow
der Fluß; Flüsse the river; rivers
französisch French
Friedrich der Große Frederick the Great
gern haben (to) like
geteilt divided
der größte the largest
die Gründung, –en the founding
die Handelsstadt, ⸚e the commercial city
hatte, hatten had
die Hauptstadt, ⸚e the capital
es heißt it is called
der Humor the humor
die Industriestadt, ⸚e the industrial city
das Jahrhundert, –e the century
seit Jahrhunderten for centuries
der Kanal, ⸚e the canal
klein small
der König, –e the king
kulturell cultural
läuft runs
das Leben the life
leicht nehmen (to) take easy
mehr more
die Menschen the people
die Million, –en the million
die Millionenstadt, ⸚e the city with a million inhabitants
das Museum; Museen the museum
neu new
nur only
der Osten the east
der Ostsektor the East Sector
Preußen Prussia
das Rathaus, ⸚er the city hall
das Reichstagsgebäude the Parliament Building
russisch Russian
schwierig difficult
der Soldat, –en the soldier
die Universität, –en the university
Unter den Linden Under the Lindens
verbunden connected
viele Jahre for many years
von by, of
war, waren was, were
der Weltkrieg the World War
der Westen the west
der Westsektor the West Sector
der Witz the wit
es wuchs it grew
es wurde; es ist geworden it became, it has become
der zweite the second

Aufgabe Sieben

PAST TENSE CONJUGATION
WEAK AND STRONG VERBS

I. Reading Selection

Gestern hatte Herr Löwenzahn Geburtstag. Er wurde sechzig Jahre alt. Wir machten ihm einen Geburtstagstisch mit vielen Blumen und Geschenken. In der Mitte des Tisches stand die Lampe von Frau Löwenzahn. Darunter lagen Geschenke, eine Krawatte von mir, eine Pfeife von Herbert, eine Armbanduhr von den Löwenzahnkindern, ein paar Flaschen Wein und viele Zigarren. Nach dem Essen kamen ein paar Freunde von Herrn Löwenzahn. Es war an diesem Abend sehr warm im Haus. So blieben wir nicht im Haus, sondern gingen auf den Balkon und in den Garten. Frau Löwenzahn hatte viel Arbeit. Herbert und ich halfen ihr. Wir trugen Stühle und zwei Tische auf den Balkon und stellten viele Gläser auf die Tische. Herr Löwenzahn ging mit seinen Gästen durch den Garten und zeigte ihnen seine Blumen. Er rief aus dem Garten: „Lisette, ist die Erdbeerbowle fertig?" und Frau Löwenzahn antwortete: „Ja, Heinrich, sie ist fertig und wartet auf dich." Nun hatte Herr Löwenzahn plötzlich kein Interesse mehr für Blumen, er nahm zwei seiner Freunde beim Arm und ging zurück zum Haus.

Herr Löwenzahn feierte seinen Geburtstag mit einer Erdbeerbowle. Ein paar Stunden vor der Ankunft der Gäste schnitt er zwei Pfund Erdbeeren mit Zucker in eine Glasschüssel und goß fünf Flaschen Wein darüber. Nach zwei oder drei Stunden war die Erdbeerbowle fertig. Sie schmeckte sehr gut und machte uns sehr lustig. Herr Löwenzahn stand auf dem Balkon, hatte ein Glas in der Hand, den Lampenschirm auf dem Kopf und sang: „Oh, wie ist es am Rhein so schön!"

Frau Löwenzahn sagte leise etwas zu ihrer Freundin, und Herr Löwenzahn rief: „Sie fragt: wird dieser Mann heute sechzig oder sechzehn Jahre alt?"

Frau Löwenzahn sagte: „Heinrich, ich denke, du hörst nicht gut."

Er kam zu ihr, gab ihr einen Kuß und sagte: „Lisette, nach einer Flasche Wein höre ich wieder gut."

Wir saßen bis spät in der Nacht auf dem Balkon, und Herr Löwenzahn sang noch oft

„Oh, wie ist es am Rhein so schön!"

II. Vocabulary

NOTE: Plurals of nouns will be indicated thus henceforth: – for no ending; ⸚ for no ending, but with umlaut; **–e** for an **–e** ending; **⸚e** for an **–e** ending with an umlaut; etc.

If the genitive singular of a masculine noun adds **–n** or **–en**, that will be indicated between the singular and plural forms.

*__der Abend, –e__ the evening
__die Ankunft, ⸚e__ the arrival
*__der Arm, –e__ the arm
__die Armbanduhr, –en__ the wrist watch
__der Balkon, –e__ the balcony
*__bei__ by
*__bis__ until
*__bleiben__ (to) remain
__die Erdbeerbowle, –n__ the strawberry punch
__die Erdbeere, –n__ the strawberry
*__etwas__ something, some
__feiern__ (to) celebrate
*__fertig__ ready
*__der Gast, ⸚e__ the guest
__der Geburtstagstisch, –e__ the birthday table
*__gestern__ yesterday
*__gießen__ (to) pour
__die Glasschüssel, –n__ the glass bowl
*__das Interesse, –n__ the interest
*__das Jahr, –e__ the year
*__das Kind, –er__ the child
__der Kuß, Küsse__ the kiss
__der Lampenschirm, –e__ the lamp shade
*__leise__ soft, quiet
*__lustig__ merry, cheerful
*__die Mitte__ the middle
*__die Nacht, ⸚e__ the night

oder or
die Pfeife, –n the pipe
das Pfund the pound
der Rhein the Rhine (River)
***schmecken** (to) taste (good)
***schneiden** (to) cut
***schön** beautiful, nice
sechzehn sixteen
sechzig sixty
***sieben** seven
***singen** (to) sing
***sondern** but (on the contrary)
***stellen** (to) place, put
***der Wein, –e** the wine
***die Zigarre, –n** the cigar
der Zucker the sugar

IDIOMS

***ein paar** couple of, a few
***kein . . . mehr** no . . . any more, no . . . any longer, no more, not . . . any more

III. Grammar

THE PAST TENSE

Like English, German has two different types of verbs (in English called regular and irregular verbs) which are distinguished by the formation of their past tense. The first group (in English: regular verbs) we call *weak* or *suffix verbs,* the second (in English: irregular verbs) *strong* or *vowel-changing verbs.*

As in the present tense (and in all other tenses), the German past tense has neither a progressive nor an emphatic form. So there is in German no difference between: *I asked, I was asking, I did ask.* (See Lesson III, Section III, A.)

A. THE PAST TENSE OF WEAK (OR SUFFIX) VERBS

In English, this group of verbs forms the past tense by adding **–ed** (or sometimes **–t**) to the stem. So the past tense of *ask* is *ask-ed.* In German, this type of verb adds the suffix **–te** to the stem. So the past tense of **frag-en** is **frag-te.** This is the basic form for the conjugation in the past tense, called **the second principal part** of the verb (the first principal part being the infinitive form). We now give you the complete conjugation of a weak verb in the past tense. You will notice that the first and third persons singular do not add any ending to the second principal part.

1.	ich frag-te	ich wart-e-te
2.	du frag-te**st**	du wart-e-te**st**
3.	er, sie, es } frag-te	er, sie, es } wart-e-te
1.	wir frag-te**n**	wir wart-e-te**n**
2.	ihr frag-te**t**	ihr wart-e-te**t**
3.	sie (Sie) } frag-te**n**	sie (Sie) } wart-e-te**n**

If the stem of a verb ends in a **–t** or **–d,** an **–e–** is inserted between the stem and the **–te** of the second principal part (see above the conjugational forms of **warten**). Of this group you have already learned the verbs **antwort-en, arbeit-en, kost-en.**

The weak verb **haben** is slightly irregular. Its second principal part is **hat-te (du hattest, er hatte,** etc.).

B. The Past Tense of Strong (or Vowel-Changing) Verbs

As in English, this group of verbs does not add an ending to the stem, but forms the past tense by changing the stem vowel. So the past tense of *sing* is *sang*. We have the same verb in German; there the past tense of **sing-en** is **sang.** In English, as in German, we just have to learn and to remember this second principal part, because we cannot otherwise know how the stem vowel will change. Here is the complete conjugation of a strong verb in the past tense. Notice: the personal endings of the past tense are identical for the weak and the strong verbs. Again the first and third persons singular do not have an ending.

1.	ich sang	1.	wir sang**en**
2.	du sang**st**	2.	ihr sang**t**
3.	er, sie, es } sang	3.	sie (Sie) } sang**en**

In future vocabularies the past tense of all strong verbs will be given, so that you can memorize the vowel change of the stem. If, for instance, you find the entry **lesen (ie), las,** you will know: a) it is a strong or vowel-changing verb; b) the stem vowel changes from **e** to **a** for the past tense; c) in the second and third persons singular of the present tense the **e** of the infinitive changes to **ie.** Unless you are given the principal parts of the verb in the vocabulary, you may assume that you are dealing with a weak verb.

So far you have learned the following strong (or vowel-changing) verbs:

INFINITIVE		PAST TENSE	
bleiben	*remain*	**blieb**	*remained*
essen (i)	*eat*	**aß**	*ate*
fahren (ä)	*ride, travel*	**fuhr**	*rode, traveled*
geben (i)	*give*	**gab**	*gave*
gehen	*go*	**ging**	*went*
gießen	*pour*	**goß**	*poured*
helfen (i)	*help*	**half**	*helped*
kommen	*come*	**kam**	*came*
lesen (ie)	*read*	**las**	*read*
liegen	*lie*	**lag**	*lay*
nehmen (nimmt)	*take* (*takes*)	**nahm**	*took*
rufen	*call*	**rief**	*called*
schlafen (ä)	*sleep*	**schlief**	*slept*
schneiden	*cut*	**schnitt**	*cut*
schreiben	*write*	**schrieb**	*wrote*
sehen (ie)	*see*	**sah**	*saw*
sein (ist)	*be* (*is*)	**war**	*was*
singen	*sing*	**sang**	*sang*
sitzen	*sit*	**saß**	*sat*
sprechen (i)	*speak*	**sprach**	*spoke*
stehen	*stand*	**stand**	*stood*
tragen (ä)	*carry, wear*	**trug**	*carried, wore*
treffen (i)	*meet*	**traf**	*met*
trinken	*drink*	**trank**	*drank*
wachsen (ä)	*grow*	**wuchs**	*grew*
werden (wird)	*become* (*becomes*)	**wurde**	*became*

C. Aber AND Sondern

German has two words for *but*: **aber** and **sondern. Sondern** is used when the English *but* means *on the contrary* and is preceded by a negative. Otherwise use **aber.** Examples: **Er saß am Tisch, aber er aß nicht. Er hat einen Bleistift, aber er schreibt nicht damit. Die Tafel ist nicht weiß, sondern schwarz. Wir blieben nicht im Haus, sondern gingen in den Garten.**

D. NOUNS OF MEASURE

In English, after nouns of measure, we use the preposition *of*, e.g., *a bottle of lemonade, four bottles of wine, two pounds of strawberries,* etc. German omits the preposition: **eine Flasche Limonade, vier Flaschen Wein, zwei Pfund Erdbeeren.**

Masculine and neuter nouns of measure do not form a plural in such cases, e.g., **zwei Pfund Erdbeeren.** (See Lesson VI, Section III, E.)

IV. Grammatical Exercises

A. Put the infinitive into the proper form of the past tense:

1. Der Mann (bleiben) im Haus. 2. Er (essen) zu viel. 3. Das Mädchen (geben) dem Studenten die Hand. 4. Die Frau (gehen) in die Stadt. 5. Du (haben) zwei Flaschen Wein. 6. Conrad (helfen) mir. 7. Du (kommen) zu spät in das Eßzimmer. 8. Was (lesen) ihr in der Zeitung? 9. Was (liegen) auf dem Tisch? 10. Was (sagen) Frau Löwenzahn? 11. Was (antworten) du? 12. Was (kosten) die Lampe? 13. Herr Löwenzahn (nehmen) zwei Pfund Erdbeeren. 14. Er (schneiden) sie in eine Schüssel. 15. Dann (gießen) er Wein darüber und (trinken) etwas. 16. Frau Löwenzahn (rufen) sehr laut. 17. Aber Herr Löwenzahn (schlafen) ruhig. 18. (Sehen) du die Aufgabe? 19. (Schreiben) du sie in dein Heft? 20. (Sein) ihr mit der Aufgabe fertig?

21. (Sitzen) du in dem Sessel? 22. Oder (stehen) du vor dem Schreibtisch? 23. Conrad (treffen) das Mädchen am Tennisplatz. 24. Er (sprechen) über dies und das. 25. Es (werden) spät. 26. Der Student (wachsen) zu schnell. 27. Der Herr (tragen) eine Brille.

B. Re-do Exercise A in the present tense.

C. Add the endings required, if any:

1. Ich aß_____ Schweinebraten. 2. Er fuhr_____ mit der Straßenbahn. 3. Du sprach_____ von einer Flasche Limonade. 4. Wir nahm_____ die Kreide in die Hand. 5. Gestern traf_____ sie mich am Tennisplatz. 6. War_____ ihr gestern in der Stadt? 7. Es lag_____ zwischen der Kirche und dem Park. 8. Ging_____ sie in den Garten? 9. Half_____ Sie ihr bei der Arbeit?

D. Place the verbs in Exercise C in the present tense.

V. Translation Exercise

1. I went downtown yesterday. 2. The salesman sold me a couple of bottles of wine. 3. This wine is not white, but red. 4. Didn't he have any more cigars? 5. He came in half an hour, didn't he? 6. That church was situated behind the park, wasn't it? 7. We remained in the garden until late in the night. 8. The guests ate and drank something. 9. Mrs. Löwenzahn was waiting for the students. 10. She met them in the garden. 11. They were carrying presents into the garden. 12. They were not pouring lemonade into these glasses. 13. They gave her something to drink. 14. Yesterday they went downtown with the street car. 15. They stood and talked with a salesman. 16. They saw many things on the tables. 17. They were helping the woman. 18. It cost four marks. 19. It was getting late. 20. They took their books and went into the house. 21. Then they sat at their

tables and read and wrote their lessons. 22. They worked very hard and then went to (*zu*) bed.

VI. Fragen

1. Warum kamen gestern viele Freunde zu Herrn Löwenzahn? 2. Wie alt wurde er? 3. Was machten wir für ihn? 4. Wie war es im Hause? 5. Was trugen wir auf den Balkon? 6. Wohin ging Herr Löwenzahn mit seinen Gästen? 7. Was wartete schon auf die Löwenzahns und ihre Freunde? 8. Wie machte Herr Löwenzahn die Erdbeerbowle? 9. Warum wurden alle sehr lustig? 10. Was sagte Frau Löwenzahn zu ihrer Freundin? 11. Wann hört Herr Löwenzahn wieder gut? 12. Was machte er bis spät in der Nacht?

VII. Lesestück

Till Eulenspiegel heilt

Till Eulenspiegel lebte vor 600 (sechshundert) Jahren, aber noch heute sprechen die Leute in Deutschland über seine lustigen Streiche.

Er kam einmal nach Nürnberg, ging zum Bürgermeister und sagte: „Ich bin ein großer Arzt, ich heile alle Kranken."

Der Bürgermeister sagte: „Du bist der Mann, den wir in Nürnberg brauchen. Unser Krankenhaus ist nicht groß genug. Wir haben zu viele Kranke und nicht genug Betten."

„In zwei Tagen sind alle Betten in eurem Krankenhaus leer", sagte Eulenspiegel.

„Wenn du die Wahrheit sagst", antwortete der Bürgermeister, „dann zahlen wir dir 100 (hundert) Gulden."

„Gut", sagte Eulenspiegel, „aber ich muß mit jedem Kranken allein sprechen."

Er ging in das Krankenhaus und sagte zu dem ersten Kranken: „Ich kann euch alle heilen, aber ich muß den

Kränksten von euch zu Pulver verbrennen, und ihr müsst dann dieses Pulver als Medizin essen. Morgen komme ich zurück und rufe ‚Wer nicht krank ist, komme heraus.' Wer als Letzter kommt, ist der Kränkste, und dann verbrennen wir ihn zu Pulver."

So ging Eulenspiegel von einem Bett zum nächsten und zum nächsten und sprach leise mit jedem Kranken allein.

Am nächsten Tag kam er mit dem Bürgermeister zurück und rief in das Krankenhaus: „Wer nicht krank ist, komme heraus."

Sofort war das Krankenhaus in großer Aufregung. Alle Kranken sprangen aus ihren Betten und liefen weg, denn keiner wollte der Kränkste und Letzte sein.

„Ich habe sie in einer Nacht geheilt", sagte Eulenspiegel zum Bürgermeister. „Alle Betten sind leer, nicht wahr?"

„Du sagtest die Wahrheit, du bist ein großer Arzt", antwortete der Bürgermeister und gab ihm die 100 (hundert) Gulden.

Nach zwei Tagen kamen alle Kranken zurück. Bald war wieder in jedem Bett ein Kranker.

„Wo ist Eulenspiegel?" rief der Bürgermeister.

Aber Till Eulenspiegel war nicht mehr da, und er kam nie wieder nach Nürnberg zurück.

VIII. Wörterverzeichnis

allein alone
als as
der Arzt, ⸚e the physician, doctor
die Aufregung the excitement
der Bürgermeister, – the mayor
den whom
einmal once
der erste the first one
genug enough
der Gulden, – the guilder (*coin*)
heilen (to) heal, cure
ich kann I can
klein small
komme heraus (*imp.*) come out!
das Krankenhaus, ⸚er the hospital
der Kränkste the sickest one
leer empty
der letzte the last one
die Medizin, –en the medicine
ich muß I must
ihr müßt you must
der Nächste the next one

nicht mehr no longer
noch still
das Pulver the powder
springen aus; sprang (to) spring out of; sprang
der Streich, –e the trick, prank
der Tag, –e the day
über about
verbrennen; verbrannte (to) burn; burned
vor sechshundert Jahren six hundred years ago
die Wahrheit the truth
wenn if
wer whoever
er wollte he wanted to

Aufgabe Acht

INTERROGATIVES AND IMPERATIVES

I. Reading Selection

Auf einer Bank im Park saß ein Mädchen. Sie war jung, hübsch und blond. Herbert und ich saßen auch auf einer Bank. Wir lasen eine Zeitung. Darin war eine Prüfung über deutsche Geschichte.

Ich las eine Frage: „Wodurch wurde Gutenberg berühmt?“

Herbert antwortete: „Durch die Erfindung der Buchdruckerkunst.“

Er las: „Wer war Buxtehude?“

Ich antwortete: „Buxtehude war ein Komponist.“

Er sagte: „Nein, Buxtehude ist eine Stadt an der Elbe, und das Mädchen ist sehr hübsch.“

Ich sagte: „Sprich nicht so dumm. Die Frage ist nicht ‚was ist‘, sondern ‚wer war‘.“

Herbert sagte leise: „Sie raucht jetzt eine Zigarette.“

Ich sagte: „Wer? Die Stadt an der Elbe? Lies die Fragen und sieh nicht immer nach der Bank. Außerdem ist es nicht richtig: man sagt auf deutsch ‚es raucht eine Zigarette‘. M ä d c h e n[1] ist ein Neutrum.“

Herbert gab mir die Zeitung und sagte: „Nimm sie, ich meine die Zeitung, und lies.“

[1] German uses letterspacing, i.e., the letters are “spaced out,” where we use italic type in English for purposes of emphasis, etc.

Ich las: „Womit warf Luther nach dem Teufel?"
„Für wen kämpfte der General Wallenstein?"
„Wann lebte der Freiherr vom Stein?"
„Mit wem war Maria Theresia verheiratet?"

Herbert unterbrach: „Sagtest du: verheiratet?—Höre! Ich habe Angst vor ihr. Gehe zu ihr und sprich zu ihr!"

Ich ging mit der Zeitung zu der Bank und fragte das Mädchen: „Mit wem war Maria Theresia verheiratet?"

Sie sagte: „Speak English. I'm from Kansas City."

Ich sagte: „Sprechen Sie deutsch, Fräulein Amerika! Wir verstehen englisch, aber wir sprechen es nicht."

Sie sagte: „Aren't you two Americans?"

Ich antwortete: „Gewiß. Ich bin aus Pennsylvania, und die Eltern meines Freundes wohnen in Colorado. Wir sind ein Jahr in Deutschland und sprechen nur deutsch. Wir lernen die Sprache und üben sie jeden Tag."

Ich glaube, sie verstand kein Wort.

„Lernen Sie nicht Deutsch?" fragte ich sie.

Sie sagte etwas zu mir auf englisch. Es war nichts für Gutenbergs Buchdruckerkunst. Not fit to print, sagen wir auf englisch.

Ich nahm Herbert beim Arm, und wir gingen nach Hause. Mit der Zeitung. Ohne das Mädchen.

„Was sagte sie?" fragte Herbert.

„Die Übersetzung ist schwer", sagte ich. „Sie sagte: ihr seid Nüsse."

Herbert war an diesem Abend sehr traurig.

II. Vocabulary

***acht** eight
***außerdem** besides, moreover
***die Bank, ⸚e** the bench
***berühmt** famous
***blond** blond
die Buchdruckerkunst the art of printing
die Elbe the Elbe (River)
***die Eltern** (*plu.*) the parents
***englisch** English
die Erfindung, –en the invention
***die Frage, –n** the question
***das Fräulein, –** the girl, miss, Miss

der Freiherr, (–n), –en the baron
***die Geschichte, –n** the story; history
***gewiß** sure, certain(ly)
***glauben** (to) believe
***hübsch** pretty
***jung** young
kämpfen (to) fight, struggle
der Komponist, (–en), –en the composer
***lernen** (to) study, learn
***meinen** (to) mean, think, believe
das Neutrum the neuter
***nichts** nothing
die Nuß, Nüsse the nut
***die Prüfung, –en** the test, quiz, examination
***rauchen** (to) smoke
***die Sprache, –n** the language, speech
***der Tag, –e** the day
der Teufel, – the devil
***traurig** sad
***über** (with *acc.*) about, concerning
***die Übersetzung, –en** the translation
***unterbrechen (i), unterbrach** (to) interrupt
verheiratet married
***wer** who
***werfen (i), warf mit** (to) throw (e.g., er wirft mit einem Ball nach ihm, he throws a ball at him)
***die Zigarette, –n** the cigaret

IDIOMS

***Angst haben vor** (to) be afraid of
***auf deutsch** in German
***auf englisch** in English
***nach Hause** home (always motion toward, e.g., ich gehe *or* komme nach Hause)

III. Grammar

A. INTERROGATIVES

An interrogative is a word we use to form questions. So far we have had as active vocabulary: **wann,** *when;* **warum,** *why;* **was,** *what;* **wie,** *how;* **wo,** *where;* and **wohin,** *where (to).* Fortunately these are not declined.

Examples: **Wann gehen wir in die Stadt? Warum wächst Conrad zu schnell? Was lag auf den Tischen des Warenhauses? Wie macht man eine Erdbeerbowle? Wo wohnten die Studenten? Wohin gingen Sie gestern?**

Note that **wohin** is used in the sense of *where to,* i.e., motion towards. **Wo** means *where, in what place.* **Wohin** means *where, to what place.*

We also had **welcher,** *which* or *what,* which is used with a noun (expressed or understood) as an interrogative. Examples: **Welches Buch lesen Sie jetzt? Auf welchem Stuhl sitzt er?**

B. Wo-Combinations

Before going on, read again what was said in Lesson V, Section III, B about the **da**-combinations.

When the interrogative **was** (which always refers to an inanimate object or an idea) is used with a preposition, German is apt to make a **wo-combination.** We again have the reversible equation:

English preposition + what = German wo + preposition.

Thus we get the **wo**-combinations: **woraus** (again the **–r–** is inserted when the preposition begins with a vowel), **wobei, womit, wonach, wovon, wozu; wodurch, wofür; woran, worauf, wohinter, worin, woneben, worüber, worunter, wozwischen.** Examples: **Worauf wartest du? Womit machte er die Erdbeerbowle? Wovon lebt er? Wodurch wurde er berühmt?**

C. Wer As Interrogative Pronoun

The word **wer** as an interrogative corresponds exactly to English *who*:

Nom.	**wer**	*who*
Gen.	**wessen**	*whose*
Dat.	**wem**	*to* or *for whom*
Acc.	**wen**	*whom*

Examples: **Wer war im Garten? Wessen Übersetzung ist das? Wem gab Conrad ein Geschenk? Wen siehst du in der Straßenbahn?**

Cf. III, B above for the difference between the examples there and such sentences as: **Auf wen wartest du? Mit wem ging Conrad in die Stadt?**

D. IMPERATIVES

A language will normally have as many forms of the imperative for giving commands as it has words for *you.* Thus English has only one imperative form, e.g., Pay! Wait! Carry! Go!

German, on the other hand, will have three forms: 1) the singular familiar; 2) the plural familiar; 3) the polite form (the same for singular and plural).

SING. FAMIL.:	Zahle!	Warte!	Trage!	Gehe!
PLUR. FAMIL.:	Zahlt!	Wartet!	Tragt!	Geht!
POLITE FORM:	Zahlen Sie!	Warten Sie!	Tragen Sie!	Gehen Sie!

The singular familiar form, used for a person you address with **du,** is the **verb stem plus –e.** (In informal, everyday conversation the final **–e** is often dropped.)

The **plural familiar** form, used with persons you address individually with **du** or collectively with **ihr,** is **identical with the second person plural of the present tense.** No personal pronoun is used for the two familiar forms of the imperative.

The **polite form** is merely the **infinitive plus Sie.** This form *must* always have the capitalized personal pronoun.

To use our sample verbs in sentences, Frau Löwenzahn would say to Conrad: **Warte auf mich! Zahle für mich!**

Talking to both Conrad and Herbert, she would say: **Tragt diese Dinge! Geht jetzt nach Hause!**

Either Conrad or Herbert, talking to either Herr or Frau Löwenzahn (or to both), would say: **Warten Sie auf mich, bitte** (*please*)! **Bitte, tragen Sie diese Dinge!**

E. IMPERATIVES WITH VOWEL CHANGES

The rules and examples listed above in III, D hold true for all imperatives except those of strong (or vowel-changing) verbs which in the present tense singular change their stem from **e** to **i** or **ie** (see Lesson III, Section III, A). **In the singular familiar imperative only, these verbs change e to i or ie, and add no e– ending.** Here are the singular familiar imperatives of all e– stem verbs with present tense vowel change that we have had so far as active vocabulary: **Iß! Gib! Hilf! Lies! Nimm! Sieh! Sprich! Triff! Unterbrich! Wirf!**

The three imperative forms of **werden** are **werde, werdet, werden Sie;** of **sein** they are **sei, seid, seien Sie!**

IV. Grammatical Exercises

A. Change the following sentences into questions, using **was, wo,** a form of **wer,** or a **wo–** combination:

Examples: a) Ich warte auf meinen Freund. Auf wen warte ich? b) Ich warte auf die Zeitung. Worauf warte ich?

1. Ein Mädchen saß auf einer Bank. 2. Die Bank war im Park. 3. Wir gingen mit der Zeitung nach Hause. 4. Wir gingen nicht mit dem Mädchen. 5. Die Geschenke lagen unter dem Tisch. 6. Die Krawatte war von mir. 7. Wir helfen Frau Löwenzahn. 8. Die Luft kam durch das Fenster. 9. Herr Löwenzahn hat kein Interesse mehr für Blumen—für mich auch nicht. 10. Du trinkst eine Erdbeerbowle. 11. Gestern war Herrn Löwenzahns Geburtstag. 12. Er wurde traurig über die Geschichte.

B. Address each of the following commands to Herr or Frau Löwenzahn, or to both:

1. (werfen) das nicht nach mir! 2. (sehen) nicht immer nach der Bank! 3. (machen) Ihre Arbeit! 4. (sagen) solche Dinge nicht! 5. (gehen) in die Stadt! 6. (geben) mir etwas Geld! 7. (nehmen) dieses Geld! 8. (rufen) mich in einer halben Stunde! 9. (sprechen) lauter! 10. (treffen) mich in

der Stadt! 11. (unterbrechen) mich nicht! 12. (tragen) dies in das Haus.

C. Re-do B, addressing each sentence to Conrad or Herbert.

D. Re-do B, addressing each sentence to *both* students, Herbert and Conrad.

V. Translation Exercise

1. Conrad, read that newspaper! 2. Where did you read the test about history? 3. On what is the city (of) Buxtehude situated? 4. Wait for your friend! (*three forms*) 5. Whose cigarets are those? 6. Who was Maria Theresia? 7. Whom are you helping? 8. Help me! 9. What are you waiting for? 10. Are you afraid of this girl? 11. How do you say that in English? 12. He came home every afternoon. 13. Whom do you see now? 14. Give (*three forms*) me something to eat. 15. When were you downtown? 16. How old is Mr. Löwenzahn? 17. Why did he suddenly hear well? 18. For whom did you buy the shirt? 19. Where are you going? 20. What does the air come through?

VI. Fragen

1. Worauf saß das Mädchen? 2. Worin war die Prüfung? 3. Wie war das Mädchen? 4. Was lasen wir? 5. Worüber lasen wir in der Zeitung? 6. Wodurch wurde Gutenberg berühmt? 7. Welche Stadt liegt an der Elbe? 8. Was raucht das Mädchen? 9. Wohin ging Conrad? 10. Was fragte er das Mädchen? 11. In welcher Sprache antwortete das Mädchen? 12. Wo wohnen Herberts Eltern? 13. Womit gingen wir nach Hause? 14. Was sagte das Mädchen? 15. Wie war Herbert an diesem Abend?

VII. Lesestück

Till Eulenspiegel kauft und verkauft

Till Eulenspiegel kam nach Quedlinburg. Da war gerade Markt, und auf dem Marktplatz saß eine Bauernfrau neben einem Korb. In dem Korb waren fünf Hühner und ein Hahn.

„Was kosten die Hühner?“ fragte Eulenspiegel.

„Der ganze Korb kostet acht Groschen“, antwortete die Bauernfrau.

„Ich kaufe die Hühner und den Hahn“, sagte Eulenspiegel, nahm den Korb und ging weg.

„Halt, junger Mann“, rief die Bauernfrau, „du mußt mir acht Groschen dafür geben.“

„Ich habe mein Geld vergessen“, sagte Eulenspiegel. „Hier, nimm den Hahn als Pfand. Ich trage den Korb mit den Hühnern nach Hause und komme mit dem Geld zurück.“

Die dumme Bauernfrau nahm ihren Hahn als Pfand und wartete. Sie saß da noch am Abend und wartete und wartete.

Als die Leute in Quedlinburg die Geschichte hörten, begannen sie, Eulenspiegel zu suchen.

Aber Till Eulenspiegel war nicht mehr da, und er kam nie wieder nach Quedlinburg zurück.

. . .

Till Eulenspiegel kam nach Leipzig. In Leipzig wohnten viele Pelzhändler, denn die Stadt war berühmt durch ihren Pelzhandel. Eulenspiegel fing eine dicke, alte Katze, nähte sie in ein schönes Hasenfell, steckte sie in einen alten Sack und ging auf den Markt.

„Ich habe einen schönen Hasen zu verkaufen“, sagte er zu einem Pelzhändler.

„Gut“, antwortete der Pelzhändler, „ich kaufe ihn für sieben Groschen.“

Er gab Eulenspiegel das Geld, nahm den Sack und ging nach Hause. Dann rief er seine Freunde.

„Kommt in den Hof hinter dem Haus und laßt die Hunde in den Hof. Ich habe einen Hasen in dem Sack. Wir werden eine lustige Jagd sehen, und am Abend werden wir den Hasen essen. Und dann habe ich noch das schöne Hasenfell."

Er öffnete den Sack und die Katze kam heraus. Die Hunde begannen zu bellen, die Katze sprang auf einen Baum, schrie „Miau, miau" und lief weg.

„Wo ist Eulenspiegel?" schrieen die Pelzhändler.

Aber Till Eulenspiegel war nicht mehr da, und er kam nie wieder nach Leipzig zurück.

VIII. Wörterverzeichnis

als as, when
der Baum, ⸚e the tree
beginnen; begann (to) begin; began
bellen (to) bark
dick fat
fangen; fing (to) catch; caught
ganz whole, entire
gerade just; just then
der Groschen, – the groschen, dime
der Hahn, ⸚e the rooster
halt! halt!
der Hase, (–n), –n the hare
das Hasenfell the rabbit pelt
heraus out
der Hof, ⸚e the yard
das Huhn, ⸚er the chicken
der Hund, –e the dog
die Jagd the chase, hunt
die Katze, –n the cat
der Korb, ⸚e the basket
lassen, (to) let, permit
der Markt, ⸚e the market
der Marktplatz, ⸚e the market place
du mußt you must
nähen (to) sew
nicht mehr no longer
noch still
öffnen (to) open
der Pelzhandel the fur trade
der Pelzhändler, – the furrier
das Pfand, ⸚er the security
der Sack, ⸚e the sack, bag
schreien; schrie (to) cry; cried
springen; sprang (to) spring; sprang
stecken (to) put
suchen (to) seek, look for
vergessen; vergaß; vergessen; vergißt (to) forget; forgot; forgotten; forgets

Aufgabe Neun

PRESENT PERFECT, PAST PERFECT TIME EXPRESSIONS

I. Reading Selection

Nachmittags gehen viele Leute in Deutschland in ein Café. Im Winter sitzt man drinnen, im Sommer draußen auf dem Bürgersteig oder im Garten. Heute treffen wir Monika Wenk und ihre Freundin Vera Sütterlin in einem Café in der Stadt.

Wir sind zu früh gekommen. Wir haben eine Zeitung gekauft, eine Zigarette geraucht, Kaffee und Kuchen bestellt, aber wir haben noch nicht gegessen. Der Kaffee ist kalt geworden, die Schlagsahne auf dem Kuchen ist geschmolzen: wir sitzen und warten.

„Wir sind zu höflich", sage ich. „Das macht das Leben zu schwer."

„Vielleicht ist etwas geschehen", sagt Herbert. „Sie sind noch nie so spät gekommen."

In diesem Augenblick kommen die Mädchen.

„Es tut uns leid, wir sind wieder zu spät gekommen. Es gab einen Verkehrsunfall."

„Was ist geschehen?" frage ich. „Erzählen Sie!"

„Ein Volkswagen ist um die Ecke gekommen und ist in unsere Straßenbahn gefahren. Man hat einen Polizisten gerufen, und er hat einen Bericht geschrieben. Der Volkswagen war ganz . . ."

„Kaputt", unterbreche ich schnell. „Sagt man das auf deutsch?"

Monika und Vera lächeln.

„Gewiß, man sagt es“, antwortet Vera, „aber man schreibt es nicht.“

„Du hast unterbrochen“, sagt Herbert. „Wir hatten noch nicht das Ende der Geschichte gehört.“

„Sie haben fast alles gehört“, berichtet Monika. „Ein Verkehrsunfall mit viel Lärm, aber ohne Blut. Wir haben dann ein Taxi genommen und sind zum Café gefahren.“

„Ich sehe, Sie haben eine Zeitung gekauft“, sagt Vera. „Was haben Sie darin gelesen?“

„Wir haben sie nur gekauft, aber nicht gelesen“, sage ich. „Die Drucktypen in dieser Zeitung sind deutsch. Das ist sehr schwer für uns. Wir haben es heute in der Schule gelernt, aber wir haben es noch nicht geübt.“

„Gestern haben wir eine Zeitung gekauft und darin Fragen über deutsche Geschichte gelesen“, sagt Herbert.

„O ja“, sage ich, „es gab etwas über Maria Theresia. Die Frage war: hat Maria Theresia in Kansas City gewohnt?“

Die Mädchen lachen. Herbert ist rot geworden.

„Nehmen Sie ihn nicht ernst“, sagt er, „er ist ein Till Eulenspiegel.“

In former centuries a great number of German books (in 1930 still more than 50 per cent) were set in Gothic letters, usually called *Fraktúr*. During the last decades the Gothic print has receded more and more, and today approximately 90 per cent of all German publications are set in Roman type, called *Antíqua*. We have used *Antiqua* for this book. However, if anyone wants to read older publications, he will have to familiarize himself with Gothic print, which is considerably easier than it may look at first glance. Many present-day German newspapers use *Fraktur* for their headlines. To give you an idea of how German *Fraktur* looks, we reprint now the Reading Selection of Lesson IX in Gothic letters.

Nachmittags gehen viele Leute in Deutschland in ein Café. Im Winter sitzt man drinnen, im Sommer draußen auf dem Bürgersteig oder im Garten. Heute treffen wir Monika Wenk und ihre Freundin Vera Sütterlin in einem Café in der Stadt.

Wir sind zu früh gekommen. Wir haben eine Zeitung gekauft, eine Zigarette geraucht, Kaffee und Kuchen bestellt, aber wir haben noch nicht gegessen. Der Kaffee ist kalt geworden, die Schlagsahne auf dem Kuchen ist geschmolzen: wir sitzen und warten.

„Wir sind zu höflich", sage ich. „Das macht das Leben zu schwer."

„Vielleicht ist etwas geschehen", sagt Herbert. „Sie sind noch nie so spät gekommen."

In diesem Augenblick kommen die Mädchen.

„Es tut uns leid, wir sind wieder zu spät gekommen. Es gab einen Verkehrsunfall."

„Was ist geschehen?" frage ich. „Erzählen Sie!"

„Ein Volkswagen ist um die Ecke gekommen und ist in unsere Straßenbahn gefahren. Man hat einen Polizisten gerufen, und er hat einen Bericht geschrieben. Der Volkswagen war ganz . . ."

„Kaputt", unterbreche ich schnell. „Sagt man das auf deutsch?"

Monika und Vera lächeln.

„Gewiß, man sagt es", antwortet Vera, „aber man schreibt es nicht."

„Du hast unterbrochen", sagt Herbert. „Wir hatten noch nicht das Ende der Geschichte gehört."

„Sie haben fast alles gehört", berichtet Monika. „Ein Verkehrsunfall mit viel Lärm, aber ohne Blut. Wir haben dann ein Taxi genommen und sind zum Café gefahren."

„Ich sehe, Sie haben eine Zeitung gekauft", sagt Vera. „Was haben Sie darin gelesen?"

„Wir haben sie nur gekauft, aber nicht gelesen", sage ich. „Die Drucktypen in dieser Zeitung sind deutsch. Das ist sehr schwer für uns. Wir haben es heute in der Schule gelernt, aber wir haben es noch nicht geübt."

„Gestern haben wir eine Zeitung gekauft und darin Fragen über deutsche Geschichte gelesen", sagt Herbert.

„O ja", sage ich, „es gab etwas über Maria Theresia. Die Frage war: hat Maria Theresia in Kansas City gewohnt?"

Die Mädchen lachen. Herbert ist rot geworden.

„Nehmen Sie ihn nicht ernst", sagt er, „er ist ein Till Eulenspiegel."

II. Vocabulary

*__alles__ (*singular*) everything
*__der Bericht, –e__ the report
*__berichten__ (to) report
*__bestellen__ (to) order
__das Blut__ the blood
__der Bürgersteig, –e__ the sidewalk

das Café, –s the cafe
draußen outside
drinnen inside
die Drucktypen (*plu.*) the type, type faces
***die Ecke, –n** the corner
***das Ende, –n** the end
***ernst** serious
***erzählen** (to) tell, narrate
***fast** almost
***früh** early
***ganz** whole, entire
***geschehen (ie), geschah, ist geschehen** (to) happen, occur
***höflich** courteous
***der Kaffee** the coffee
***kalt** cold
kaputt broken, ruined, "all shot"
***der Kuchen, –** the cake, pastry, cookie
der Lärm the noise
***das Leben** the life
***man** one, they, people, (*3rd person indefinite*)
***nachmittags** afternoons, in the afternoon, of an afternoon
***neun** nine
***nie** never
***noch nie** never yet
***nur** only
der Polizist, (–en), –en the policeman
die Schlagsahne the whipped cream
schmelzen (i), schmolz, ist geschmolzen (to) melt
***der Sommer, –** the summer
das Taxi, –s the taxi
der Verkehrsunfall, ⸚e the traffic accident
der Volkswagen, – the Volkswagen
***der Winter, –** the winter

IDIOMS

***es gibt** (*takes acc.*) there is, there are

III. Grammar

The perfect tenses (present perfect and past perfect) are generally formed as in English: the proper form of the auxiliary "have" *plus the past participle* of the verb. **The past participle is the third principal part of the verb.**

A. PAST PARTICIPLES OF WEAK VERBS

Weak verbs form their past participle by adding **–t** to the stem and prefixing the syllable **ge–.** So the three principal parts of fragen are: **fragen, fragte, gefragt.** With verbs whose stem ends in a **–t** or **–d** you will, of course, again insert an **–e–**

between stem and **t**–ending. Here are a few examples of weak past participles: **gelebt, gesagt, gewartet, geantwortet.**

B. PAST PARTICIPLES OF STRONG (OR VOWEL-CHANGING) VERBS

Strong verbs form their past participle (i.e., the third principal part) by three simultaneous devices:

1. change of stem vowel
2. adding the ending **–en**
3. prefixing **ge–**

Since the change of the stem vowel cannot be predicted, you absolutely have to learn and then memorize the vowel change through all the three principal parts. Here are a few examples of the principal parts of strong verbs: **trinken, trank, getrunken; rufen, rief, gerufen; schreiben, schrieb, geschrieben.** From now on you will find all three principal parts listed in the vocabulary.

If no principal parts are given for a verb, you may assume that it is weak and that you can form the principal parts according to the rules given in Section A above.

C. THE AUXILIARIES OF THE PERFECT TENSES

In English, all verbs use the auxiliary *have* to form the perfect tenses. In German, most verbs do the same, i.e., they use forms of **haben** for the perfect tenses. There are, however, some verbs which instead of **haben** use the corresponding forms of the auxiliary **sein.** These verbs are all intransitive and indicate motion or change of condition. He **has** come: er **ist** gekommen; they **had** gone: sie **waren** gegangen; you **have** grown: du **bist** gewachsen; she **has** become: sie **ist** geworden. To this group also belong the two verbs **sein** and **bleiben,** e.g., you **have** been: ihr **seid** gewesen; we **had** remained: wir **waren** geblieben. From now on our vocabularies will list such verbs with **ist** before the past participle.

D. PRINCIPAL PARTS OF STRONG (OR VOWEL-CHANGING) VERBS

The following is a list of the principal parts of all the strong verbs we have had so far (together with the vowel change in the present tense and with an indication whether they use *sein* for the perfect tenses).

INFINITIVE	PAST	PAST PARTICIPLE
bleiben	**blieb**	**ist geblieben**
essen (i)	**aß**	**gegessen**
fahren (ä)	**fuhr**	**ist gefahren**
geben (i)	**gab**	**gegeben**
gehen	**ging**	**ist gegangen**
geschehen (ie)	**geschah**	**ist geschehen**
gießen	**goß**	**gegossen**
helfen (i)	**half**	**geholfen**
kommen	**kam**	**ist gekommen**
lesen (ie)	**las**	**gelesen**
liegen	**lag**	**gelegen**
nehmen (nimmt)	**nahm**	**genommen**
rufen	**rief**	**gerufen**
schlafen (ä)	**schlief**	**geschlafen**
schneiden	**schnitt**	**geschnitten**
schreiben	**schrieb**	**geschrieben**
sehen (ie)	**sah**	**gesehen**
sein (ist)	**war**	**ist gewesen**
singen	**sang**	**gesungen**
sitzen	**saß**	**gesessen**
sprechen (i)	**sprach**	**gesprochen**
stehen	**stand**	**gestanden**
tragen (ä)	**trug**	**getragen**
treffen (i)	**traf**	**getroffen**
trinken	**trank**	**getrunken**
unterbrechen (i)	**unterbrach**	**unterbrochen** *
wachsen (ä)	**wuchs**	**ist gewachsen**
werden (wird)	**wurde**	**ist geworden**
werfen (i)	**warf**	**geworfen**

* Omission of the prefix ge– for this form will be explained later.

E. WORD ORDER FOR PERFECT TENSES

A very important feature of German word order is that **the past participle stands at the end** of the clause (except after subordinating conjunctions). Examples: sie haben den Kuchen gegessen; er ist in die Stadt gegangen; gestern habe ich meinem Freund einen Brief geschrieben.

F. THE PRESENT PERFECT TENSE

Here is a table of the conjugation of two verbs (one weak, one strong—one using haben, one sein) in the present perfect tense:

1.	ich habe ein Buch gekauft	ich bin nach Hause gekommen
2.	du hast ein Buch gekauft	du bist nach Hause gekommen
3.	er hat ein Buch gekauft	er ist nach Hause gekommen
1.	wir haben ein Buch gekauft	wir sind nach Hause gekommen
2.	ihr habt ein Buch gekauft	ihr seid nach Hause gekommen
3.	sie haben ein Buch gekauft	sie sind nach Hause gekommen

In German the present perfect tense always denotes an event completed in the past; in most cases it is more or less equivalent to the German past tense. It is very hard to define precisely in which case the German will prefer the past to the present perfect tense or vice versa. However, it may roughly be said that in conversation the present perfect tense is used with preference, while in an objective narration of past events the past tense is indicated.

In German the present perfect tense can never be used as in English to indicate an action that has started in the past and is still going on. "I have lived in this city for five years" means you are still living there. For this, German must use the present tense, usually in combination with **schon** (*already*). So the above sentence would be: **ich wohne schon seit fünf Jahren in dieser Stadt.** The German sentence **ich habe fünf**

Jahre in dieser Stadt gewohnt means you are no longer living there.

G. THE PAST PERFECT TENSE

The German past perfect tense fortunately corresponds exactly to the English (except that some verbs, as noted, use **sein** as their auxiliary). Again we give you the full conjugation for two verbs:

1.	ich hatte eine Zigarette geraucht	ich war schnell gegangen
2.	du hattest eine Zigarette geraucht	du warst schnell gegangen
3.	er hatte eine Zigarette geraucht	er war schnell gegangen
1.	wir hatten eine Zigarette geraucht	wir waren schnell gegangen
2.	ihr hattet eine Zigarette geraucht	ihr wart schnell gegangen
3.	sie hatten eine Zigarette geraucht	sie waren schnell gegangen

H. THE IDIOM **Es gibt**

Es gibt is in some cases the proper translation for *there is, there are.* It is followed by the noun in the accusative case and does not go into the plural, no matter whether the following noun is in the singular or plural. **Es gibt einen Amerikaner in der Stadt; es gibt viele Amerikaner in der Stadt.**

There is a distinction, although not easy to define, when to use **es gibt,** and when **es ist, es sind. Es gibt** is a statement of general, unspecified existence or of a broad general truth, e.g., **es gibt viele Geschichten über Till Eulenspiegel. Es ist (es sind)** refers to a more specific situation, limited to a circumscribed space and location, e.g., **es ist ein Geschenk für Sie auf dem Tisch,** or **es sind fünf Zimmer in diesem Haus.** The noun followed by **es ist** or **es sind** is, of course, in the nominative case.

I. TIME EXPRESSIONS

1. To express customary action for parts of the day, e.g., *mornings* or *in the morning,* German forms adverbs in the same manner as English: **morgens, vormittags, nachmittags,**

abends, nachts. Examples: Ich gehe morgens (*or* vormittags) in die Schule. Nachmittags gehe ich in die Stadt. Ich schreibe abends meine Aufgabe in mein Heft. Nachts schlafen wir.

2. Time expressions indicating definite time or extent o. time are put into the accusative case. *Every evening:* **jeden Abend;** *every day:* **jeden Tag;** *the entire day:* **den ganzen Tag.**

3. All the names of the days, months, seasons, and points of the compass are masculine. All are regularly used with the definite article (which English often omits in these cases). Note the following prepositional uses: *on Tuesday* is **am Dienstag;** *on Wednesday:* **am Mittwoch;** *on this day:* **an diesem Tag.**

For the months, seasons, and points of the compass we use the prepositional contraction **im: im September, im Mai, im Winter, im Sommer, im Frühling** (*spring*), **im Herbst** (*autumn*), **im Norden** (*north*), **im Süden** (*south*), **im Westen** (*west*), **im Osten** (*east*). Remember that the German names of days, months, seasons, and points of the compass are all masculine.

IV. Grammatical Exercises

A. Put into the present perfect tense:

1. Viele Leute gehen in ein Café. 2. Im Winter sitzt man drinnen. 3. Heute trafen wir die Freundinnen in der Stadt. 4. Wir warten auf sie. 5. Wir sind zu höflich. 6. Das macht das Leben zu schwer. 7. Dann kommen die Mädchen. 8. Es tat ihnen leid. 9. Es gab einen Verkehrsunfall. 10. Sagt sie das auf deutsch? 11. Schreibt er das auf englisch? 12. Was berichtet Monika? 13. Was sieht Vera? 14. Herbert bleibt im Haus. 15. Conrad fährt in die Stadt. 16. Herr Löwenzahn liest in der Zeitung. 17. Dann liegt er auf dem Sofa und schläft. 18. Später ruft ihn seine Frau. 19. Dann nimmt er zwei Pfund Erdbeeren, steht vor dem Tisch und schneidet sie in eine Schüssel. 20. Er gießt Wein darüber.

21. Du hilfst ihm bei dieser Arbeit. 22. Wir gehen in den Garten, trinken etwas und sprechen über dies und das.

B. Re-do A, putting the verbs into the past perfect tense.

V. Translation Exercise

(Use the present perfect where English has the past)

1. A girl sat on a bench. 2. She read a newspaper and smoked a cigaret. 3. I saw a quiz in it. 4. Herbert read the questions. 5. Buxtehude wasn't a teacher. 6. Herbert gave me the paper. 7. What did Luther throw? 8. What did Herbert ask the girl? 9. Where had his parents lived? 10. I had taken Herbert by the arm. 11. Then we went home. 12. It had become very late. 13. We slept well (*gut*). 14. We stayed in Germany one year. 15. Herbert had eaten too much and grown too fast. 16. Many things had lain on the tables in our kitchen. 17. A salesman had come to us. 18. We went home by trolley. 19. Yesterday we met the girls downtown. 20. They were standing and talking, and we had been waiting for them. 21. In the afternoon I worked, but at night (*nachts*) I slept. 22. In the winter it was not warm, but cold. 23. What did Monika report yesterday? 24. Who interrupted her? 25. We have bought an easy chair for Mrs. Löwenzahn.

VI. Fragen

1. Wohin gehen viele Leute nachmittags? 2. Wo sitzen sie im Sommer? 3. Und im Winter? 4. Wen treffen die Studenten heute? 5. Wo treffen sie sie? 6. Was haben sie gekauft? 7. Und was haben sie bestellt? 8. Warum haben sie nicht sofort gegessen? 9. Warum sind die Mädchen wieder spät gekommen? 10. Wen hat man gerufen? 11. Was ist mit dem Volkswagen geschehen? 12. Womit sind die Mädchen zum Café gefahren?

VII. Lesestück

Die Schweiz

In drei Ländern spricht man die deutsche Sprache: in Deutschland, in Österreich und in der Schweiz. In Deutschland und Österreich sprechen alle Leute deutsch. In dem Lande zwischen Deutschland, Frankreich, Italien und Österreich sprechen nur dreiviertel der Schweizer deutsch, die anderen sprechen französisch oder italienisch.

Im deutschen Teil der Schweiz finden wir einen Unterschied zwischen geschriebener und gesprochener Sprache. Die geschriebene Sprache ist die gleiche, die man in Deutschland und Österreich braucht; die gesprochene Sprache in der Schweiz ist verschieden. Es ist ein Dialekt, das sog. „Schwyzerdütsch." Alle Schweizer im deutschen Teil des Landes verstehen Hochdeutsch, sie lesen auch hochdeutsche Bücher und Zeitungen, aber sie sprechen ihr Schwyzerdütsch. Es gibt in der Schweiz viele Leute, die mehr als eine Sprache fließend sprechen. Sie wissen, daß es sehr wichtig ist, viele Sprachen zu lernen.

Im Mittelalter war die Schweiz ein Teil des Deutschen Reiches. Die Trennung begann im 14. (vierzehnten) Jahrhundert, aber erst in der Mitte des 17. (siebzehnten) Jahrhunderts wurde die Schweiz ein selbständiger Staat. In früheren Jahrhunderten waren die Schweizer berühmt als die besten Soldaten in ganz Europa. Bis heute hat der Papst in Rom eine Garde von Schweizer Soldaten. Die Schweiz aber ist seit 1815 (achtzehnhundertfünfzehn) ein neutrales Land. Seit der Zeit von Napoleon sind die Schweizer in allen Kriegen neutral geblieben.

Es hat in der Schweizer Geschichte nie einen Kaiser oder König gegeben. Die Schweiz ist heute die älteste Republik Europas. In der Verfassung des Landes findet man viele Ähnlichkeiten mit der Verfassung der Vereinigten Staaten.

Die Schweiz ist ein Bundesstaat. In unserem Lande haben wir 48 (achtundvierzig) Staaten, in der Schweiz gibt es 22 (zweiundzwanzig) Kantone. Hier sind ein paar Namen von Schweizer Kantonen: Uri, Glarus, Aargau, Luzern, Basel, Graubünden, Genf. Jeder Kanton hat eine Hauptstadt. Bern ist die Hauptstadt des Kantons Bern und die Hauptstadt des ganzen Landes. Von dem Kanton Schwyz hat das ganze Land seinen Namen und seine Fahne genommen: ein weißes Kreuz in einem roten Feld.

Eine berühmte internationale Organisation wurde von dem Schweizer Henri Dunant gegründet. Diese Organisation brauchte die Schweizer Farben für ihre Fahne: ein rotes Kreuz in einem weißen Feld. Es gibt heute gewiß nicht viele Leute auf der Welt, die noch nie vom Roten Kreuz gehört haben.

VIII. Wörterverzeichnis

die Ähnlichkeit, –en the similarity
als as
die älteste the oldest
die anderen the others
beginnen; begann; begonnen (to) begin; began; begun
die besten the best
der Bundesstaat, –en the federated state
das Deutsche Reich the German Empire
der Dialekt, –e the dialect
dreiviertel three-quarters
erst only, not until
die Fahne, –n the flag
das Feld, –er the field
fließend fluently
Frankreich France
französisch French
früher former
die Garde, –n the guard
wurde . . . gegründet was . . . founded
das gleiche the same
die Hauptstadt, ⸚e the capital
Hochdeutsch High German
Italien Italy
italienisch Italian
das Jahrhundert, –e the century
der Kaiser, – the emperor
der Kanton, –e the canton
der König, –e the king
das Kreuz, –e the cross
der Krieg, –e the war
mehr more
das Mittelalter the Middle Ages
der Name, (–ns), –n the name
neutral neutral
oder or
die Organisation, –en the organization
Österreich Austria
der Papst, ⸚e the Pope
die Schweiz Switzerland
der Schweizer, – the Swiss
Schwyzerdütsch Swiss German
seit since, for
selbständig independent

sogenannt, *abbr.* **sog.** so-called
der Soldat, (–en), –en the soldier
der Staat, –en the state
der Teil, –e the part
die Trennung, –en the separation
der Unterschied, –e the difference
die Verfassung, –en the constitution
verschieden different
verstehen; verstand; verstanden (to) understand; understood; understood
die Welt the world
wichtig important
wissen (to) know

Aufgabe Zehn

MODAL AUXILIARIES IN THE PRESENT AND PAST

I. Reading Selection

Wir blieben mit den Mädchen bis fünf Uhr im Café. Dann machten wir einen Spaziergang durch den Park und kamen zum Zoologischen Garten.

„Sollen wir in den Zoo gehen?" fragte Herbert.

„Ich muß um sieben Uhr zu Hause sein", sagte Monika. „Haben wir genug Zeit?"

„Gewiß", sagte ich. „In einer Stunde können wir viel sehen."

Vor dem Käfig mit dem Affen stand eine Frau mit ihrem Sohn. Der Junge war vielleicht zehn Jahre alt. Er warf mit einem Stein nach dem Affen. Ein Mann kam und sagte: „Du darfst nicht nach den Tieren werfen." Der Junge sagte: „Der Affe soll etwas tun. Er sitzt da und tut nichts."

Der Affe beachtete weder die Mutter noch den Sohn. Er saß still in einer Ecke, sah in die Luft und fraß eine Banane.

Wir gingen durch den Zoo und sahen Elefanten, Tiger und Löwen. Wir kamen dann an einen Teich. Herbert las laut: „Man soll die Tiere nicht füttern!" In dem Wasser schwamm ein Walroß.

Herbert und ich mußten lachen.

„Warum lachen Sie?" fragte Vera Sütterlin.

„Das Walroß gleicht Herrn Löwenzahn", sagte ich.

„Sie sind nicht sehr höflich", meinte Monika.

„Ich wollte nicht unhöflich sein“, sagte ich. „Ich mag Herrn Löwenzahn. Ich mag auch das Walroß.“

„Ich wollte Sie und Herbert immer etwas fragen“, sagte Monika. „Sie beide sind achtzehn Jahre alt. Da soll man in Deutschland die Sie-Form brauchen. Warum sprechen die Löwenzahns zu Ihnen in der Du-Form?“

„Ich will es Ihnen erklären“, antwortete Herbert. „Nur unser Lehrer und die Löwenzahns sprechen zu uns in der Du-Form. Wir wollen die Du-Form üben. Nach drei Monaten und nach Aufgabe vierzehn sprechen sie alle in der Sie-Form zu uns.“

Wir waren wieder zu dem Käfig mit dem Affen gekommen. Der Affe fraß jetzt eine Tomate. Sie war groß, rot und sehr reif. Der Junge stand noch vor dem Käfig und rief: „Er soll etwas tun! Komm aus deiner Ecke! Ich will dich sehen.“

„Darf man zu einem Affen ‚du‘ sagen?“ fragte ich Monika.

„Nein“, antwortete sie. „Vor Darwin durfte man es. Jetzt muß man ‚Sie‘ sagen.“

Wieder warf der Junge einen Stein in den Käfig. Plötzlich nahm der Affe die Tomate und warf sie schnell nach dem Jungen. Sie traf ihn auf den Kopf. Er schrie laut.

„Sagtest du nicht, er sollte etwas tun?“ fragte seine Mutter.

II. Vocabulary

NOTE: In this lesson, new meanings are used for three words: **da,** *then, in that case;* **meinen,** (*to*) *say;* **treffen,** (*to*) *hit*. Such meanings will be given in the end vocabulary.

achtzehn eighteen
der Affe, (–n), –n the ape, monkey
die Banane, –n the banana
beachten (to) notice, pay attention to
***beide** (*plu.*) both
***dürfen (darf), durfte, gedurft** (to) be permitted; may
der Elefant, (–en), –en the elephant
***erklären** (to) explain, declare
fressen (i), fraß, gefressen (to) eat (*used of animals*)
füttern (to) feed
gleichen, glich, geglichen (*takes dative*) (to) resemble, be like
***der Junge, (–n), –n** the boy

der Käfig, –e the cage
***können (kann), konnte, gekonnt** (to) be able; can
***laut** loud
der Löwe, (–n), –n the lion
***mögen (mag), mochte, gemocht** (to) like; may
***der Monat, –e** the month
***müssen (muß), mußte, gemußt** (to) have to; must
***die Mutter, ⸚** the mother
reif ripe
***schreien, schrie, geschrieen** (to) cry, shout
***schwimmen, schwamm, ist geschwommen** (to) swim
***der Sohn, ⸚e** the son
***sollen (soll), sollte, gesollt** (to) be to, ought to; shall, should
***der Spaziergang, ⸚e** the walk
***der Stein, –e** the stone
der Teich, –e the pond
***das Tier, –e** the animal
der Tiger, – the tiger
die Tomate, –n the tomato
***tun, tat, getan** (to) do
unhöflich impolite, discourteous
***vielleicht** perhaps
vierzehn fourteen
das Walroß, Walrosse the walrus
***das Wasser** the water
***weder . . . noch** neither . . . nor
***wollen (will), wollte, gewollt** (to) want to, wish to, will
***zehn** ten
***die Zeit, –en** the time
der Zoo, –s (*abbreviation*) the zoo
***der Zoologische Garten** the zoological garden

IDIOMS

***einen Spaziergang machen** (to) take a walk
***zu Hause** home (*only in the sense of* at home)

III. Grammar

MODAL AUXILIARIES

In German, as in English, there are several verbs which are called "modal auxiliaries." They do not express (as other verbs do) an "activity," but indicate the manner or mode in which the "activity" is undertaken. Normally a modal auxiliary is accompanied by the infinitive of another verb which conveys the action.

The decisive difference between English and German modals is the fact that the German modals are full-fledged verbs, capable of forming all the tenses. The English modals, however, are defective, i.e., they offer only a few of the tenses and have to be replaced by circumlocutions in the missing forms. Thus, the modal *must* exists only in the present tense (I must, etc.) while all other tenses have to be replaced by the respective forms as *to have to*. In German, the modal **müssen** has an infinitive and all possible tense forms.

A. Meaning of the Modals

German has six modal auxiliaries: **müssen, können, dürfen, wollen, sollen, mögen.** In the following we give you a list of these verbs together with their basic meanings and the way they can usually be translated:

müssen *to have to, must.* Its basic meaning is **physical necessity.** Note that **nicht müssen** means *don't have to.*

können *to be able to, can.* Its basic meaning is **physical ability.**

dürfen *may, to be permitted to.* Its basic meaning is **permission.** In English *must not* is used to render the idea "ought not to, is not permitted to." In this case German uses the modal **nicht dürfen. Du darfst hier nicht rauchen,** *you must not smoke here.*

wollen *wish to, want to.* Its basic meaning is **volition** or **intention.**

sollen *shall* (not future!), *be supposed to, be to, be said to; ought to, should.* Its basic meaning is **moral obligation.** The present tense is rather forceful and corresponds to "Thou *shalt* not steal!" or to "You *are to* go home!" In its past tense it is weaker and more polite, e.g., "You *should* do that" or "You really *ought to* see this."

mögen *may* (not permission!), *like.* Its basic meaning is **inclination.** The past tense **mochte** means *might* when it refers to past time, e.g., "he *might* have been walking an hour." The most prevalent use of this verb is in the form **möchte** which means *would* or *should like* (*to*), e.g., **ich möchte ein Glas Limonade,** *I'd like a glass of lemonade,* or **ich möchte nach Hause gehen,** *I'd like to go home.* **Mögen** (without an infinitive) is often used as a verb for the English (*to*) *like:* **ich mag ihn nicht,** *I don't like him.*

B. Present Tense of the Modals

The present tense of the modal auxiliaries is as follows:

INFINITIVE	müssen	können	dürfen	wollen	sollen	mögen
1. ich	muß	kann	darf	will	soll	mag
2. du	mußt	kannst	darfst	willst	sollst	magst
3. er	muß	kann	darf	will	soll	mag
1. wir	müssen	können	dürfen	wollen	sollen	mögen
2. ihr	müßt	könnt	dürft	wollt	sollt	mögt
3. sie	müssen	können	dürfen	wollen	sollen	mögen

Note that they have no endings in the first and third singular and that all plural forms are perfectly regular.

C. Past Tense of the Modals

The past tense is formed in the usual way from the second principal part and will resemble the past tense of any weak verb. Those modals which have an umlaut in the infinitive drop it in the past tense. Here are the second principal parts (past tenses) of our modals: **mußte, konnte, durfte, wollte, sollte, mochte.**

D. The Infinitive Connected with the Modals

As in English, **never use *zu* with an infinitive depending on a modal auxiliary.** Whether we say in English "I **must** go" or "I **have to** go," German says "ich muß **gehen.**" Watch out particularly when the English sentence tends to lead you astray with a *to* plus infinitive; this *to* is not translated in German whenever an infinitive combines with a modal auxiliary.

German is apt to omit an infinitive after a modal if the sense is perfectly clear without it. This corresponds to the colloquial English "The dog wants out" from which the infinitive *to go* has been omitted. Thus, German will say the following: a) **Vor Darwin konnte man es;** b) **Er will mit;** c) **Mußt du schon**

nach Hause? d) **Ich kann es.** In these cases the infinitives **sagen, kommen, gehen,** and **tun** respectively have been omitted.

The infinitive is normally placed at the very end of its clause. We use the phrase "very end" because we have previously said that past participles come at the end of their clauses. If we remember that the past participles stand at the end of the clause, but infinitives at the very end of the clause, we will be all right. Note that in **er mochte eine Stunde gegangen sein,** *he might have been wandering an hour,* the infinitive gets the favored position at the end of the clause while the past participle has to be content with second best.

IV. Grammatical Exercises

A. Supply the proper present tense of the verb in parentheses:

1. Du (sollen) etwas tun. 2. Er (dürfen) mit den Mädchen bis fünf Uhr bleiben. 3. Ich (wollen) einen Spaziergang machen. 4. Das (mögen) ich nicht. 5. In einer Stunde (können) der Student nicht viel sehen. 6. Er (müssen) sein Haus verkaufen. 7. Der Junge (wollen) mit einem Stein nach dem Affen werfen. 8. Das (dürfen) du nicht. 9. Der Junge (können) die Tiere füttern, aber er (sollen) es nicht. 10. Der Student (wollen) nicht unhöflich sein, aber er (müssen) in einer halben Stunde zu Hause sein.

B. Re-do A, putting all the subjects and verbs into the plural by changing 1st person singular to 1st person plural, etc.

C. Re-do A, putting all the verbs into the past tense.

D. Translate the words in parentheses:

1. Sie (doesn't have to) so bald nach Hause gehen. 2. Sie (is to) noch eine halbe Stunde hier bleiben. 3. Er (can) nicht lauter rufen. 4. Man (mustn't) hier rauchen. 5. (You may) die Zeitung lesen (*three forms*). 6. (Are you able to) dieses

Deutsch lesen? (*three forms*). 7. Ich (must) jetzt in die Schule gehen. 8. Er (wants to) mit. 9. Das Mädchen (likes) diese Geschichte nicht.

E. Re-do D, putting the verbs in the past tense.

V. Translation Exercise

1. Conrad can have a room with this family. 2. He is not permitted to smoke in the dining room. 3. That he must not do. 4. He is to go to bed every evening at ten o'clock. 5. He doesn't have to eat with the family. 6. He does want to talk German with them. 7. He is not able to talk it very well. 8. He has to work very hard. 9. Perhaps he doesn't like that. 10. He does not want to laugh but he has to. 11. She does not like to stay at home. 12. I am supposed to tell the story in German.

B. Re-do the above twelve sentences in the past tense.

VI. Fragen

1. Bis wann sind die Studenten mit den Mädchen im Café? 2. Wohin sind sie danach gegangen? 3. Wann muß Monika zu Hause sein? 4. Wer hat vor dem Käfig mit dem Affen gestanden? 5. Wie alt war der Junge? 6. Womit hat er nach dem Affen geworfen? 7. Was hat ein Mann zu ihm gesagt? 8. Warum hat der Junge Steine geworfen? 9. Warum mußten die Studenten lachen? 10. Was hat der Affe am Ende der Geschichte getan?

VII. Lesestück

Wilhelm Tell schießt zwei Pfeile

Am Anfang der Schweizer Geschichte steht die Figur von Wilhelm Tell. Damals gehörte das Land um den Vierwaldstättersee den Herzögen von Österreich. Der Landvogt Geßler herrschte für den Herzog. Geßler war ein Tyrann, der die Schweizer grausam unterdrückte. Sie alle hofften auf das Ende seiner Herrschaft.

Eines Tages sagte der Landvogt zu seinen Soldaten: „Stellt eine Stange auf die Straße in der Mitte der Stadt Altdorf und hängt meinen Hut darauf. Jeder Schweizer, der den Hut sieht, muß ihn grüßen. Wenn der Mann den Hut nicht grüßen will, werft ihn ins Gefängnis."

An diesem Tage kam Wilhelm Tell mit seinem jungen Sohn in die Stadt. Er sah die Stange und den Hut, aber er tat nichts.

„Halt!" riefen die Soldaten. „Willst du den Hut des Landvogts nicht grüßen?"

„Nein", sagte Tell. „Ich bin ein freier Mann, ich grüße weder den Landvogt noch seinen Hut."

In diesem Augenblick kam Geßler selbst, und die Soldaten erzählten ihm, was geschehen war.

„Ich kann dich ins Gefängnis werfen, ich kann dich für deinen Ungehorsam töten", sagte Geßler zu Tell. Er sah, daß ein Junge neben Tell stand, und fragte: „Ist dies dein Sohn?"

„Ja", antwortete Tell und legte seinen Arm um den Jungen, „dies ist mein Sohn."

„Ich habe gehört, daß du als guter Schütze berühmt bist. Du sollst uns zeigen, ob du schießen kannst. Wenn du diesen Apfel vom Kopf deines Sohnes schießen kannst, darfst du dein Leben behalten."

Wilhelm Tell zeigte ihm, daß er ein guter Schütze war. Der Pfeil traf den Apfel auf dem Kopf des Jungen. Tell glaubte, er wäre jetzt ein freier Mann und wollte gehen.

„Halt!", rief Geßler. „Ich sah, du nahmst zwei Pfeile in die Hand, bevor du den Apfel schossest. Was wolltest du mit dem zweiten Pfeil?"

„Der zweite Pfeil war für dich", sagte Tell. „Wenn ich meinen Jungen getroffen hätte, würdest du jetzt nicht mehr leben."

„Werft ihn ins Gefängnis", befahl Geßler seinen Soldaten. „Ich habe ihm sein Leben versprochen, aber nicht seine Freiheit."

Aber Wilhelm Tell entkam. Auf einer engen Straße im Wald wartete er auf den Landvogt, und nun schoß er den zweiten Pfeil. Er traf den Tyrannen mitten ins Herz.

Dies war der Anfang der Schweizer Freiheit.

VIII. Wörterverzeichnis

der Anfang, ⸚e the beginning
der Apfel, ⸚ the apple
der Augenblick, –e the moment
befehlen (ie), befahl, befohlen (*with dat.*) (to) command
behalten (ä), behielt, behalten (to) keep
bevor before
damals then
daß that
eng narrow
entkommen, entkam, ist entkommen (to) escape
die Figur, –en the figure
frei free
die Freiheit the freedom
das Gefängnis, –se the jail
gehören (*with dat.*) (to) belong to
grausam cruelly
grüßen (to) greet
Halt! Halt!
hängen (to) hang
ich hätte (*subjunctive*) I would have
die Herrschaft the rule, dominion
herrschen (to) rule
das Herz, (–ens), –en the heart
der Herzog, ⸚e the duke
der Hut, ⸚e the hat
der Landvogt, ⸚e the governor
legen (to) place
mitten in in the middle of
nicht mehr no longer
ob if, whether
Österreich Austria
der Pfeil, –e the arrow
schießen, schoß, geschossen (to) shoot
der Schütze, –n the marksman, shot
der Schweizer, – the Swiss (**Schweizer** *is also used as adjective*)
der Soldat, (–en), –en the soldier
die Stange, –n the pole
eines Tages one day
töten (to) kill
treffen (trifft), traf, getroffen (to) hit
der Tyrann, (–en), –en the tyrant
der Ungehorsam the disobedience
unterdrücken (to) oppress
versprechen (i), versprach, versprochen (to) promise
der Vierwaldstättersee Lake Lucerne
er wäre (*subjunctive*) he would be
wenn if
Wilhelm William
du würdest you would
der zweite the second

Aufgabe Elf

FUTURE TENSES • ADVERBS IRREGULAR WEAK VERBS

I. Reading Selection

Wir saßen mit den Löwenzahns im Garten hinter dem Haus.

„In ein paar Wochen werdet ihr Ferien haben", sagte Frau Löwenzahn. „Was werdet ihr dann tun? Wollt ihr hier bleiben oder eine Reise machen?"

„Wir werden eine Radtour durch das Rheinland machen", antwortete Herbert. „Wir wollen von Mainz bis Köln mit dem Rad fahren."

„Ihr werdet eine schöne Landschaft sehen", sagte Herr Löwenzahn. „Dort wächst der beste Wein in Deutschland."

Frau Löwenzahn lächelte. „Daran denkt unser Papa immer zuerst", meinte sie.

„Du weißt", sagte er, „der Wein ist sehr wichtig für die Ausfuhr unseres Landes."

„Natürlich", sagte seine Frau, „nur daran hast du gedacht. Doch es ist richtig: das Rheinland ist ein Weinland. Dort brennt die Sonne bis spät im Herbst heiß auf die Berge. Davon wird der Wein so gut. Werdet ihr auch zur Loreley gehen?"

„Wer ist die Loreley?" fragte ich.

„Conrad!" rief Herbert. „Willst du sagen, du kennst die Geschichte von der Loreley nicht?"

„Ich kenne ein Restaurant Loreley in Philadelphia", antwortete ich.

„Die Loreley war eine sehr schöne Frau. Sie saß auf einem Berg über dem Rhein, kämmte ihr Haar, sang und brachte die Schiffer auf dem Rhein in Gefahr. Sie dachten nur an die Frau und nicht an die Felsen im Wasser. Später hat man den Berg Loreley genannt."

„Die Geschichte ist sehr traurig", sagte ich. „Vielleicht werden auch wir die Loreley sehen. Ich hoffe, sie wird dann nicht singen und dich in Gefahr bringen."

„Ihr dürft nicht die ganze Reise mit dem Rad machen", sagte Frau Löwenzahn. „Von Rüdesheim bis Koblenz müßt ihr mit einem Dampfer fahren. In Koblenz kenne ich eine Familie. Dort könnt ihr über Nacht bleiben. Morgen werde ich an die Leute schreiben und ihnen von euch erzählen."

Herr Löwenzahn war ins Haus gegangen. Jetzt kam er zurück. Er trug eine Flasche Wein und zwei Gläser. „Ihr habt zu viel vom Rhein und vom Wein gesprochen", meinte er. „Das hat mich durstig gemacht." Er goß Wein in ein Glas und gab es seiner Frau. „Prost, Mutter!"

„Prost", antwortete sie. „Ich dachte, der Wein ist für die Ausfuhr unseres Landes. Darum sollten wir ihn nicht trinken."

„Gewiß", sagte Herr Löwenzahn. „Das ist alles richtig, aber dies hier nennt man den inneren Markt."

II. Vocabulary

die Ausfuhr the export, foreign trade
der beste the best
***brennen, brannte, gebrannt** (to) burn
***bringen, brachte, gebracht** (to) bring
der Dampfer, – the steamer
***darum** therefore, for this reason
***denken, dachte, gedacht (an** *with acc.*) (to) think (of)
***doch** yet, still; but, however; really
***dort** there
***durstig** thirsty
***elf** eleven
der Felsen, – the rock
***die Ferien** (*plu.*) vacation

***die Gefahr, –en** the danger
***heiß** hot
***der Herbst, –e** the fall, autumn
der innere Markt the domestic market, local consumption
kämmen (to) comb
***kennen, kannte, gekannt** (to) know, be acquainted with
***die Landschaft, –en** the scenery, landscape
***natürlich** naturally, of course
***nennen, nannte, genannt** (to) name, call
der Papa, –s papa
***Prost** (*abbreviation of Latin* **prosit**) Here's to your health!
***das Rad, ⸚er** the wheel, bicycle
die Radtour, –en the bicycle tour
***die Reise, –n** the trip
***das Restaurant, –s** the restaurant
***der Rhein** the Rhine (River)
***das Rheinland** the Rhineland
der Schiffer, – the boatman
***die Sonne** the sun
***später** later
über Nacht bleiben (to) stay overnight
das Weinland, ⸚er the wine country
***wichtig** important
***wissen (weiß), wußte, gewußt** (to) know (*facts*)
***die Woche, –n** the week
***zuerst** first

IDIOMS

***eine Reise machen** (to) take a trip
***fahren mit** (to) travel by *or* with, e.g., **man fährt mit dem Rad, mit dem Auto, mit dem Dampfer, mit der Straßenbahn.**

III. Grammar

A. THE FUTURE TENSE

1. The future tense in English is formed by using an auxiliary (*shall* or *will*) plus the infinitive: I shall go home, you will go home, etc. German forms its future tense the same way—by using as an auxiliary the present tense of **werden** plus the infinitive:

1. **ich werde** nach Hause **gehen**
2. **du wirst** nach Hause **gehen**
3. **er wird** nach Hause **gehen**

1. **wir werden** nach Hause **gehen**
2. **ihr werdet** nach Hause **gehen**
3. **sie werden** nach Hause **gehen**

Again the infinitive goes to the very end of the clause, as explained in Lesson X, Section III. D.

2. In English we use occasionally the present tense instead of the more formal-sounding future tense: "There's a dance tonight," "I'm taking a trip tomorrow," and so forth. In German, this usage is much more frequent. Thus our examples in German would be: **Heute abend gibt's einen Tanz** and **Ich mache morgen eine Reise.** Whenever an adverbial phrase contains a future time element (such as **heute abend, morgen, in ein paar Wochen,** etc.), you may in such a sentence use the future or simply the present tense.

3. German also has the so-called future perfect tense. Its forms resemble closely the corresponding forms in English, the only difference being in the word order. One comforting feature the two languages have in common is that they use the future perfect tense very seldom. Here are two examples: **ich werde das Buch gelesen haben** (*I shall have read the book*); **er wird in die Stadt gegangen sein** (*he will have gone into the city*).

B. Irregular Weak Verbs

There are several verbs in German which are weak (or suffix) verbs, but which in the infinitive have a vowel different from the vowel in the two last principal parts. Once you know their principal parts, there are no irregularities in their conjugation: they will form the present tense from the infinitive and their past tense from the second principal part. The conjugational endings are the same as for any other weak verb.

The list of these verbs (used actively so far) is as follows:

bringen	**brachte**	**gebracht**	(to) bring
denken	**dachte**	**gedacht**	(to) think
brennen	**brannte**	**gebrannt**	(to) burn
kennen	**kannte**	**gekannt**	(to) know, be acquainted with
nennen	**nannte**	**genannt**	(to) name, call
wissen	**wußte**	**gewußt**	(to) know a fact

[There are three other verbs in this group which we have not used so far: rennen—rannte—gerannt, (*to*) *run;* senden—

sandte—gesandt, (*to*) *send;* and wenden—wandte—gewandt, (*to*) *turn.*]

C. **Wissen, Kennen, Können**

All three (**wissen, kennen, können**) may stand for the English verb (*to*) *know*. **Wissen** means *to know* in the sense of *factual knowledge*. **Kennen** means *to know* in the sense of *to be acquainted with* someone or something. **Können** is used idiomatically as *to know a language*. Examples: **Wissen Sie, wo er wohnt? Kennen Sie seine Mutter? Können Sie Deutsch?**

Wissen is irregular in the present tense singular: **ich weiß, du weißt, er weiß;** the plural is regular.

D. GERMAN ADVERBS

Most adjectives can be used as adverbs. In German, the uninflected form of the adjective and the adverb are identical: Der Lehrer ist gut; er schläft gut. Dieser Wein ist schlecht; wir spielten heute sehr schlecht. Das Mädchen ist sehr schön; es singt auch sehr schön.

Notice that if we translate these adjective-adverb couplets into English, we generally have to add *–ly* in case the word is an adverb. However, **in German adverbs have no endings.**

In our vocabularies, we normally list the English adjective form. You may have to add *–ly* when it is used as an adverb. Thus, **schlecht** *means bad* or *badly,* **schön** *beautiful* or *beautifully;* **gut** means *good* or *well.*

IV. Grammatical Exercises

A. Put the following sentences into the future tense:

1. Wir sitzen im Garten hinter dem Haus. 2. Ich mache eine Reise durch das Rheinland. 3. Dort findet man guten Wein. 4. Er wächst gut, denn die Sonne brennt heiß auf die Berge. 5.

Dann wird der Wein gut. 6. Woran denkt Papa Löwenzahn zuerst? 7. Was weiß er? 8. Wofür ist der Wein sehr wichtig? 9. Die Frau sitzt auf einem Berg. 10. Sie kämmt ihr Haar. 11. Sie singt sehr schön. 12. Damit bringt sie die Schiffer in Gefahr. 13. Dort kannst du über Nacht bleiben (*when you change* **kannst** *into the infinitive, just put it at the end, as you have been doing*). 14. Machst du die ganze Reise mit dem Rad? 15. Herr Löwenzahn ist nicht hier. 16. Er geht ins Haus. 17. Dann kommt er wieder. 18. Er trägt eine Flasche Wein. 19. Die Geschichte macht ihn durstig. 20. Er gießt Wein in ein Glas. 21. Er gibt seiner Frau das Glas. 22. Dann sagt man „Prost" und trinkt.

B. Put the sentences in A into the past tense.

C. Put the sentences in A (except number 13) into the present perfect tense.

D. Put the sentences in A (except number 13) into the past perfect tense.

E. Supply the proper present-tense form for the verb in parentheses:

1. Was (bringen) Herr Löwenzahn? 2. Er (denken) zuerst an den Wein. 3. (Kennen) Sie das Rheinland? 4. Dort (brennen) die Sonne sehr heiß. 5. Wie (nennen) man diesen Berg am Rhein? 6. Das (wissen) er so gut wie ich. 7. (Können) du Deutsch?

F. Re-do E, putting the sentences into the future tense.

G. Re-do E, putting the sentences into the past tense.

H. Re-do E, putting the verbs into the present perfect tense.

I. Re-do E, putting the verbs into the past perfect tense.

V. Translation Exercise

1. I know this garden behind the house. 2. Naturally the scenery in the Rhineland will be very beautiful. 3. In the summer the sun will burn very hot on the mountains. 4. That will be good for the wine. 5. It will really get very hot. 6. Are you going to take a trip by bicycle? 7. What do you know about the Loreley? 8. You knew the story about her, didn't you? 9. He knows where he is going (to). 10. He is thinking of a trip through the Rhineland. 11. Later they named this mountain the Loreley. 12. The men thought only of her, for she sang so beautifully. 13. Therefore she brought them into danger. 14. In this summer the sun was burning hot in the Rhineland. 15. They will not think of her again. 16. We will have our vacation in a couple of days. 17. We get very thirsty and go into a restaurant.

VI. Fragen

1. Wo sitzen die Studenten? 2. Mit wem sitzen sie? 3. Wessen Garten ist das? 4. Was haben die Studenten bald? 5. Wohin wollen sie gehen? 6. Wie ist die Landschaft am Rhein? 7. Was wächst dort auf den Bergen? 8. Warum wird der Wein so gut im Rheinland? 9. Wer ist die Loreley? 10. Wo hat sie gesessen? 11. Was hat sie dort getan? 12. Woran haben die Schiffer gedacht? 13. Womit werden unsere Studenten von Rüdesheim bis Koblenz fahren? 14. Wo werden sie über Nacht bleiben? 15. Was wird Frau Löwenzahn tun?

VII. Lesestück

Basel

Basel liegt an der nördlichen Grenze der Schweiz. Hier kommen die Grenzen von drei Ländern zusammen, von Deutschland, Frankreich und der Schweiz. Vom Marktplatz der Stadt kann man in einer halben Stunde mit der Straßenbahn nach Frankreich oder nach Deutschland fahren.

Basel war im Mittelalter eine sehr berühmte Stadt. Noch in unserer Zeit gibt es hier viele Häuser, die 300 (dreihundert) oder 400 (vierhundert) Jahre alt sind. Auf einem Felsen über dem Rhein steht eine schöne, alte Kirche, das Münster. Von dem Platz hinter dem Münster hat man eine wunderbare Aussicht über die Stadt, den Fluß und die Schwarzwaldberge. Viele berühmte Männer haben in Basel gewohnt, z.B. die Maler Conrad Witz, Albrecht Dürer und Hans Holbein und der größte Gelehrte des 16. (sechzehnten) Jahrhunderts, Erasmus von Rotterdam.

Seit dem Mittelalter ist Basel eine wichtige europäische Handelsstadt gewesen. Hier kreuzten sich zwei große europäische Handelswege, von Osten nach Westen und von Süden nach Norden. Darum wurde Basel auch eine wichtige Industriestadt. Im 16. (sechzehnten) Jahrhundert war Basel bekannt als die Stadt der Buchdrucker, im 19. (neunzehnten) Jahrhundert wurde die Seidenindustrie sehr wichtig, und in unserer Zeit ist die Stadt berühmt als ein Zentrum der chemischen Industrie. Auch in den Vereinigten Staaten kennen wir die Produkte der Ciba. CIBA ist nur eine Abkürzung für C hemische I ndustrie B a sel. Durch den Rhein hat Basel eine gute Wasserverbindung mit dem Atlantischen Ozean.

Der Rhein fließt durch die Mitte der Stadt. Auf fünf Brücken kann man über den Fluß gehen. Wenn man viel Zeit hat, kann man auch mit der Fähre über den Rhein fahren. Dann erzählt der Fährmann vielleicht eine Geschichte. Man nennt diese Geschichten in der Schweiz „Baseler Fährmannsgeschichten.“ Hier ist eine der berühmten Geschichten, die der Fährmann auf dem Rhein erzählt.

Eine Baseler Fährmannsgeschichte

In der Gerbergasse in Basel steht noch heute ein altes Haus, das im Mittelalter plötzlich berühmt wurde. Dort geschah es im Jahre 1479 (vierzehnhundertneunundsiebzig), daß ein Hahn ein Ei legte. Wenn ein Hahn ein Ei legt—so glaubte man im Mittelalter—dann wird aus diesem Ei ein großes Ungetüm kommen, das allen Leuten Tod und Verderben bringt. Darum wurde der Hahn vor Gericht gestellt und wegen Hexerei zum Tode verurteilt. Das Ei wurde verbrannt und der Hahn wurde öffentlich enthauptet. So wurde die Stadt Basel gerettet.

VIII. Wörterverzeichnis

die **Abkürzung, –en** the abbreviation
der **Atlantische Ozean** the Atlantic Ocean
die **Aussicht über** the view of
bekannt known
die **Brücke, –n** the bridge
der **Buchdrucker, –** the book printer
chemisch chemical
daß that
ein Ei legen (to) lay an egg
enthaupten (to) behead
europäisch European
die **Fähre, –n** the ferry
der **Fährmann** the ferryman
die **Fährmannsgeschichte, –n** the ferryman's tale
der **Felsen, –** the cliff
fließen, floß, ist geflossen (to) flow
der **Fluß, Flüsse** the river
Frankreich France
der **Gelehrte, (–n), –n** the scholar
die **Gerbergasse** Gerber St., Tanner St.
vor Gericht before the court
die **Grenze, –n** the border
der **größte** the greatest
der **Hahn, ⸚e** the rooster
halb half
die **Handelsstadt, ⸚e** the commercial city
der **Handelsweg, –e** the trade route
die **Hexerei** the witchcraft
die **Industrie** industry
die **Industriestadt, ⸚e** the industrial city
das **Jahrhundert, –e** the century
sich kreuzen (to) cross
der **Maler, –** the painter
der **Marktplatz, ⸚e** the market place
das **Mittelalter** the Middle Ages
das **Münster, –** the minster, cathedral
der **Norden** the north
nördlich northern
öffentlich public
der **Osten** the east
der **Platz, ⸚e** the square
das **Produkt, –e** the product
retten (to) save
die **Schwarzwaldberge** the Black Forest Mountains
die **Schweiz** Switzerland
die **Seidenindustrie** the silk industry
der **Süden** the south
der **Tod** the death

zum Tode verurteilt condemned to death
das Ungetüm, –e the monster
verbrennen, verbrannte, verbrannt (to) burn
das Verderben the destruction, ruin
die Wasserverbindung, –en the water connection
wegen on account of
wenn if
der Westen the west
wunderbar wonderful
z.B.; zum Beispiel e.g., for example
das Zentrum the center
zusammen together

Aufgabe Zwölf

CONJUNCTIONS
DEPENDENT CLAUSES

I. Reading Selection

Am Sonntag haben Herbert und ich eine Reise nach Frankfurt gemacht. Da wir so viel von der Stadt gehört hatten, wollten wir sie einmal sehen. Obgleich es vormittags regnete, wurde es später ein sehr schöner Tag. Am Bahnhof kauften wir einen Führer, um darin zu lesen, was man über Frankfurt wissen muß. Dann gingen wir durch die Stadt, um alles zu sehen.

Frankfurt war bis vor hundert Jahren eine Freie Reichsstadt. Reichsstädte waren frei, weil sie nicht unter einem Fürsten standen, sondern direkt unter dem Kaiser. In diesen Städten regierte nicht ein Graf oder ein Herzog, sondern die Bürger selbst, d.h. sie wählten einen Bürgermeister und einen Rat. Wenn der Bürgermeister die Räte zu einer Sitzung rief, kamen sie in das Rathaus, um dort über die Geschäfte der Stadt zu sprechen. Das Rathaus in Frankfurt ist sehr berühmt. Wenn ein Kaiser gestorben war, kamen die sieben Kurfürsten des Reiches im Rathaus von Frankfurt zusammen, um den nächsten Kaiser zu wählen. Weil früher hier ein „Gasthaus zum Römer" gestanden hatte, nannte man das Rathaus den „Römer." Nachdem die Kurfürsten gewählt hatten, ging der neue Kaiser auf den Balkon des Rathauses, um sich dem Volk zu zeigen. Alle Leute schrieen „Hurra" oder „Vivat" und zeigten damit dem Kaiser, daß sie mit der Wahl zufrieden waren. Ich weiß nicht, ob sie auch etwas tun konnten, wenn sie den Kaiser nicht mochten. Darüber stand nichts in unserm Führer, obwohl wir zwei Mark dafür gezahlt hatten.

Nicht alles in Frankfurt ist alt. Als wir einen Spaziergang durch die Stadt machten, sahen wir, daß viele Häuser ganz neu und modern sind.

Nachdem wir alles gesehen hatten, gingen wir zum Essen in ein Restaurant. Ehe wir mit der Straßenbahn zum Bahnhof fuhren, schrieben wir eine Ansichtskarte an Herberts Vater. Er hat vor vielen Jahren in Frankfurt an der Universität studiert.

Als wir an diesem Abend nach Hause kamen, waren die Löwenzahns noch im Wohnzimmer. Ehe wir zu Bette gingen, erzählten wir ihnen von Frankfurt, vom Römer und vom Heiligen Römischen Reich.

„Nichts ist geblieben", sagte Herr Löwenzahn, „kein Kurfürst, kein Kaiser, kein Reich."

„Doch das deutsche Verb steht auch heute noch am Ende des Nebensatzes", sagte ich. „Gute Nacht!"

II. Vocabulary

*__als__ when
__die Ansichtskarte, –n__ the picture postcard
*__der Bahnhof, ⸚e__ the railroad station
__der Balkon, –e__ the balcony
__der Bürger, –__ the citizen; *plu.*: citizens, people
__der Bürgermeister, –__ the mayor
*__da__ (*conj.*) since
*__daß__ (*conj.*) that
__direkt__ direct
*__ehe__ before
__Frankfurter__ of Frankfurt (*–er is usually added to names of cities in German to mean pertaining to. Cf.* New Yorker *in English*)
*__frei__ free, independent
__die Freie Reichsstadt__ the Independent Imperial City
*__früher__ formerly
__der Führer, –__ the guide; leader; guide book
__der Fürst, (–en), –en__ the prince (*i.e., a ruling prince*)
__das Gasthaus zum Römer__ the Roman Inn
__die Geschäfte__ (*plu.*) the business
__der Graf, (–en), –en__ the count

*heilig holy
das Heilige Römische Reich the Holy Roman Empire
der Herzog, ⸗e the duke
hundert a hundred
hurra hurrah
der Kaiser, – the emperor
der Kurfürst, (–en), –en the elector
modern modern
***nachdem** after
der nächste the next
der Nebensatz, ⸗e the dependent clause
***neu** new
noch still
***ob** whether, if
***obgleich** although
***obwohl** although
***oder** or
der Rat, ⸗e the council, councillor
***das Rathaus, ⸗er** the city hall
***regieren** (to) reign, rule, govern
***regnen** (to) rain
das Reich, –e the empire, nation
der Römer the Römer (*old city hall of Frankfurt*)
***selbst** even; -self, e.g., himself, herself, etc.
sich himself
die Sitzung, –en the session, meeting
***der Sonntag, –e** Sunday
***sterben (i), starb, ist gestorben** (to) die
***studieren** (to) study
***um . . . zu** in order to
die Universität, –en the university
***der Vater, ⸗** the father
das Verb, –en the verb
vivat (*Latin word*) Long may he live!
***das Volk, ⸗er** the people, folk
***vormittags** mornings, in the morning
die Wahl, –en the choice, selection, election
wählen (to) choose, select, elect
***weil** because
***wenn** when(ever)
***zufrieden** content, satisfied
zusammen together
***zwölf** twelve

IDIOMS

***d.h.** (*abbreviation for* **das heißt**) that is, i.e.
***vor vielen Jahren** (*dat.*) many years ago (**vor** *with time expressions always means* ago: **vor hundert Jahren, vor zwei Monaten, vor vier Wochen**)

III. Grammar

A. MAIN CLAUSES AND DEPENDENT CLAUSES—INTRODUCTORY MATERIAL

1. A **clause** normally consists of a subject, expressed or implied, and a finite verb.

2. A **finite verb** is one that has person and number, i.e., it is inflected. Infinitives and past participles are not finite verbs

since they have neither person (first, second, third) nor number (singular or plural).

3. A **conjunction** is literally a "joining word": it can join together words (Herbert *and* Conrad), phrases (behind the house *or* in the garden), or clauses (He came late *but* we still had time).

4. There are two kinds of **conjunctions: coordinating** and **subordinating.** They are discussed in B and C below.

5. There are also two kinds of clauses: **main clauses** and **dependent clauses.** A main clause can stand alone and will still mean something, while a dependent clause needs something besides itself to complete its meaning. For example: It was hot because the sun was shining. "It was hot" is the main clause—it is meaningful, and could stand alone as a sentence all by itself. On the other hand, "because the sun was shining" is the dependent clause—it is not meaningful by itself but needs something to complete its meaning, and it could not stand alone as a sentence.

B. COORDINATING CONJUNCTIONS

The coordinating conjunctions (most of them known to us from previous lessons) are: **und, aber, sondern, denn, oder. They do not affect the word order of the verbs.**

Let us see how this works out with a few examples:

1. Wir sind in Deutschland. Wir haben ein Zimmer bei einer deutschen Familie.

2. Die Aufgabe ist schwer. Die Geduld des Lehrers ist groß.

3. Wir blieben nicht im Haus. Wir gingen in den Garten.

4. Wir aßen sehr viel. Wir waren sehr hungrig.

5. Gehen die Studenten in die Stadt? Bleiben sie zu Hause?

If we combine the above examples with coordinating conjunctions, we have no change in word order:

1. Wir sind in Deutschland, und wir haben ein Zimmer bei einer deutschen Familie.

2. Die Aufgabe ist schwer, aber die Geduld des Lehrers ist groß.

3. Wir blieben nicht im Haus, sondern wir gingen in den Garten.

4. Wir aßen sehr viel, denn wir waren sehr hungrig.

5. Gehen die Studenten in die Stadt, oder bleiben sie zu Hause?

The subject in the second clause is often implied rather than expressed. We may say: Wir sind in Deutschland und haben ein Zimmer bei einer deutschen Familie.

C. SUBORDINATING CONJUNCTIONS AND DEPENDENT CLAUSES

If we memorize the five coordinating conjunctions above, there will be no problem since **all other conjunctions are subordinating and send the finite verb to the end of the dependent clause** (even beyond past participles and infinitives). Examples: Ich weiß, daß er nach Hause kommt; ich weiß, daß er nach Hause kommen wird; ich weiß, daß er nach Hause kommen will; ich weiß, daß er nach Hause gekommen ist; etc.

The most frequently needed subordinating conjunctions are: **als, da, daß, ehe, nachdem, obgleich, obwohl, weil, wenn.**

Indirect questions beginning with such words as **wann, wer, was, wo, wohin, wie,** or **ob** are dependent clauses and therefore have the finite verb at the end.

Let us join two sentences with **nachdem:** Wir gingen in ein Restaurant. Wir hatten alles gesehen. The result is: Wir gingen in ein Restaurant, nachdem wir alles gesehen **hatten.** The subordinate conjunction has sent the finite verb to the end of its clause, but nothing else has been changed.

Now, let us take the same two sentences and put the subordinating clause first: Nachdem wir alles gesehen **hatten, gingen wir** in ein Restaurant. Again the subordinating conjunction has sent the finite verb to the end of its clause.

However, something else has happened: in the main clause subject and verb have exchanged positions. Thus, **if a dependent clause comes ahead of the main clause, the verb of the main clause precedes the subject.** We call this the "inverted order" (verb before subject).

With regard to word order of the finite verb, remember: Normally the finite verb is the second element in a sentence (the first element may be the subject, an adverb, an adverbial phrase of time, place or manner, or even an entire dependent clause).

In questions without an interrogative and in imperative forms, the finite verb is in first position.

Interpunctuation: **All dependent clauses in German are set off by commas.** Never forget to put in these commas; they act as a sort of reminder to realize where the dependent clause starts or ends.

D. Infinitive Phrases

1. In German the infinitive phrase is felt to be a dependent clause, which means that the verb (in this case the infinitive) will be placed at the very end. **I hope to buy** a lamp for my mother in this city: **ich hoffe,** eine Lampe für meine Mutter in dieser Stadt **zu kaufen.**

2. We use **um . . . zu with the infinitive** to express purpose, e.g., Er saß am Tisch, **um** einen Brief **zu schreiben,** He sat at the table *in order to write* a letter. Wir gingen durch die Stadt, **um** alles **zu sehen,** We went through the city *in order to see* everything. Again the infinitive with **zu** goes to the end of the clause.

E. Als, Wann, Wenn, Ob

Notice the following usages of these words:

1. **als** (*when*) is used for a single event in the past: Als wir nach Frankfurt fuhren, regnete es.

2. **wann** (*when*) is used for questions, direct or indirect: Wann ist er nach Hause gegangen? Können Sie mir sagen, wann er nach Hause gegangen ist?

3. **wenn** (*when*) is used only for repeated, customary action in the sense of *whenever*: Wenn sie diese Geschichte las, wurde sie immer sehr traurig.

4. **wenn** also means *if* (in a conditional sense): Wenn ich Zeit habe, werde ich Ihnen schreiben.

5. But *if,* in the sense of *whether,* is **ob**: Können Sie mir sagen, ob Herr Löwenzahn zu Hause ist?

F. Selbst, Selber

Note the following usages of **selbst** (*himself, herself; even*); **selber** (*himself, herself,* etc.).

1. Mein Vater selbst (*or* selber) war da—*My father himself was there.* Meine Mutter selbst (*or* selber) schrieb den Brief—*My mother herself wrote the letter.*

2. Selbst mein Vater war da—Even my father was there. Both, **selbst** and **selber,** are indeclinable. In the meaning of a) they are synonymous and exchangeable. **Selbst** or **selber** after a word will mean *himself, herself, itself, myself, themselves,* etc. But **selbst** preceding a word intensifies it and is equivalent to English *even.*

G. Verbs Ending in **–ieren**

There is a considerable number of verbs which after the stem have the infinitive ending **–ieren. Such verbs never take the ge– prefix in the past particle.** Regieren—er hat **regiert;** studieren—ich habe **studiert.** All these verbs are of foreign origin and they are all weak. When you come across them, you will never have trouble in knowing their meanings: alarmieren, atomisieren, experimentieren, illuminieren, produzieren, reformieren, etc.

IV. Grammatical Exercises

A. Combine the following sentences with the German conjunctions equivalent to the English in parentheses:

1. Wir haben ein Zimmer bei einer deutschen Familie. Wir sind nun in Deutschland. (*since, and, for, because*) 2. Ich sehe ein Schulbuch. Ich bin sofort krank. (*when, for, and, because*) 3. Herbert hat die Aufgabe an die Tafel geschrieben. Der Lehrer findet alles sehr gut. (*and, after*) 4. Die Fenster sind offen. Die Luft kommt dadurch. (*because, and, since*) 5. Conrads Aufgabe ist schwer. Die Geduld des Lehrers ist groß. (*and, but*) 6. Ich ging zu Bett. Ich schrieb meiner Mutter einen Brief. (*before*) 7. Es wird jetzt spät. Ich werde sehr hungrig. (*and, because, since*) 8. Ich frage Frau Löwenzahn: "Werden wir bald essen?" (*whether*) 9. Ich frage sie: „Werden wir essen?" (*when*) 10. Ich frage Herbert: „Liest Herr Löwenzahn in der Zeitung?" (*what*) 11. Er trägt eine Brille. Er sieht nicht gut. (*because, for, since*) 12. Wir hatten Tennis gespielt. Wir wurden durstig und bestellten ein Glas Limonade. (*since, after, because*) 13. Ich will dieses Kleid nicht kaufen. Es kostet zu viel. (*for, because*) 14. Wir waren auf den Balkon gegangen. Herr Löwenzahn brachte uns etwas zu trinken. (*after*) 15. Er wurde alt. Er konnte ganz gut hören. (*before*) 16. Ich sage: „Ich muß um sieben Uhr zu Hause sein." (*that*)

B. Use **wenn, wann, als,** or **ob:**

1. ____ es spät wird, wird Conrad hungrig. 2. ____ die Studenten an diesem Sonntag nach Frankfurt gingen, sahen sie den Römer. 3. Ich möchte wissen, ____ man im Bahnhof ein Glas Limonade bestellen kann. 4. Im Führer steht nichts darüber, ____ der Kaiser gestorben ist. 5. ____ machen wir wieder einen Spaziergang? 6. ____ Herr Löwenzahn etwas Wein trank, dann sang er immer.

C. Use **aber** or **sondern:**

1. Die Tafel ist nicht schwarz, ____ weiß. 2. Ich bin nicht hungrig, ____ ich bin durstig. 3. Er ist sehr alt, ____ er lehrt noch immer. 4. Ich gehe nicht in die Stadt, ____ nach Hause. 5. Die Mädchen sprechen gut deutsch, ____ sie spielen nicht so gut Tennis.

D. Just for fun—try to unscramble the following sentences (based on the Reading Selection from Lesson X):

1. Nachdem im Café wir machten hatten einen Spaziergang gegessen wir und getrunken. 2. Obgleich Zeit um sieben Uhr sein wir genug wir zu Hause mußten hatten. 3. Da wir viel hatten konnten sehen eine Stunde wir. 4. Ein Junge einen Stein und vor dem Käfig warf stand nach dem Affen. 5. In seiner Ecke ruhig obgleich mit einem Stein den Affen der Junge saß warf er. 6. Obwohl die Tiere zu fressen soll füttern man etwas dem Affen wir nicht geben. 7. Wir das Walroß lachen denn Herrn Löwenzahn gleicht müssen. 8. Ich fragen die Löwenzahns Sie zu Ihnen sprechen wollte in der Du-Form warum.

V. Translation Exercise

1. Since Herbert and Conrad don't have any (= *have no*) school on Sunday, they will go to Frankfurt on this day. 2. I believe that they will travel by car. 3. Although he has never studied in Germany, he knows German. 4. The students, that is Herbert and Conrad, went to buy something for Mrs. Löwenzahn. 5. We can ask that man if he knows where the Römer is. 6. He says that it is situated in the middle of the city. 7. Not all of it is old because it burned many years ago.

8. When my father was a student in Frankfurt, many houses in the city were very old. 9. Can you tell me when your father studied here? 10. After they had taken a walk through the city, they went into a restaurant in order to eat something. 11. Before they went home, they also drank a glass of Coca Cola. 12. Although we had read much about Frankfurt, we wanted to see the city ourselves. 13. Because the city hall is so famous, we wanted to see it. 14. The father of my friend told us that many years ago he had studied in Frankfurt. 15. The Frankfurt station is old, but the station in Heidelberg is entirely new. 16. Do you know who this man is? 17. Can you tell me why he is going downtown?

VI. Fragen

1. Warum wollten Conrad und Herbert Frankfurt sehen? 2. An welchem Tage fuhren sie dahin? 3. Wie wurde es an diesem Tag? 4. Warum haben sie einen Führer gekauft? 5. Warum sind sie durch die Stadt gegangen? 6. Warum nennt man eine Reichsstadt „frei?“ 7. Wer hat in diesen Städten regiert? 8. Warum kamen die Räte in das Rathaus? 9. Wie nennt man das Frankfurter Rathaus? 10. Warum ist der neue Kaiser auf den Balkon des Römers gegangen? 11. Wieviel hatten die Studenten für ihren Führer gezahlt? 12. Wie sind viele Frankfurter Häuser? 13. Wann hat Herberts Vater an der Universität Frankfurt studiert? 14. Wo waren die Löwenzahns am Abend?

VII. Lesestück

Münchhausen erzählt

Wenn man in Deutschland von einem Mann sagt: „Er erzählt wie der Freiherr von Münchhausen“, dann will man damit sagen: „Er kann viele gute Geschichten erzählen, aber sie sind alle nicht wahr. Er ist ein unterhaltsamer Lügner."

Münchhausen, so hören wir, lebte im 18. (achtzehnten) Jahrhundert. Er war in vielen Kriegen, machte lange Reisen, er war oft in großer Gefahr, aber er wußte immer Rat.

Hier mag er uns selbst eine seiner Geschichten erzählen. Denken wir daran, daß das Wort „lügen" nicht in seinem Wörterbuch steht.

„Vor vielen Jahren war ich ein Matrose in der Flotte des Kaisers. Der Kaiser und seine Flotte waren in großer Gefahr, denn der Feind hatte mehr Matrosen als wir, mehr Schiffe und eine große Kanone. Am Abend vor der Schlacht kam der Kaiser zu mir. Als er in mein Zimmer kam, war er sehr besorgt und traurig. Nachdem er mit mir gesprochen und meinen Rat gehört hatte, ging er glücklich nach Hause, denn er wußte, daß wir morgen den Feind schlagen würden.

Als die Schlacht begann, stand ich hinter unserer großen Kanone und wartete auf den ersten Schuß des Feindes. Ich schoß im gleichen Augenblick wie der Feind. Die beiden großen Kanonenkugeln trafen sich in der Mitte zwischen uns und dem Feind. Weil unsere Kugel stärker war, ging die Kugel des Feindes zurück; sie enthauptete den Kanonier des Feindes und zwölf andere Matrosen, die in einer Reihe hinter ihm standen, zerstörte die Maste von drei Schiffen und fiel dann auf das Dach eines Hauses auf dem Land. In dem Haus war nur eine alte Frau. Sie lag auf einem Bett und schlief mit offenem Munde. Es war ein altes Haus, ein altes Dach und eine schwere Kugel. Weil die Kugel zu schwer war, brach sie durch das Dach, fiel in den offenen Mund der alten Frau und zerstörte ihren letzten Zahn.

Unsere Kugel aber zerstörte die große Kanone des Feindes und das Schiff des Admirals mit 1000 (tausend) Matrosen. Sie alle ertranken. Muß ich noch sagen, daß wir die Schlacht gewannen, und daß ich ein Admiral in der Flotte des Kaisers wurde?"

VIII. Wörterverzeichnis

der Admiral, ⸚e the admiral
ander other
beginnen, begann, begonnen (to) begin
besorgt worried, apprehensive
brechen (i), brach, gebrochen (to) break
das Dach, ⸚er the roof
enthaupten (to) behead
der erste the first
ertrinken, ertrank, ist ertrunken (to) drown
fallen (ä), fiel, ist gefallen (to) fall
der Feind, –e the enemy
die Flotte, –n the fleet
der Freiherr, (–n), –en the baron
gewinnen, gewann, gewonnen (to) win
im gleichen Augenblick in the same moment
glücklich happily
das Jahrhundert, –e the century
der Kaiser, – the emperor
die Kanone, –n the cannon
die Kanonenkugel, –n the cannon-ball
der Kanonier, –e the gunner
der Krieg, –e the war
die Kugel, –n the ball
der letzte the last
lügen, log, gelogen (to) lie, tell a lie
der Lügner, – the liar
der Mast, –e the mast
der Matrose, (–n), –n the sailor
mehr . . . als more . . . than
der Mund, ⸚er the mouth
noch still, in addition
oft often
der Rat the counsel, advice
Rat wissen (to) know what to do
die Reihe, –n the row
das Schiff, –e the ship
die Schlacht, –en the battle
schlagen (ä) schlug, geschlagen (to) defeat
der Schuß, Schüsse the shot
sich themselves, each other
stärker stronger
unterhaltsam entertaining
wahr true
wie as
das Wort, –e *or* **⸚er** the word
das Wörterbuch, ⸚er the dictionary
wir würden we would
der Zahn, ⸚e the tooth
zerstören (to) destroy

Aufgabe Dreizehn

PREFIX VERBS
TIME EXPRESSIONS

I. Reading Selection

Heute ist Monika Wenk abgefahren, um Freunde in Bremen zu besuchen. Wir waren am Bahnhof, weil wir ihr „Auf Wiedersehn" sagen wollten. Wir waren zu spät aufgestanden, und wir mußten laufen, um vor acht am Bahnhof anzukommen.

Als wir dann am Bahnhof waren, wußten wir nicht, auf welchem Bahnsteig der Zug abfuhr. Wir wußten nur, es war der Hansa-Expreß nach Bremen, und er sollte um acht Uhr abfahren. Wir hatten gerade angefangen, den Fahrplan zu lesen, als wir hinter uns Vera Sütterlins Stimme hörten: „Bahnsteig vier. Kommen Sie mit mir! Ich brauche es nicht nachzusehen, weil ich oft mit diesem Zug aus der Schweiz hier angekommen bin."

Gerade als wir auf den Bahnsteig hinausgingen, kam der Zug an. Monika war schon da und Herbert half ihr nun, ihre Koffer in den Zug hineinzutragen.

Leider blieb Monika nicht allein in ihrem Abteil. Eine Dame kam. Sie war sehr dick und furchtbar aufgeregt. Sie stieg ein und aus, machte das Fenster auf und zu, nahm ihren Hut ab und setzte ihn wieder auf. „Wo sind meine Koffer? Wo ist mein Mann?" schrie sie. Es war alles da: ihre fünf Koffer waren schon im Abteil, und ihr Mann stand vor dem Zug auf dem Bahnsteig. Er sprach gerade mit dem Schaffner:

„Meine Frau fährt allein. Sie muß in Köln umsteigen. Bitte, helfen Sie ihr mit den Koffern."

„Wir werden Sie vermissen", sagte ich zu Monika. „Herbert wird Sie sogar sehr vermissen. Wann werden Sie zurückkommen?"

„In einer Woche komme ich zurück", sagte sie. „Ich werde Ihnen auch schreiben." Ich gebe zu, daß sie es mehr zu Herbert als zu mir sagte.

Die Dame hatte das Fenster aufgemacht und sprach zu ihrem Mann:

„Die Blumen brauchen jeden Tag Wasser.
Vergiß nicht, jeden Abend alle Fenster zuzumachen.
Denk daran, den Staubsauger zu reparieren."

Der Zug fuhr ab, es wurde sehr laut auf dem Bahnsteig. Noch einmal gaben wir Monika die Hand und riefen „Auf Wiedersehn! Gute Reise! Kommen Sie bald zurück!" Alle Leute im Zug und auf dem Bahnsteig winkten.

„Du darfst im Bett nicht rauchen", schrie die dicke Dame noch. „In der Küche darfst du nicht . . ."

Doch dann konnte man sie nicht mehr hören.

„So," sagte ihr Mann laut. „Jetzt fangen meine Ferien an."

II. Vocabulary

NOTE: Separable prefixes will be indicated by a hyphen between the prefix and the verb for the convenience of the student in both the lesson and the end vocabularies. Thus we list **ab-fahren** as an aid to the student who should not make any other use of the hyphen, but should write **abfahren.**

***ab-fahren (ä), fuhr ab, ist abgefahren** (to) leave, depart
***ab-nehmen (nimmt ab), nahm ab, abgenommen** (to) take off
***das Abteil, –e** the compartment
***allein** alone
***an-fangen (ä), fing an, angefangen** (to) begin
***an-kommen, kam an, ist angekommen** (to) arrive
aufgeregt excited, stirred up
***auf-machen, machte auf, aufgemacht** (to) open
auf-setzen, setzte auf, aufgesetzt (to) put on (*glasses, hat, etc.*)

*__auf-stehen, stand auf, ist aufgestanden__ (to) get up, stand up
*__aus-steigen aus, stieg aus, ist ausgestiegen__ (to) get out, get off
*__der Bahnsteig, –e__ the platform, track
*__besuchen__ (to) visit
*__bitte__ please
__dick__ thick, fat
*__dreizehn__ thirteen
*__ein-steigen in, stieg ein, ist eingestiegen__ (to) get on, board (*a vehicle*)
__der Expreß__ the express
__der Fahrplan, ¨–e__ the time table
__furchtbar__ frightful, fearful
*__gerade__ just
__hinaus-gehen, ging hinaus, ist hinausgegangen__ (to) go out
*__hinein-tragen in (ä), trug hinein, hineingetragen__ (to) carry in
*__der Hut, ¨–e__ the hat
__der Koffer, –__ the trunk; suitcase, valise
*__laufen (äu), lief, ist gelaufen__ (to) run
*__leider__ unfortunately
*__mehr__ more; __nicht mehr__ no longer, not any more
*__nach-sehen (ie), sah nach, nachgesehen__ (to) look up (*in a phone book, time table, etc.*)
__noch einmal__ once more, again
__reparieren__ (to) repair, fix
__der Schaffner, –__ the conductor
*__die Schweiz__ Switzerland
*__sogar__ even
__der Staubsauger, –__ the vacuum cleaner
*__die Stimme, –n__ the voice
__um-steigen, stieg um, ist umgestiegen__ (to) transfer, change trains
*__vergessen (i), vergaß, vergessen__ (to) forget
__vermissen__ (to) miss
__wieder-sehen (ie), sah wieder, wiedergesehen__ (to) see again
__winken__ (to) wave
*__der Zug, ¨–e__ the train
__zu-geben (i), gab zu, zugegeben__ (to) admit
*__zu-machen, machte zu, zugemacht__ (to) shut, close
*__zurück-kommen, kam zurück, ist zurückgekommen__ (to) come back, return

IDIOMS

*__Auf Wiederseh(e)n__ good-bye, au revoir
*__Gute Reise__ pleasant journey
__sehr__ *is used in German often when we say* very much: Ich vermisse Sie sehr, I miss you very much. *German uses* viel *only for amounts that can be measured in standard units of measure.*

III. Grammar

We have in German a great number of compound verbs, i.e., composed of an original verb plus a prefix. The vast majority of prefixes may be divided into two groups: inseparable and separable prefixes.

A. INSEPARABLE PREFIXES

The inseparable prefixes are: be–, ge–, emp–, ent–, er–, ver–, zer–. As active vocabulary we have had the verbs **berichten, bestellen, besuchen, erklären, erzählen, geschehen, vergessen, verkaufen.** We have also used **beachten** (*notice*), **vermissen** (miss), **verstehen** (understand). **Inseparable prefixes never have the accent on the prefix.**

These verbs follow all the rules which we have established so far for the conjugation of verbs, except one: **they never take the ge- prefix in the past participle.**

Using **bestellen** as an example, we see that verbs with inseparable prefixes are treated the same way as any verb ending in **–ieren:**

PRES.	ich **bestelle** ein Glas Limonade
PAST	ich **bestellte** ein Glas Limonade
FUT.	ich **werde** ein Glas Limonade **bestellen**
PRES. PERF.	ich **habe** ein Glas Limonade **bestellt**
PAST PERF.	ich **hatte** ein Glas Limonade **bestellt**

The imperatives are **bestelle, bestellt, bestellen Sie!** If we use an **infinitive with zu,** there again is no variation from what we had before: **Ich ging in ein Restaurant, um ein Glas Limonade zu bestellen.**

B. SEPARABLE PREFIXES

Most prepositions and also some adverbs may appear as separable prefixes. As active vocabulary we have had so far the following separable prefix verbs: **abfahren, abnehmen, anfangen, ankommen, aufmachen, aufstehen, aussteigen, einsteigen, zumachen, zurückkommen. Separable prefixes are always accented.**

When these verbs (or any other separable prefix verbs) are used in a main clause in the so-called "simple tenses" (present tense, past tense, imperative) **the prefix separates** from the main body of the verb **and goes to the very end of the clause.** In the past participle these verbs use the **ge–** prefix, but the **ge–** comes between the prefix and the stem syllable. Thus the past participles of the above mentioned verbs are **abgefahren, abgenommen, angefangen, angekommen, aufgemacht, aufgestanden, ausgestiegen, eingestiegen, zugemacht, zurückgekommen.**

Using **abnehmen** as an example, we get the following sequence:

PRES.	Conrad **nimmt** den Hut **ab**
PAST	Conrad **nahm** den Hut **ab**
FUT.	Conrad **wird** den Hut **abnehmen**
PRES. PERF.	Conrad **hat** den Hut **abgenommen**
PAST PERF.	Conrad **hatte** den Hut **abgenommen**

The imperatives are **nimm den Hut ab, nehmt den Hut ab, nehmen Sie den Hut ab!** When we use an **infinitive with zu,** the **zu** goes between the prefix and the main part of the verb: **Monika ging ins Schlafzimmer, um den Hut abzunehmen.**

Separable prefix verbs never separate in dependent clauses after a subordinating conjunction or a relative pronoun. Examples: Wenn er **zurückkommt,** werde ich mit ihm sprechen. Als er das Fenster **aufmachte,** wurde es kalt im Zimmer. Obgleich er früh **aufstand,** kam er zu spät an.

C. DOUBTFUL PREFIXES

A few prepositional prefixes may be used as either separable or inseparable prefixes; in such cases the separable form has one meaning and the inseparable another one.

Let's take the verb **übersetzen.** In its original meaning, pronounced **ü'bersetzen,** it stands for *to ferry over.* **Der Fährmann setzte sie über,** *The ferryman ferried them over.* The past participle would be **ü'bergesetzt.** In its figurative meaning **übersétzen** stands for *to translate.* **Herbert übersétzte den Satz,** *Herbert translated the sentence.* The past participle is now **übersétzt.**

The literal meaning of **wiederholen** is *to fetch again;* past: **er holte wieder;** past participle: **wiédergeholt.** The derived (and much more frequently used) verb is **wiederhólen,** *to repeat*; past tense: er **wiederhólte;** present perfect: er hat **wiederhólt.**

Very often such verbs have lost their original, literal meaning, but frequently are used in their derived, figurative meaning. We have used actively the verb **unterbréchen,** *to interrupt,* which belongs in this category. Examples: **Er unterbrícht mich; unterbrích mich nicht!; er hat mich unterbróchen,** etc.

Fortunately the number of these doubtful prefix verbs is very limited. Our vocabulary will always clearly indicate the character of the prefix verbs.

D. hin—her, aus—ein, auf—ab

The prefixes **hin–** and **her–** are really only directional signals. **Hin** means *away from the speaker;* **her** means *toward the speaker.* They are used a great deal, both alone, and in combination with **ein** and **aus** (*in* and *out*) and **auf** and **ab** (*up* and *down*).

Suppose I am in a room and you are outside of it, and Conrad enters the room. I say: **Conrad kommt in das Zimmer herein.** You say: **Conrad geht in das Zimmer hinein.**—But Herbert leaves the room. I say: **Herbert geht aus dem Zimmer hinaus.** You say: **Herbert kommt aus dem Zimmer heraus.**

E. Time Expressions

1. When no preposition is used, **indefinite time takes the genitive case: Eines Tages (eines Abends)** fuhren die Freunde nach Frankfurt, *One day* (*one evening*) the friends went to Frankfurt.

2. When no preposition is used, **definite time** or **duration of time takes the accusative:** Die Blumen brauchen **jeden Tag** Wasser, The flowers need water *every day.* Parallel expressions are: **alle Tage, jeden Abend, jede Nacht.** Sie arbeiteten

eine Stunde (lang), They worked (*for*) *an hour.* Sie saßen **den ganzen Abend** auf dem Balkon, They sat on the balcony (*for*) *the whole evening.*

For other time expressions see Lesson IX, Section III, I.

F. TELLING TIME WITH um, vor, nach

In telling the hour of the day, **um** means *at;* **nach** means *after;* and **vor** means *before, until,* or *to.*

Wie spät ist es? or **Wieviel Uhr ist es?** *What time is it?* **Es ist fünf Minuten vor acht,** *It is five minutes to eight.* **Es ist gerade sieben (Uhr),** *It is exactly seven* (*o'clock*). **Kommt der Zug um neun (Uhr) an?** *Does the train arrive at nine* (*o'clock*)? **Es ist schon zehn Minuten nach zwölf,** *It is already ten minutes after twelve.*

G. INFINITIVES AS NOUNS

Practically any German infinitive can be used as a neuter noun. **Das Arbeiten macht mich hungrig,** *Working makes me hungry.* **Sein Beten half,** *His praying helped.* **Rauchen verboten,** *Smoking forbidden.* **Sehen ist Glauben,** *Seeing is Believing.* So **Auf Wiedersehen** means literally *until seeing* (*each other*) *again.*

IV. Grammatical Exercises

A. Put the following into the present, past, future, and perfect tenses:

1. Heute (abfahren) Monika Wenk. 2. Sie (hoffen), Freunde zu besuchen. 3. Sie (besuchen) Freunde in Bremen. 4. Wir (aufstehen) zu spät. 5. Wir (ankommen) vor acht am Bahnhof. 6. Auf welchem Bahnsteig (abfahren) der Zug? 7. Wir (anfangen) gerade, den Fahrplan zu studieren. 8. Wir (lesen) den Fahrplan. 9. Was (geschehen) nun? 10. Ich (ankommen) oft aus der Schweiz hier. 11. Er (hinausgehen) auf

den Bahnsteig. 12. Dann (ankommen) der Zug. 13. Herbert (hineintragen) Monikas Koffer in den Zug. 14. Die Dame (einsteigen) sofort. 15. Dann (aussteigen) sie wieder. 16. Sie (aufmachen) das Fenster. 17. Dann (zumachen) sie es wieder. 18. Meine Frau (umsteigen) in Köln. 19. Wir (bestellen) etwas. 20. Wann (zurückkommen) Sie? 21. Herbert (unterbrechen) mich. 22. Er (vergessen) das nicht.

B. Make sentences with three forms of the imperative, using the verbs: besuchen, aufstehen, abnehmen, aufmachen, vergessen, zurückkommen, erzählen, unterbrechen.

C. Use **zu** with the infinitive, if and where needed:

1. Ich gehe in ein Restaurant, um etwas bestellen. 2. Wir brauchen nicht in Köln umsteigen. 3. Ich möchte das Fenster aufmachen. 4. Das darf ich nicht tun. 5. Ich bin hier, um Ihnen das erzählen. 6. Hier darf man nicht rauchen. 7. Wir sind um acht Uhr hier, um mit diesem Zug abfahren.

V. Translation Exercise

1. Monika is leaving today and we must not get up too late. 2. We must get up earlier in order to say good-bye to her. 3. Do you know when the train leaves? 4. Don't get up too early! (*three forms*) 5. Herbert was on the platform in order to carry Monika's suitcase (*Koffer*) into the compartment. 6. When he arrived at the station, the train had just left. 7. It happened one day. 8. Do you know her? 9. Before she got into the compartment she bought a newspaper for the trip. 10. He is to open the windows every afternoon. 11. We hoped to arrive in Düsseldorf at nine o'clock (*Uhr*). 12. Please help me (to) close the windows (*three forms*). 13. He shakes hands with the girl. 14. He becomes sick because he opens the window. 15. The lady gets on the train and then she gets off again. 16. When is Herbert's girl friend

coming back? 17. She is visiting friends of her family in Bremen. 18. After she had returned, she began to learn English.

Re-do sentences 3, 8, 14, 15, 16, 17 in the past, future and perfect tenses.

VI. Fragen

1. Wo will Monika Freunde besuchen? 2. Warum sind wir am Bahnhof gewesen? 3. Womit fährt Monika nac Bremen? 4. Auf welchem Bahnsteig fuhr der Zug ab 5. Wann ist der Zug angekommen? 6. Was hat Herbert getan? 7. Wer ist auch in Monikas Abteil eingestiegen? 8. Wieviele Koffer hatte die Dame? 9. Wo stand ihr Mann? 10. Wo soll die Dame umsteigen? 11. Muß Monika auch umsteigen? 12. Was sagte der Mann, als der Zug abfuhr? 13. Was soll er zu Hause tun?

VII. Lesestück

Der Rattenfänger von Hameln

Nicht viele Leute in Deutschland kennen die kleine, alte Stadt Hameln an der Weser, aber jedes deutsche Kind kennt die Geschichte vom Rattenfänger von Hameln.

Es geschah im Mittelalter, daß die Zahl der Ratten in Hameln erschreckend wuchs. Man sah sie in allen Häusern und auf allen Straßen. Nicht nur in der Nacht, sondern auch am hellen Tage liefen sie durch die Stadt. Die Bürger von Hameln legten Gift, sie töteten Hunderte und Tausende von Ratten, doch ihre Zahl wuchs mit jedem Tage.

An einem schönen Tag im Sommer kam ein junger Mann in die Stadt, den niemand kannte. Er ging zum Rathaus und fragte den Bürgermeister: „Wieviel wollt ihr mir zahlen, wenn ich euch von den Ratten befreie?"

Der Bürgermeister rief seine Räte und erzählte ihnen von dem Angebot des jungen Mannes.

„Wenn du uns von den Ratten befreien kannst“, sagte der Bürgermeister dann zu dem jungen Mann, „werden wir dir tausend Gulden zahlen und ich, meine Räte und alle Bürger der Stadt werden dir ewig dankbar sein.“

Der junge Mann war damit zufrieden. Er nahm aus seiner Tasche eine Flöte und, während er langsam durch alle Straßen von Hameln ging, spielte er seltsame Melodien darauf. Aus allen Häusern kamen nun die Ratten und folgten ihm. Als alle Ratten aus den Häusern herausgekommen waren, ging der junge Mann zur Weser, gefolgt von Tausenden von Ratten. Er führte sie ins Wasser, und alle Ratten ertranken in der Weser.

Am Abend ging der junge Mann zum Rathaus, um sein Geld zu holen. Doch der Bürgermeister und die Räte lachten. „Wir wußten nicht, daß es so einfach war. Tausend Gulden? Hier, nimm zehn Gulden, das ist genug für dein Flötenspiel.“

Der junge Mann sagte nichts. Er warf die zehn Gulden auf den Tisch und ging.

Doch an einem Abend im Herbst kam er zurück. Wieder ging er langsam durch die Straßen von Hameln, und wieder spielte er auf seiner Flöte seltsame Melodien. Jetzt kamen die Kinder von Hameln aus ihren Häusern, alle Kinder zwischen sechs und dreizehn. Sie alle folgten dem jungen Mann mit seiner Flöte. Sie hörten nicht die Stimmen der Eltern, sie hörten nur das Flötenspiel des jungen Mannes. Er führte sie aus der Stadt, in den Wald und in die Berge über der Weser. Sie kamen nie zurück und niemand weiß, was aus ihnen geworden ist.

VIII. Wörterverzeichnis

das Angebot, –e the offer
befreien (to) free
der Bürger, – the citizen
der Bürgermeister, – the mayor
dankbar grateful
einfach simple

erschreckend frightfully, startlingly
ertrinken, ertrank, ist ertrunken (to) drown
ewig forever, eternally
die Flöte, –n the flute
das Flötenspiel the flute-playing
folgen (*with dative*) (to) follow
führen (to) lead
genug enough
das Gift, –e the poison
der Gulden, – the guilder
hell bright
heraus-kommen, kam heraus, ist herausgekommen (to) come out
holen (to) get
Hunderte hundreds
klein small
langsam slowly
legen (to) place, set out
die Melodie, –n the melody, tune
das Mittelalter the Middle Ages
niemand no one
der Rat, ¨–e the councillor, alderman
die Ratte, –n the rat
der Rattenfänger, – the rat catcher
seltsam strange
spielen (to) play
Tausend, –e a thousand
töten (to) kill
während (*conj.*) while
die Weser the Weser (River)
wieviel how much
die Zahl, –en the number

Aufgabe Vierzehn

RELATIVE PRONOUNS
GENITIVE PREPOSITIONS

I. Reading Selection

Liebe Vera!

Gestern bin ich nach einer Reise, von der man nicht viel berichten kann, hier in Bremen angekommen. Die Dame, deren Mann mit Euch am Bahnsteig stand, wurde später sehr nett. Während der Reise machte sie vier Schachteln mit Süßigkeiten auf und bot allen Leuten im Zug davon an. „Bitte essen Sie", sagte sie immer wieder. „Ich selbst sollte wegen meiner Figur nichts davon nehmen. Ich weiß nicht, warum ich so viel Schokolade esse. Mein Arzt sagt, es ist alles psychologisch, aber was wissen die Ärzte?"

Unser Zug kam um drei Uhr in Bremen an. Meine Freundin Anna und ihre Eltern, die ich bis jetzt noch nicht kannte, waren am Bahnhof. Sie haben sogar ein Auto, womit wir sofort eine Rundfahrt durch die Stadt machten. Es ist eine Stadt, die viele Jahrhunderte alt und sehr interessant ist, mit einem Hafen, von dem Schiffe in alle Länder der Welt fahren. Annas Vater hat mir viel aus der Geschichte Bremens erzählt, wovon ich leider nicht alles verstanden habe. Ich bin in Geschichte nicht so gut wie Herbert. Heute sind wir in die Stadt gegangen, um das Rathaus zu sehen. Unten im Rathaus ist der Ratskeller, wo wir zu Mittag gegessen haben. Vor dem Rathaus steht eine Statue, ein Mann, der in den Händen ein

Courtesy of the German Tourist Information Office, New York

Der Dom zu Speyer (11. Jahrhundert)

Courtesy of the German Tourist Information Office, New York

Rathaus und St. Petrikirche in Bremen

Schwert hält. Diese Statue ist der Roland von Bremen, ein Symbol der Gerechtigkeit. Ich mußte an etwas denken, was ich in der Schule gelernt hatte:

> Roland, der Riese, am Rathaus zu Bremen,
> Steht er ein Standbild, standhaft und starr.[1]

Vom Rathaus gingen wir zum Dom, dessen Dach im Lauf der Zeit ganz grün geworden ist, was mir sehr gut gefällt.

Die Landschaft ist nicht wie zu Hause. Anstatt der Berge und Wälder, wie wir sie kennen, gibt es hier Felder und Wiesen, die alle ganz flach sind. Weil das Land so flach ist, fahren fast alle Leute mit den Rädern. Herbert (Du weißt, er kommt von Colorado) sagt immer, eine Landschaft ohne Berge gefällt ihm nicht.

Wie geht es Dir? Wie geht es unseren Freunden aus Amerika? Hilfst Du ihnen, wenn sie ihre Aufgaben übersetzen müssen? Hast Du Herbert gesehen? Hat er von mir gesprochen? Schreib mir darüber. (Ich weiß nicht, warum Du jetzt lächelst. Kann ich nicht fragen, was meine Freunde tun?)

Es ist spät in der Nacht, und ich will zu Bett gehen. Ich hoffe, von Dir zu hören, ehe ich hier wieder abfahre.

Herzlich, Deine Monika.

II. Vocabulary

***an-bieten, bot an, angeboten** (to) offer
***anstatt** (*prep. with gen.*) instead of
***der Arzt, ⸗e** the physician, doctor
das Dach, ⸗er the roof
der Dom, –e the cathedral
***das Feld, –er** the field
die Figur, –en the figure
***flach** flat, level
***gefallen (ä), gefiel, gefallen** (*takes dative*) (to) be pleasing to, to like
die Gerechtigkeit justice
der Hafen, – the harbor

[1] Roland, the giant, at Bremen's town hall
Stands as a statue, steadfast and stern.

***halten (hält), hielt, gehalten** (to) hold
***herzlich** cordial
***interessant** interesting
***das Jahrhundert, –e** the century
der Lauf the course
***lieb** dear
nett nice
psychologisch psychological
der Ratskeller the *rathskeller,* basement restaurant in city hall
die Rundfahrt, –en the drive, sightseeing trip
die Schachtel, –n the box
***das Schiff, –e** the ship
die Schokolade the chocolate
das Schwert, –er the sword
die Statue, –n the statue
die Süßigkeiten (*plu.*) sweets, candies
das Symbol, –e the symbol
***übersetzen, übersetzte, übersetzt** (to) translate
***unten** below, downstairs
***verstehen, verstand, verstanden** (to) understand
***vierzehn** fourteen
***während** (*prep. with gen.*) during
***wegen** (*prep. with gen.*) on account of
***die Welt** the world
***wie** (*conj.*) as, like
***die Wiese, –n** the meadow

IDIOMS

***es gefällt mir, es gefällt ihm,** etc. I like it, he likes it, etc.
***immer wieder** again and again
***Wie geht es dir? Es geht mir gut.** How are you? I'm fine.
***zu Mittag essen** (to) have dinner, eat dinner (*at noon*)

III. Grammar

A. DEFINITE RELATIVE PRONOUNS

1. **The definite relative pronoun is identical with the definite article, except in all forms of the genitive, and the dative plural.**

	MASCULINE	FEMININE	NEUTER	PLURAL
NOM.	**der**	**die**	**das**	**die**
GEN.	**dessen**	**deren**	**dessen**	**deren**
DAT.	**dem**	**der**	**dem**	**denen**
ACC.	**den**	**die**	**das**	**die**

In place of **der, die, das** German sometimes uses **welcher, welche, welches,** etc., which, however, has no forms for the genitive case (sing. and plu.). For the genitive we must always use **dessen** and **deren.**

2. The definite relative pronoun always has a specific antecedent, i.e., a word or words to which the relative pronoun refers. **The relative pronoun must agree with its antecedent in number and gender.** The antecedent determines whether the relative pronoun is singular or plural; masculine, feminine, or neuter.

3. The case we use for the relative pronoun is determined by its grammatical function in its own subordinate clause, i.e., in the relative clause. Examples: Der Mann, **der** mit ihm spricht, ist sein Lehrer. Der Mann, **dessen** Haus wir kauften, ist Amerikaner. Der Mann, **dem** ich das Buch gab, ist Conrads Freund. Der Mann, **den** Sie sahen, war unser Arzt.

4. Since all relative clauses are dependent clauses, we must use the dependent word order, as explained in Lesson XII. **In a relative clause the finite verb stands at the end.**

5. The relative pronoun is never omitted in German. If the English sentence omits it you will have to add it in German. The car *he bought* was new; Das Auto, **das er kaufte,** war neu.

6. German relative clauses are always set off by commas.

7. **If the relative pronoun is preceded by a preposition and refers to an inanimate antecedent, a** *wo + preposition* **combination may be used,** similar to the one explained for interrogatives in Lesson VIII, Section III, B. So we may say: Der Bleistift, **womit** ich schreibe, ist grün. Das Zimmer, **worin** ich schlafe, ist groß. Die Gläser, **woraus** wir trinken, sind sehr schön. However, these relative **wo**-combinations are less frequently used than the interrogative **wo**-combinations (see Lesson VIII) or the personal pronoun **da**-combinations (see Lesson V). The interrogative **wo**-combination and the pronoun **da**-combination are normally a *must*; the relative **wo**-combination is a *maybe*.

B. Indefinite Relative Pronouns

1. It may happen that a relative clause has no specific antecedent. In that case the indefinite relative pronouns **wer** and **was** are used, which in their declensional forms are completely identical with the interrogative pronoun (see Lesson VIII). The corresponding English forms are *whoever* (*he who*) and *whatever* (*that which*). The indefinite relative pronoun shows neither gender nor number, but it carries the distinction of persons **(wer)** and things **(was).** Examples: **Wer krank ist, kann nicht arbeiten,** *Whoever is sick, cannot work;* **Wer das getan hat, ist nicht mein Freund,** *Whoever has done that, is not my friend;* **Wen wir mögen, (den) besuchen wir,** *Whomever we like, we visit;* **Was schön ist, ist auch gut;** *Whatever is beautiful, is also good.*

2. **Was** is also used:

a) if it refers to such indefinite neuter pronouns as **alles, etwas, nichts, viel. Er erzählte mir nichts, was ich nicht schon wußte;** *He told me nothing that I didn't know already.*

b) if it refers not to a specific word but to an entire clause. **Er lag zwei Stunden in der Sonne, was ihn sehr durstig machte;** *He was lying in the sun for two hours, which made him very thirsty.*

C. Prepositions with the Genitive

We have used in the reading of this lesson three prepositions which take the genitive case: **anstatt** (or **statt**), **während,** and **wegen.** (Other genitive prepositions, not used so far, are: **trotz,** *in spite of;* **außerhalb,** *outside of;* **innerhalb,** *inside of;* **diesseits,** *this side of;* **jenseits,** *the other side of*).

D. Capitals in Correspondence

In writing letters, not only the polite form but also the familiar form of personal pronouns and possessive adjectives are capitalized **(Du, Ihr, Dein,** etc.).

IV. Grammatical Exercises

A. Fill in the proper relative pronoun:

1. Herbert und Conrad, ____ aus Amerika sind, wohnen nun in Deutschland. 2. Ist das alles, ____ Sie von ihm wissen? 3. Ich sehe ein Schulbuch, ____ mich krank macht. 4. Die Aufgabe, ____ ich schreibe, ist schwer. 5. Er gab mir etwas, ____ ich gut brauchen konnte. 6. Meine Mutter, ____ ich einen Brief schreibe, ist alt. 7. Die Arbeit, ____ ich mache, macht mich hungrig. 8. Herr Löwenzahn schläft auf dem Sofa, ____ sie im Wohnzimmer haben. 9. Die Mädchen, ____ Tennis schlecht ist, sind unsere Freundinnen. 10. Das Mädchen, ____ Herbert die Hand gibt, ist Monika. 11. Der Mann, in ____ Haus wir wohnen, hatte gestern Geburtstag. 12. Die Mädchen sprechen sehr gut deutsch, ____ uns sehr gefällt. 13. Der Mann, ____ Geburtstag heute ist, hört nicht gut. 14. Der Student, ____ ich dieses Geschenk gebe, ist sehr jung. 15. Der Mann, ____ Sie sehen, ist mein Freund. 16. Die Leute, ____ ich diesen Brief schreibe, sind Freunde meiner Eltern. 17. Die Frau, ____ Mann auf sie wartet, hat auch Ferien. 18. Der Mann, ____ Frau auf Ferien ist, muß jeden Tag die Fenster aufmachen. 19. Der Kaffee, ____ er mir brachte, war kalt. 20. ____ ich die Hand gebe, ist ein Freund von mir. 21. Der Stuhl, ____ in meinem Zimmer steht, gefällt mir. 22. Die Bücher, ____ ich lese, sind sehr dick.

B. Fill in the proper relative pronoun:

1. Das Fenster, durch ____ die Luft kommt, ist offen. 2. Die Tafel, an ____ (*acc.*) ich schreibe, ist schwarz. 3. Die Brille, durch ____ Herr Löwenzahn sieht, ist sehr groß. 4. Der Sessel, auf ____ ich sitze, ist grün. 5. Das Buch, in ____ ich lese, ist schwarz. 6. Das Geld, mit ____ ich für uns zahle,

ist in meiner Tasche. 7. Das Zimmer, aus ____ ich komme, ist das Wohnzimmer. 8. Dieser Zug, mit ____ ich oft fahre, kommt aus der Schweiz. 9. Die Kirche, vor ____ ich stehe, ist nicht sehr alt. 10. Die Geschichte, über ____ wir sprechen, haben wir gestern in der Zeitung gelesen. 11. Das Restaurant, in ____ wir aßen, war der Ratskeller. 12. Unsere Studenten haben eine Reise gemacht, von ____ ich Ihnen etwas erzählen will. 13. Eine Dame stieg nun in das Abteil ein, in ____ Monika saß.

C. Re-do B, making a **wo–** combination with the prepositions in place of the relative pronoun in sentences 4, 5, 6, 8, 11, and 12.

V. Translation Exercise

1. Monika has reported about a trip which she took to Bremen. 2. Whoever takes a trip to Germany, must see the Rhineland. 3. The lady with whom she traveled was not very beautiful. 4. The man, whose wife was on this train, had gone home. 5. The woman, whose husband stood on the platform, said good-bye. 6. The city hall, in which we ate our noon dinner yesterday, is many centuries old. 7. Is that all you know about it? 8. Anna's parents, in whose house we are living, are very cordial. 9. During the evening she spoke about history in which she is not as good as her husband. 10. The doctor I visited knows almost everything. 11. On account of her trip Monika went to bed early. 12. I explained it to him again and again, which did not please him. 13. She wants to know how her friends, who have stayed home, are. 14. You have done everything you could. 15. Instead of the mountains of the Rhineland Monika now saw fields and meadows which were flat and green. 16. He translates every day which is very good for him.

VI. Fragen

1. Wann ist Monika in Bremen angekommen? 2. Wie wurde die dicke Dame während der Reise? 3. Warum sollte sie keine Süßigkeiten essen? 4. Was sagt ihr Arzt immer wieder? 5. Wer hat Monika am Bahnhof getroffen? 6. Was haben sie dann alle gemacht? 7. Was hat Annas Vater dem Mädchen erzählt? 8. Wohin sind die Freundinnen heute gegangen? 9. Wo steht die Statue vom Roland? 10. Wohin sind die Freundinnen dann gegangen? 11. Wie ist das Dach der Kirche geworden? 12. Wie gefällt das dem Mädchen? 13. Wie ist die Landschaft um Bremen? 14. Womit fahren fast alle Leute hier? 15. Warum will Monika nun zu Bett gehen?

VII. Lesestück

Deutsche Klöster

Bis zum 8. (achten) Jahrhundert waren die deutschen Stämme, die in dem Land zwischen Weser und Rhein wohnten, heidnisch. Sie verehrten heidnische Götter, deren Namen noch heute in den Namen der Wochentage leben, z.B. in den deutschen Namen Donnerstag und Freitag oder in den englischen Namen W e d n e s d a y und T h u r s d a y.

In der Mitte des 8. (achten) Jahrhunderts kam Bonifatius nach Deutschland, ein englischer Mönch, dem die deutsche Geschichte den Namen „Apostel der Deutschen" gegeben hat. Er predigte die christliche Religion und bekehrte Tausende von Heiden zum Christentum. In den Wäldern von Deutschland gab es oft große, alte Bäume. Viele dieser Bäume (so glaubten die heidnischen Deutschen) waren heilig und den Göttern geweiht. Es war ein wichtiger Tag in der deutschen Geschichte, als Bonifatius eine große, alte, heilige Eiche fällte.

Er wollte den Deutschen zeigen, daß kein heidnischer Gott protestierte oder ihn strafte, und daß darum ihre heidnische Religion falsch war.

Es dauerte noch mehr als 100 (hundert) Jahre, bis alle Deutschen das Christentum angenommen hatten. Die christlichen Mönche gründeten Klöster in allen Gegenden Deutschlands. Diese Klöster wurden bald die Zentren christlicher Kultur. In diesen Zeiten vor der Erfindung der Buchdruckerkunst war es sehr wichtig, daß in allen Klöstern die Mönche alte Manuskripte abschrieben. So retteten sie viele Werke der alten, deutschen Literatur. Fast alle Klöster hatten Schulen, in denen die Mönche lehrten. Man hat oft die 200 (zweihundert) Jahre von 900 (neunhundert) bis 1100 (elfhundert) „die Zeit der Klosterkultur" genannt. Berühmt waren das Kloster St. Gallen in der Schweiz, das Kloster Reichenau auf einer Insel im Bodensee, oder die Klöster Fulda, Hersfeld, Gandersheim, Tegernsee, Maulbronn, Weißenburg, St. Blasien, Eberbach. Dies sind nur ein paar Namen aus der Geschichte berühmter, deutscher Klöster.

Eine Klostergeschichte

Die Mönche des alten Klosters Eberbach waren berühmt, nicht nur wegen ihrer Frömmigkeit und Gelehrsamkeit, sondern auch weil in ihrem Weinberg der beste Wein am Rhein wuchs. Eberbach gehörte zu dem großen Kloster Fulda. Jedes Jahr, wenn der Wein zu reifen anfing, mußte ein Bote zum Abt nach Fulda gehen und fragen, ob sie jetzt die Trauben schneiden dürften. Für die Reise von Eberbach nach Fulda brauchte man drei oder vier Tage. Es geschah in einem Herbst, daß der Bote auf dieser Reise krank wurde. Die Trauben wurden reif und überreif, aber der Bote kam nicht. Es war nun Ende Oktober. Die meisten Trauben waren in der warmen Sonne trocken geworden oder halbverfault. Die guten Mönche waren verzweifelt, als endlich, endlich der Bote aus Fulda ankam. Die Eberbacher Mönche schnitten traurig

Courtesy of Landesverkehrsverband Hessen, Wiesbaden

Kloster Eberbach im Rheingau

Kloster Birnau am Bodensee

Courtesy of the German Tourist Information Office, New York

Courtesy of the German Tourist Information Office, New York

Klosterkirche in Eichstädt, Bayern

Kloster Ettal in Bayern

Courtesy of the German Tourist Information Office, New York

ihre überreifen und halbverfaulten Trauben, doch sieh da: nie zuvor hatte man einen so guten Wein getrunken. Seit dieser Zeit wissen die Leute am Rhein, daß man aus den späten, überreifen Trauben den besten Wein macht.

VIII. Wörterverzeichnis

ab-schreiben, schrieb ab, abgeschrieben (to) copy
der Abt, ⸗̈e the abbot
an-nehmen (nimmt an), nahm an, angenommen (to) accept
der Apostel, – the apostle
der Baum, ⸗̈e the tree
bekehren (to) convert
der beste the best
der Bodensee Lake Constance
Bonifatius Boniface
der Bote, (–n), –n the messenger
die Buchdruckerkunst the art of printing
das Christentum Christianity
christlich Christian
dauern (to) last, take
der Donnerstag Thursday
die Eiche, –n the oak (tree)
endlich finally
die Erfindung, –en the invention
fällen (to) fell, cut down
falsch false
der Freitag Friday
die Frömmigkeit piety
die Gegend, –en the region
die Gelehrsamkeit learning
geweiht dedicated
der Gott, ⸗̈er the god
gründen (to) found
halbverfault half rotten
der Heide, (–n), –n the heathen, pagan
heidnisch heathen
die Insel, –n the island
das Kloster, ⸗̈ the cloister, monastery
die Klosterkultur the cloister culture
die Kultur the culture
die Literatur the literature
die meisten most of the
der Mönch, –e the monk
der Name, (–ns), –n the name
nie zuvor never before
noch still
predigen (to) preach
protestieren (to) protest
reif ripe
reifen (to) ripen
die Religion, –en the religion
retten (to) save
St.; Sankt St.; Saint
sieh da lo and behold
der Stamm, ⸗̈e the tribe
strafen (to) punish
Tausende thousands
die Traube, –n the grape
trocken dry
überreif over-ripe
verehren (to) venerate
verzweifelt desperate, in despair
der Weinberg, –e the vineyard
das Werk, –e the work (of art)
der Wochentag, –e the day of the week
das Zentrum; Zentren the center; centers
z.B.; zum Beispiel e.g.; for example

Aufgabe Fünfzehn

DECLENSION OF ADJECTIVES
TIME EXPRESSIONS

I. Reading Selection

„Wollen Sie heute abend mit mir kommen?" fragte mich Herr Löwenzahn. „Ich gehe zur Probe meines Gesangvereins."

„Das ist nichts Interessantes", sagte Frau Löwenzahn.

„Es ist etwas sehr Deutsches", meinte Herr Löwenzahn. „Wir singen alte deutsche Volkslieder, und manchmal haben wir ein großes Fest, zu dem wir unsere Familien und Freunde einladen."

„Ich komme gern", sagte ich.

Wir gingen zusammen in die Stadt. Der Gesangverein hatte seine Proben in einem alten Wirtshaus. Als wir ankamen, hatte die Probe schon angefangen. Weil Herr Löwenzahn zu spät kam, mußte er sofort fünfzig Pfennig Strafe zahlen. „Wir haben hier sehr strenge Gesetze", sagte er ernst. Dann ging er auf die Bühne, wo seine Freunde schon standen. Sie fingen gerade ein neues Lied an. Es berichtete eine traurige Geschichte von einem grünen Wald, in dem viele freundliche Tiere lebten, unter ihnen ein hübsches, junges Reh. Ein böser Mann kam in den Wald, ein Jäger mit einem Gewehr. Sein Hut hatte die grüne Farbe des Waldes, doch er hatte ein schwarzes Herz. In der Mitte des dunklen Waldes traf der Jäger das junge Reh und nun geschah, was geschehen mußte: er schoß es und brachte damit das Leben des Rehes und das traurige Lied zu einem schnellen Ende. Die Männer sangen die letzten Worte des Liedes mit solch leiser Stimme, daß man sie kaum verstehen konnte. Doch sofort danach wurden sie sehr laut, kamen von der Bühne und bestellten Bier. „Nichts macht so durstig wie ein trauriges Lied", sagten sie.

Es gab eine Pause von fünfzehn Minuten, in der ich mit einem alten Mann sprach, der vor vielen Jahren in Baltimore gelebt hatte. „Ich habe gern in Baltimore gewohnt", erzählte er mir, „aber wegen der heißen, feuchten Monate im Sommer konnte ich dort nicht leben. Hier in Deutschland ist es zu kalt, und es regnet zu viel. Man ist nie zufrieden."

Nun gingen die Männer wieder auf die Bühne und sangen einige berühmte deutsche Lieder, traurige und lustige, Lieder von schönen Mädchen, von gutem Wein, von heißer Liebe, von hohen Bergen, von einer blauen Blume und immer wieder von dunklen, grünen Wäldern. Dann sangen sie auch das Lied von der Loreley, von dem wir in Aufgabe elf sprachen.

Wieder ein sehr trauriges Lied, dachte ich, es wird sie wieder sehr durstig machen. Doch sofort danach kam das letzte Lied des Abends, „Das Schweigen im Walde", in dem sie so laut und hoch schrieen, daß sie alle rote Köpfe hatten.

„Wie hat Ihnen unser letztes Lied gefallen?" fragte mich Herr Löwenzahn, als wir später nach Hause gingen.

„Es war ein sehr lautes Schweigen", sagte ich.

II. Vocabulary

das Bier the beer
***blau** blue
böse bad, evil
die Bühne, –n the stage
***dunkel** dark
***einige** some
ein-laden (ladet ein or **lädt ein), lud ein, eingeladen (zu)** (to) invite (to)
das Fest, –e festival, celebration
feucht humid
freundlich friendly, kind
***fünfzehn** fifteen
fünfzig fifty
der Gesangverein, –e the singing society, choral group
das Gesetz, –e the law
das Gewehr, –e the gun
***das Herz, (ens), –en** the heart
***hoch** high

der Jäger, – the hunter
***kaum** scarcely, hardly
***der letzte** the last
***das Lied, –er** the song
***manchmal** sometimes
***mehrere** several
die Pause, –n the pause, recess, intermission
die Probe, –n the rehearsal, trial
das Reh, –e the deer
schießen, schoß, geschossen (to) shoot
das Schweigen the silence
die Strafe, –n the punishment, fine
streng strict
***unter** among
das Volkslied, –er the folksong
***wenig** little
***wenige** few
das Wirtshaus, ⸚er the inn, tavern
***das Wort, ⸚er** or **–e** the word
***zusammen** together

IDIOMS

***ich komme gern** I like to come, I'd like to come
***heute abend** this evening

III. Grammar

An adjective may be used **predicatively** (*the shirt is blue*) or **attributively** (*the blue shirt*). For the simple rules of the predicate adjective see Lesson I, Section III, D. If the adjective precedes a noun, (i.e., if it is used attributively), its ending depends 1) on the case, gender, and number of the following noun, and 2) on the type of the word which precedes the adjective.

A. DECLENSION OF ADJECTIVES AFTER **Der** WORDS

1. We learned the **der words** and how to decline them in Lesson IV: **der, dieser, jeder, mancher, solcher, welcher,** and **all** (when it has an ending). We need to remember them in order to know what endings to put on adjectives that follow them. Before you go on, review the grammar of Lesson IV.

2. **Adjectives preceded by "der words" end in –en in all except five cases, and here they end in –e.** The five exceptional cases are: nominative singular of the masculine-feminine-neuter; and accusative singular of the feminine-neuter.

ADJECTIVES AFTER **DER** WORDS

	MASCULINE	FEMININE	NEUTER
NOM.	**der gute Mann**	**diese gute Frau**	**jedes gute Kind**
GEN.	des guten Mannes	dieser guten Frau	jedes guten Kindes
DAT.	dem guten Mann	dieser guten Frau	jedem guten Kind
ACC.	den guten Mann	**diese gute Frau**	**jedes gute Kind**

PLURAL

NOM.	manche guten Leute
GEN.	mancher guten Leute
DAT.	manchen guten Leuten
ACC.	manche guten Leute

B. DECLENSION OF ADJECTIVES AFTER **Ein** WORDS

1. Again we refer to Lesson IV where we learned the declension of the **ein words.** We repeat the words here: **ein, kein; mein, dein, sein, ihr, sein; unser, euer, ihr, Ihr.** (Remember: **ein** has no plural).

2. **Adjectives preceded by "ein words" end in –en in all except five cases, and here the ending shows the gender** (**–er** for masculine, **–e** for feminine, and **–es** for neuter). The five exceptional cases are the same as in A, 2 above.

ADJECTIVES AFTER **EIN** WORDS

	MASCULINE	FEMININE	NEUTER
NOM.	**ein guter Mann**	**deine gute Frau**	**ihr gutes Kind**
GEN.	eines guten Mannes	deiner guten Frau	ihres guten Kindes
DAT.	einem guten Mann	deiner guten Frau	ihrem guten Kind
ACC.	einen guten Mann	**deine gute Frau**	**ihr gutes Kind**

PLURAL

NOM.	keine guten Leute
GEN.	keiner guten Leute
DAT.	keinen guten Leuten
ACC.	keine guten Leute

Note that **the two sets of endings** (i.e., after **der** or **ein** words) **are identical except in three cases: nominative masculine, nominative neuter, and accusative neuter.** In these three cases there is a discrepancy between the two sets and we should carefully memorize the difference.

C. Declension of Plain Adjectives

Plain descriptive adjectives, i.e., adjectives not preceded by **der** or **ein words,** take the same endings as **dieser** (except in two cases).

PLAIN ADJECTIVES

	Masculine	Feminine	Neuter
Nom.	guter Wein	gute Frau	gutes Kind
Gen.	guten * Weines	guter Frau	guten * Kindes
Dat.	gutem Wein	guter Frau	gutem Kind
Acc.	guten Wein	gute Frau	gutes Kind

Plural

Nom.	gute Leute
Gen.	guter Leute
Dat.	guten Leuten
Acc.	gute Leute

For all situations given above (whether after **der** words, after **ein** words, or plain): two or more descriptive adjectives in front of a noun regularly take the same endings: **ein schönes, altes Haus; guter, roter Wein.**

Remember for all three basic combinations as outlined in A, B, C: **the descriptive adjective used attributively (i.e., in front of a noun) must agree in case, gender, and number with the noun to which it belongs.**

D. Declensional Details

1. Adjectives are frequently used as nouns, and, being nouns, are capitalized but still declined as adjectives with their proper adjective endings: **der Deutsche,** *the German;* **ein**

* The two exceptions are the genitive masculine and genitive neuter where the expected ending **–es** normally changes to **–en.** Actually these forms are rarely used.

Deutscher, *a German;* **die Deutschen,** *the Germans;* **die Alte,** *the old woman;* **der Kranke,** *the sick man* (*the patient*); **das Gute,** *that which is good.*

2. The neuter form of these capitalized adjectives often designates an abstract (**das Schöne,** the beautiful = that which is beautiful) and frequently combines with quantitative adjectives such as **viel, wenig, etwas,** and **nichts.** The declension of this abstract adjective follows the pattern of the plain adjective (in its neuter form, of course), as given in section C above. Example: *much that is interesting,* **viel Interessantes;** *something blue,* **etwas Blaues;** we talked *of something gay,* wir sprachen **von etwas Lustigem.**—When such an abstract neuter follows the quantitative adjective **alles** (*sing.*), *all* or *everything,* it takes the endings (neuter, of course) given in section A above. Examples: *everything new* (*all that is new*), **alles Neue;** we talked *of everything interesting,* wir sprachen **von allem Interessanten.**

3. If the quantitative adjectives **viele, wenige, einige, mehrere** and **andere** (*others*) appear in the plural and are followed by one or more descriptive adjectives, these adjectives again follow the declensional pattern in section C above (plural, of course.) Examples: *few pretty things,* **wenige hübsche Dinge;** the reports of *some German students,* die Berichte **einiger deutscher Studenten;** they lived *in many old cities,* sie wohnten **in vielen alten Städten.**—If **alle** (*plur.*) is followed by one or more descriptive adjectives, these adjectives take the endings given in section A above (**–en** in all cases). Example: *all good people,* **alle guten Leute.**

4. We have two words for *some*: **etwas** and **einige.** We generally use **etwas** for the singular **(etwas Kaffee)** and **einige** for the plural **(einige Bücher.)** The two plurals **einige** and **mehrere** are synonyms.

5. German puts endings on adjectives referring back to a noun previously used but not repeated: Die Männer sangen einige berühmte Lieder, **traurige und lustige; über die lustigen**

lachten wir. The men sang some famous songs, *sad ones and gay ones;* we laughed *about the gay ones.* The endings in such cases thus correspond to the words *one* or *ones* in English to compensate for not repeating the noun (**Lieder** or *songs*).

6. The adjective **hoch** drops the **c** when it adds the letter **–e.** Der Berg ist **hoch,** but der **hohe** Berg, ein **hohes** Haus.—Adjectives ending in **–el, –en, –er** also frequently drop the **e** of the last syllable when they add the letter **–e.** Die Nacht ist **dunkel,** but die **dunkle** Nacht; das Fenster ist **offen,** but das **offne** Fenster.

7. We repeat that German adverbs (always identical with the form of the predicate adjective) take no endings; see Lesson XI, Section III, D.

E. Das Herz

Herz appears as an active word in this lesson. Remember its unusual declension: Sing.: **das Herz, des Herzens, dem Herzen, das Herz.** Plur.: **die Herzen.**

F. The Adverb Gern

The German adverb **gern** equals not only the English *gladly,* but also the English phrase (*to*) *like to.* **Er arbeitet gern,** *he likes to work.* **Sie erzählten gern Geschichten,** *they liked to tell stories.* **Ich habe gern mit ihm gesprochen,** *I liked to talk with him,* or *I was glad to talk with him.*

G. Gestern, Heute, Morgen

1. The words **gestern, heute,** and **morgen** carry no difficulty when used alone. We also use them, as in English, with parts of the day: **gestern vormittag, gestern nachmittag, gestern abend, gestern nacht.**

2. For such expressions referring to today, English uses *this,* i.e., *this morning, this afternoon,* etc. For this purpose German uses the adverb **heute: heute vormittag, heute mittag, heute nachmittag, heute abend, heute nacht.**

3. For *tomorrow morning* we say **morgen vormittag** (or **morgen früh**), for *tomorrow afternoon* **morgen nachmittag,** etc. (German has two words for *morning*: **der Vormittag** and **der Morgen.** The word **Morgen** cannot combine with **morgen** in such expressions as above.)

4. Note that when **gestern, heute, morgen** combine with a part of the day, neither word is capitalized. German treats them both as adverbs.

IV. Grammatical Exercises

A. Fill in the proper adjective endings where needed:

1. Dies____ alt____ Männer sangen ein alt____, deutsch____ Lied. 2. Einig____ von unser____ berühmt____ Liedern sind sehr traurig. 3. Nach d____ letzt____ Probe gingen wir in ein alt____ Restaurant. 4. Heute abend wird er uns ein____ interessant____ Bericht über sein____ Reise geben. 5. Wer ist dies____ jung____ Dame? 6. Sie ist ein____ gut____ Freundin mein____ lieb____ Mutter. 7. Sein____ gut____ Mutter schreibt oft ernst____ Briefe an ihn. 8. Wir sind die ganz____ Zeit mit ein____ sehr schnell____ Zug gefahren. 9. Kalt____ Luft kam durch das offen____ Fenster in sein Zimmer. 10. D____ dumm____ Kind hat laut geschrieen. 11. Ich weiß nichts Gut____ von ihm. 12. All____ höflich____ Kinder haben den Hut abgenommen, als sie ins Zimmer kamen. 13. Weiß____ und rot____ Blumen wuchsen in sein____ still____ Garten. 14. Einig____ jung____ Leute sangen mit leis____ Stimme alt____ deutsch____ Lieder. 15. Sie dachten an schön____ Mädchen, gut____ Wein und hoh____ Berge. 16. D____ Deutsch____ gehen gern in dunkl____, grün____ Wälder. 17. Er erzählte mit laut____ Stimme eine englisch____ Geschichte. 18. D____ flach____ Feld ist gut für d____ Radfahren. 19. Dies____ neu____ Schiffe fahren nach all____ groß____ Ländern d____ Welt

20. Unser neu____ Rathaus ist nicht so schön wie das alt____. 21. „Nichts Neu____ ist schön", sagen viel____ alt____ Leute. 22. „Aber alles Alt____ ist schön." 23. D____ hübsch____ Mädchen, das so spät ankam, stieg in d____ letzt____ Abteil des Zuges. 24. In dies____ frei____ Land wohnt ein zufrieden____ Volk.

B. Decline in the singular and plural: der schwarze Schuh; diese frühe Stunde; welches hübsche Kind; ein durstiger Gast; unsere alte Kirche; sein großes Heft; guter Wein; grüne Lampe; schnelles Tier; das warme Herz.

C. Translate the following expressions: last night; yesterday noon; this morning; tomorrow afternoon; this evening; tomorrow morning; something true; everything old; nothing new; little that is interesting; much that is famous; some wine; some boys.

V. Translation Exercise

1. Young man, do you like to play tennis? 2. His green chair stands in the middle of this dark room. 3. There is nothing difficult for him. 4. They have red heads, for they have been singing too loudly. 5. Many famous songs are very gay. 6. A week ago she wrote me a very sad letter. 7. He read many interesting stories in his German book, gay ones and serious ones. 8. Conrad saw a pretty blonde girl in a blue dress, who was sitting on a bench in the park. 9. We were very satisfied because we were allowed to swim in the warm water. 10. My friend's children asked me: "Do you have something good for us in your pocket?" 11. Although it was not yet late, the old lady got on the train quickly. 12. Tomorrow morning we shall meet an important man from America. 13. Our beautiful white flowers need some water every day. 14. After my dear friend had arrived in Bremen, he wrote me a very cordial letter. 15. The sick (man) was sitting in an

easy chair in front of his house near (*bei*) the beautiful, old, high forest. 16. Like our fathers we want to be free people.

VI. Fragen

1. Wohin geht Herr Löwenzahn heute abend? 2. Was sagt Frau Löwenzahn darüber? 3. Was singt man im Gesangverein? 4. Wer kommt zu den Festen des Gesangvereins? 5. Warum muß Herr Löwenzahn eine Strafe zahlen? 6. Wo standen schon Herrn Löwenzahns Freunde? 7. Welche Geschichte berichtete das neue Lied, das sie gerade angefangen hatten? 8. Wie sangen die Männer die letzten Worte dieses Liedes? 9. Was taten die Männer in der Pause? 10. Wo hatte der alte Mann, mit dem Conrad sprach, früher gelebt? 11. Warum hatte er es dort nicht gern? 12. Wie gefällt es ihm jetzt in Deutschland? 13. Wie waren die Lieder, die die Männer nach der Pause sangen? 14. Welches Lied haben sie auch gesungen? 15. Können Sie uns die Geschichte von der Loreley erzählen? 16. Wie haben sie das letzte Lied gesungen? 17. Was haben Conrad und Herr Löwenzahn nach dem letzten Lied getan?

VII. Lesestück

Deutsche Universitäten

Unter den deutschen Universitäten, die heute noch existieren, ist die Universität Heidelberg die älteste. Sie wurde im Jahre 1386 (dreizehnhundertsechsundachtzig) gegründet. In den Vereinigten Staaten haben oft reiche Leute das Geld für die Gründung einer Schule oder einer Universität gegeben. Darum tragen viele amerikanische Universitäten die Namen ihrer Gründer: Harvard, Yale, Cornell, Stanford und viele andere. In Deutschland wurden alle frühen Universitäten von Fürsten gegründet, deren Namen noch heute in den Namen der Universitäten leben: die Ludwig-Maximilians Universität in München, die Ruprecht-Karls Universität in Heidelberg, die Philipps Universität in Marburg. Die Johann Wolfgang Goethe Universität in Frankfurt und die Johannes Gutenberg Universität in Mainz tragen die Namen von zwei großen Söhnen der beiden Städte.

Viele deutsche Universitäten entstanden in der Zeit der Renaissance oder in der Zeit der Aufklärung, d.h. im 15. (fünfzehnten) oder im 18. (achtzehnten) Jahrhundert. Später übernahmen die deutschen Staaten die Universitäten. Einige der neuen Universitäten, die im 20. (zwanzigsten) Jahrhundert entstanden, wurden von Städten gegründet. So geschah es in Hamburg, Frankfurt oder Köln. Es gibt in Deutschland keine privaten Universitäten.

Während des 19. (neunzehnten) Jahrhunderts wurden die deutschen Universitäten sehr berühmt. Einige von ihnen waren führend in Philosophie, Geschichte, Philologie, Naturwissenschaften und Medizin. Von den großen Professoren nennen wir nur solche Namen wie den Philosophen Friedrich Hegel, die Historiker Leopold von Ranke und Theodor Mommsen, die Philologen Jacob und Wilhelm Grimm, die Mediziner Rudolf Virchow und Paul Ehrlich, den Chemiker Robert Bunsen, den Physiker Wilhelm Röntgen, der die Röntgenstrahlen entdeckte.

Studenten kamen aus allen Ländern der Welt, um in Deutschland zu studieren. Bei amerikanischen Studenten war besonders die Universität Göttingen beliebt. Viele der jungen Intellektuellen von Neu-England haben im frühen 19. (neunzehnten) Jahrhundert an der Universität Göttingen studiert. Auch in unserer Zeit studieren noch viele junge Amerikaner an deutschen Universitäten, doch ehe sie nach Deutschland gehen, müssen sie an ihren amerikanischen Universitäten die deutsche Sprache lernen.

Deutsche Universitäten liegen meistens in der Mitte der Stadt. Sie haben nicht das, was wir in Amerika den „Campus" nennen. Deutsche Studenten wohnen nicht in der Universität.

Ein Student in Deutschland hat ein Zimmer bei einer Familie in der Stadt, oder er wohnt bei seinen Eltern. Von dort fährt er jeden Tag mit der Straßenbahn oder mit dem Zug zur Universität.

In vielen anderen Einrichtungen und Gewohnheiten sind deutsche Universitäten anders als amerikanische. Doch das kann man nicht in wenigen Worten erklären. Vielleicht können Sie ein Buch darüber lesen oder noch besser: studieren Sie an einer deutschen Universität!

VIII. Wörterverzeichnis

der älteste the oldest
anders als different from
die Aufklärung the Enlightenment
beliebt bei popular with
besonders especially
der Chemiker, – the chemist
die Einrichtung, –en the institution, arrangement
entdecken (to) discover
entstehen, enstand, ist entstanden (to) originate
existieren (to) exist
der Fürst, (–en), –en the ruling prince
die Gewohnheit, –en the custom
gründen (to) found
der Gründer, – the founder
die Gründung, –en the foundation, founding
der Historiker, – the historian
der Intellektuelle, (–n), –n the intellectual
Köln Cologne
der Mediziner, – the medical man
meistens mostly, usually, for the most part
der Name, (–ns), –n the name
die Naturwissenschaften the natural sciences
noch still
oft often
der Philologe, (–n), –n the philologist
die Philologie language and literature, philology
der Philosoph, (–en), –en the philosopher
die Philosophie philosophy
der Physiker, – the physicist
privat private
der Professor, –en the professor
reich rich
die Röntgenstrahlen the X-rays
der Staat, –en the state
übernehmen (übernimmt), übernahm, übernommen (to) take over, assume
die Universität, –en the university
wurde, wurden *plus past participle form passive voice; translate* was *and* were

Aufgabe Sechzehn

COMPARISON OF ADJECTIVES

I. Reading Selection

Eines Abends besuchte uns Klaus Ebert, ein Neffe von Frau Löwenzahn, der an der Universität Heidelberg Physik studiert. Er ist ein freundlicher, junger Mann, vielleicht zwei oder drei Jahre älter als Herbert und ich. Er ist noch nie in Amerika gewesen, doch er wollte viel über unser Land wissen.

„In Europa hat man Amerika oft das Land der Superlative genannt", sagte er. „Ich weiß nicht, ob es so ist, aber viele Amerikaner, die uns besucht haben, haben uns erzählt, daß zu Hause alles am besten, am schönsten, am größten und am höchsten ist."

„Wir sind ein jüngeres Volk als die Völker Europas", meinte Herbert. „Wir sind vielleicht noch nicht so skeptisch wie Sie. Sie lesen in der Zeitung, daß ein Bäcker den größten Kuchen der Welt gebacken hat, aber Sie fragen sofort: hat nicht (vielleicht zur Zeit von Nebukadnezar oder später) ein anderer Bäcker einen noch größeren gebacken? Wir in Amerika lesen es und glauben es."

„O nein", widersprach ich. „Auch wir sind nicht so naiv, alle Superlative ernst zu nehmen. Wir lesen in der Politik, daß dies ‚der beste Mann' ist oder daß ein anderer ‚die größte Tat des Jahrhunderts' getan hat, aber wir wissen, daß wir davon nur die Hälfte oder noch weniger glauben dürfen. Doch weil wir, wie Herbert sagt, ein junges Volk sind, haben wir ein größeres Interesse für alles Alte, das in die frühste Geschichte unseres Landes zurückgeht. Wir sind stolz auf das älteste Haus in Massachusetts oder die älteste Kirche in Maryland."

„Das kann ich verstehen", meinte Klaus Ebert. „Hier ist so viel alt, älter und am ältesten, daß das Alte für uns nichts Neues und nichts Interessantes ist."

„Wir sprechen auch oft in Superlativen, ohne darauf stolz zu sein", sagte ich. „Immer wieder nennt man Rhode Island den kleinsten Staat des Landes. Wir sagen von einem Sommer: es war der heißeste des Jahrhunderts. In meinem Staat Pennsylvania gibt es einen großen Fluß, auf dem keine Schiffe fahren können und wir sagen darum: der Susquehanna ist der längste nutzlose Fluß der Welt. Wir wollen damit nicht sagen, daß wir stolz darauf sind. Wir lächeln darüber, anstatt es ernst zu nehmen."

„Wenn wir vom Klima sprechen", meinte Herbert, „können wir vielleicht sagen: Amerika ist nicht das Land des ‚am meisten', sondern das Land des ‚mehr'. Wir haben kältere Winter und wärmere Sommer. In Chicago ist der Wind stärker, in Seattle regnet es öfter, in Texas brennt die Sonne heißer als in anderen Städten und Ländern der Welt.—Da wir von Texas sprechen", fragte Herbert mich, „kennst du Leute aus Texas, die über ihren Staat nicht im Superlativ sprechen?"

„Halt!" unterbrach ich ihn schnell. „Sprich freundlich über die Leute in Texas, sonst werden die Studenten und Lehrer dort dies Buch nicht kaufen."

„Nun", sagte Klaus Ebert, als er aufstand, um nach Hause zu gehen, „es war ein höchst interessanter Abend. Sie haben die längsten, schönsten und schwersten Superlative geübt, und ich habe viel über Ihr Land gelernt. Auf Wiedersehen!"

II. Vocabulary

***als** (*after comparative*) than
***(der) ander(e)** (the) other
backen (ä), buk, gebacken (to) bake

der Bäcker, – the baker
***Europa** Europe
***der Fluß, (Flusses), Flüsse** the river
***freundlich** friendly
***die Hälfte** (the) half
***höchst** highly, very
***klein** small, little
das Klima the climate
***lang** long
naiv naive
Nebukadnezar Nebuchadnezzar
der Neffe, (–n), –n the nephew
***noch** still
nutzlos useless
***oft** often
die Physik physics
die Politik politics
***sechzehn** sixteen
skeptisch skeptical
***sonst** otherwise
***der Staat, –en** the state
***stark** strong
***stolz auf** (*with acc.*) proud of
der Superlativ, –e the superlative
***die Tat, –en** the act, deed
widersprechen (i), widersprach, widersprochen (to) contradict
***der Wind, –e** the wind
zurückgehen, ging zurück, ist zurückgegangen (to) go back

IDIOMS

***Halt!** Halt! Stop!
***zur Zeit** at the time

III. Grammar

A. COMPARISON OF ADJECTIVES AND ADVERBS

Introductory: English compares adjectives by adding *–er* to form the comparative, and *–est* to form the superlative, e.g., *dark—darker—darkest.*

English with longer adjectives, and with adverbs, may also use *more* and *most* with the simple form, e.g., *cordial—more cordial—most cordial*—**but German never does this.**

1. The normal way for German adjectives and adverbs to form the comparative and superlative is by adding **–er** and **–st** respectively to the simple form:

SIMPLE FORM	COMPARATIVE	SUPERLATIVE
dunkel, *dark*	dunkler	dunkelst–
durstig, *thirsty*	durstiger	durstigst–
flach, *flat*	flacher	flachst–
freundlich, *friendly*	freundlicher	freundlichst–
früh, *early*	früher	frühst–

SIMPLE FORM	COMPARATIVE	SUPERLATIVE
grün, *green*	grüner	grünst–
heilig, *holy*	heiliger	heiligst–
herzlich, *cordial*	herzlicher	herzlichst–
höflich, *courteous*	höflicher	höflichst–
klein, *small*	kleiner	kleinst–
leise, *soft*	leiser	leisest–
lieb, *dear*	lieber	liebst–
lustig, *merry*	lustiger	lustigst–
offen, *open*	offener	offenst–
schnell, *fast*	schneller	schnellst–
schön, *beautiful*	schöner	schönst–
schwer, *hard*	schwerer	schwerst–
still, *quiet*	stiller	stillst–
traurig, *sad*	trauriger	traurigst–
wichtig, *important*	wichtiger	wichtigst–
zufrieden, *contented*	zufriedener	zufriedenst–

2. German adjectives or adverbs ending in t, d, s, z, sch, or sometimes a vowel form the superlative, as in English with **–est**:

SIMPLE FORM	COMPARATIVE	SUPERLATIVE
berühmt, *famous*	berühmter	berühmtest–
blau, *blue*	blauer	blauest–
blond, *blond*	blonder	blondest–
deutsch, *German*	deutscher	deutschest–
ernst, *serious*	ernster	ernstest–
frei, *free*	freier	freiest–
heiß, *hot*	heißer	heißest–
hübsch, *pretty*	hübscher	hübschest–
interessant, *interesting*	interessanter	interessantest–
laut, *loud*	lauter	lautest–
neu, *new*	neuer	neuest–
spät, *late*	später	spätest–
stolz, *proud*	stolzer	stolzest–
weiß, *white*	weißer	weißest–

3. Some very common adjectives and adverbs of one syllable add umlaut in the comparative and superlative:

SIMPLE FORM	COMPARATIVE	SUPERLATIVE
alt, *old*	älter	ältest–
dumm, *stupid*	dümmer	dümmst–
groß, *big*	größer	größt–

SIMPLE FORM	COMPARATIVE	SUPERLATIVE
hoch, *high*	höher	höchst–
jung, *young*	jünger	jüngst–
krank, *sick*	kränker	kränkst–
kalt, *cold*	kälter	kältest–
lang, *long*	länger	längst–
oft, *often*	öfter	öftest–
rot, *red*	röter	rötest–
schwarz, *black*	schwärzer	schwärzest–
stark, *strong*	stärker	stärkst–
warm, *warm*	wärmer	wärmst–

4. A very few are irregular:

SIMPLE FORM	COMPARATIVE	SUPERLATIVE
gut, *good*	besser	best–
viel, *much*	mehr	meist–
gern, *gladly*	lieber	am liebsten

B. USE OF THE COMPARATIVE AND SUPERLATIVE

1. The comparative and superlative as well as the simple forms of the adjective take the adjective endings which were studied in the preceding lesson, e.g., **ein guter Mann, ein besserer Mann, der beste Mann,** etc.

2. In comparing two persons or things with the simple form of the adjective or adverb, we use **so . . . wie**: Conrad ist gerade **so** alt **wie** ich; Conrad is just *as* old *as* I. Vera ist nicht **so** alt **wie** ich; Vera is not *as* old *as* I.

3. In comparing two persons or things with the comparative form, we use in English *than*, in German **als**: Mein Freund ist **älter als** ich; my friend is *older than* I. Ich laufe **schneller als** er; I run *faster than* he.

4. **We never use the "bare forms" of the superlative as given in the lists above** (except for a few words such as **höchst** which is the adverb *highly*). We practically always find the superlative form either 1) preceded by the definite article, or 2) combined with **am** and ending in **–sten**, e.g., **am dunkelsten.**

5. If the superlative stands at the end of a sentence, not followed by a noun expressed or understood, i.e., if it is used predicatively or as an adverb, we use the **am form,** always with the same ending **–sten.** Examples: **Im Winter sind die Tage am kältesten;** *in winter the days are coldest.* **Die Tage sind im Sommer am heißesten;** *in summer the days are hottest.* **Diese Dame sang am schönsten;** *this lady sang most beautifully.*

6. Note how the two adverbs **lieber** and **am liebsten** are used with verbs: Ich trinke **gern** Limonade; I *like to* drink lemonade. Herbert trinkt **lieber** Frau Löwenzahns Kaffee; Herbert *prefers to* drink Mrs. Löwenzahn's coffee. Conrad trinkt **am liebsten** Herrn Löwenzahns Erdbeerbowle; Conrad *likes best of all* to drink Mr. Löwenzahn's strawberry punch. Cf. also: Er hat heiße Tage **gern**; he *likes* hot days. Ich habe kalte Tage **lieber;** I *prefer* cold days. Sie haben warme Tage **am liebsten**; they *like* warm days *best of all.*

7. **German immer + comparative = English comparative + comparative.** Examples: **immer dunkler,** *darker and darker;* **immer schneller,** *faster and faster;* also **immer wieder,** *again and again.*

C. Anstatt . . . Zu, Ohne . . . Zu

We have previously (Lesson XII, Section III, E) used **um . . . zu** with the infinitive: Conrad ging in die Stadt, **um** ein Geschenk **zu kaufen;** Conrad went downtown *in order to buy* a present.

German uses **anstatt . . . zu** and **ohne . . . zu** in the same way. Whereas English combines these prepositions with the present participle, German uses the infinitive. The infinitive, of course, must go to the end of the clause. **Anstatt** eine Reise **zu machen,** sind die Studenten zu Hause geblieben; *instead of taking* a trip, the students stayed home. Der Mann stand auf dem Bahnsteig, **ohne** in den Zug **einzusteigen;** the man stood on the platform *without getting on* the train.

D. Nun

We have had **nun** meanmg *now*. At the beginning of a sentence, **nun + comma = well + comma: Nun,** was sollen wir tun? *Well,* what shall we do?

IV. Grammatical Exercises

A. Decline in the singular and plural:

1. sein jüngerer Sohn
2. ihre ältere Freundin
3. kein besseres Volk
4. der stärkste Mann
5. die freundlichste Verkäuferin
6. das längste Leben

B. Make complete sentences out of the following fragments using the comparative and changing the infinitive to the proper form: 1. Im Winter — (sein) es — kalt — im Herbst. 2. Coca Cola — (schmecken) — gut — Limonade. 3. Ich — (fahren) — gern — mit dem Rad — mit der Straßenbahn. 4. Sommertage — (sein) — heiß — Wintertage. 5. Der Wind — (sein) — in Chicago — stark — in Frankfurt. 6. Es — (regnen) — in Seattle — oft — in Texas. 7. Der Staat Texas — (sein) — groß — Deutschland. 8. Das Geschenk — (kosten) — viel — ich dachte. 9. Einige Lieder — (sein) — lustig — andere. 10. In Texas — (brennen) — die Sonne — heiß — in anderen Staaten. 11. Am Rhein — (wachsen) — der Wein — gut — an anderen Flüssen der Welt. 12. Die Amerikaner — (sein) — jung — Volk — die Deutschen. 13. In Deutschland — (geben) — es — alt — Kirchen — in Amerika. 14. In Amerika — (machen) — die Leute — lang — Reisen — in Deutschland.

C. Fit the proper form of the superlative of the adjective or adverb in parenthesis:

1. Unsere Studenten wohnen bei den Löwenzahns (gern). 2. Sie haben das Zimmer in diesem Haus (groß). 3. Sein

Vater ist der Mann von allen Leuten, die ich kenne (stolz). 4. Die Arbeit in der Schule macht Conrad (hungrig). 5. Herbert arbeitet spät in der Nacht (gern). 6. Dieses Bier ist (gut). 7. Es ist auch (dunkel). 8. Rhode Island ist der Staat in unserm Land (klein). 9. Wissen Sie, welches Land in der Welt die Berge hat (hoch)? 10. Nachmittags schläft Herr Löwenzahn auf dem Sofa (gern). 11. Der Amerikaner kaufte mehr als der Deutsche, aber seine Frau kaufte (viel). 12. Manchmal denke ich, ich bin von allen Studenten in der Schule (dumm). 13. Wissen Sie, in welcher Stadt das Haus in Deutschland steht (alt)? 14. Ich glaube, die Landschaft am Rhein ist (schön).

V. Translation Exercise

1. This big river is perhaps the longest in Germany. 2. The best wine grows on the higher mountains on the Rhine. 3. There one has the hottest sun until late in autumn. 4. The American (*amerikanisch*) students like best of all to visit the Rhineland. 5. One evening, when they sat in a restaurant, an old man sang the saddest songs. 6. Conrad got more and more thirsty. 7. Instead of going home, he went back into the restaurant and ordered something to drink. 8. Herbert went to bed earlier without eating. 9. In fall it is not as hot as in summer, but it rains more often. 10. In summer the days are longest. 11. In the last year we had the coldest winter in this century. 12. Perhaps it rains in Seattle more than in other cities, but one sees there highly interesting scenery. 13. His German friend is the most polite young man I have met on my trip. 14. Monika will go to Bremen by a later train. 15. During the last half of their trip they saw the oldest and most famous churches in Europe. 16. Theodore Roosevelt said: "Speak softly, but carry a big stick." (*der Stock*) 17. Perhaps one should say today: "Speak still more softly, but carry a still bigger stick." 18. Or, perhaps: "Speak most

loudly, and carry the biggest stick." 19. Who knows in this century what is best! 20. Ohio is a larger state than Maryland, but Ohio is smaller than Texas. 21. Which state is smallest?

VI. Fragen

1. Wer besuchte die Studenten eines Abends? 2. Was tut Klaus Ebert in Heidelberg? 3. Wie alt ist er? 4. Ist er schon in Amerika gewesen? 5. Worüber sprachen sie an diesem Abend? 6. Hat Klaus Ebert schon früher andere Amerikaner getroffen? 7. Was haben sie ihm über ihr Land erzählt? 8. Welches Wort gebrauchen die Deutschen oft für Amerika? 9. Was sagt Herbert über die Völker Europas? 10. Nehmen die Amerikaner ihre Superlative immer ernst? 11. Was wissen Sie über Texas? 12. Was wissen Sie über Rhode Island? 13. Warum ist Klaus sehr zufrieden mit diesem Abend? 14. Warum können Conrad und Herbert mit diesem Abend sehr zufrieden sein?

VII. Lesestück

Das Rheinland

Kein anderer deutscher Fluß hat eine solch lange und ruhmreiche Geschichte wie der Rhein, kein anderer ist heute so wichtig für den Verkehr und den Handel Deutschlands und vieler anderer Länder in Europa.

Auf beiden Ufern ist der Fluß von schönen Landschaften umgeben. Da ist im Süden der Bodensee mit alten Städten, Klöstern und Burgen. Da ist der Schwarzwald mit hohen Bergen und dunklen Wäldern. Viele der alten Städte auf dem linken Ufer des Rheins wurden von den Römern gegründet. Vor 2 000 (zweitausend) Jahren gehörte das Rheinland zum römischen Reich. Es war der erste Teil Deutschlands, in den die römische Kultur eindrang. Noch heute kann man im Rheinland die Überreste römischer Tore, Theater und Bäder

Courtesy of the German Tourist Information Office, New York

Die Kölner Universität

Ein Städtchen am Rhein: Aßmannshausen

Courtesy of the German Tourist Information Office, New York

Courtesy of the German Tourist Information Office, New York

Burg Katz am Rhein, im Hintergrund die Loreley

sehen. Später, im Mittelalter, war das Rheinland der wichtigste Teil des Heiligen Römischen Reiches. Karl der Große lebte viele Jahre in Aachen; in Frankfurt wurden die Kaiser gewählt; im Dom von Speyer sind die Gräber von acht deutschen Kaisern des Mittelalters; die Erzbischöfe von Mainz, Köln und Trier gehörten zu den wichtigsten Fürsten des Heiligen Römischen Reiches. Im Museum von Mainz steht die alte Buchdruckerpresse von Johannes Gutenberg, der aus einer alten Mainzer Familie kam. Überall sehen wir Zeichen einer großen Vergangenheit: alte Burgen, die von hohen Bergen auf den Fluß herabsehen, alte Klöster, die versteckt in grünen Tälern liegen, alte Tore, Brücken, Kirchen, Städte. „Neu" nennt man im Rheinland ein Haus, das nur 100 (hundert) Jahre alt ist. Das älteste Haus Deutschlands steht in Winkel, einer kleinen Stadt am Rhein. Es ist mehr als 1 000 (tausend) Jahre alt, und noch heute wohnen Leute darin.

Zwischen den Wäldern und dem Fluß, zwischen den alten Burgen und den kleinen Städten liegen die Weinberge. Seit mehr als 1 000 (tausend) Jahren wachsen hier die Weine, deren Namen man in der Welt besser kennt als die Namen der Erzbischöfe und Kaiser des Heiligen Römischen Reiches: der Johannisberger, der Niersteiner, der Marcobrunner. Karl der Große, so erzählt die Sage, hat hier die ersten Weinberge gepflanzt, und noch heute geht der Kaiser in warmen Nächten im Sommer durch die Gärten und Weinberge und segnet die Reben.

Doch der Rhein und das Rheinland leben nicht nur in ihrer Vergangenheit. Auf dem Wasser des Flusses, zwischen seinen Ufern mit den Weinbergen, unter seinen Brücken mit den Toren fahren die Schiffe, von der Schweiz bis zum Atlantischen Ozean. Der Rhein zwischen Mainz und Rotterdam ist der belebteste Fluß der Welt, die wichtigste Nord-Süd-Verbindung in Europa. 300 (dreihundert) Schiffe fahren an jedem Tag im Jahr auf dem Rhein über die Grenze zwischen Holland und Deutschland.

Wir kennen keine andere Landschaft mit einer solch glücklichen Verbindung von Vergangenheit und Gegenwart, von Geschichte und Leben.

VIII. Wörterverzeichnis

der Atlantische Ozean the Atlantic Ocean
das Bad, ⸚er the bath, spa
belebt busy, crowded
der Bodensee Lake Constance
die Brücke, –n the bridge
die Buchdruckerpresse, –n the printing press
die Burg, –en the castle
der Dom, –e the cathedral
ein-dringen, drang ein, ist eingedrungen (to) penetrate
der erste the first
der Erzbischof, ⸚e the archbishop
der Fürst, (–en), –en the (ruling) prince
die Gegenwart the present
gehören zu (to) belong to
glücklich fortunate, happy
das Grab, ⸚er the grave
die Grenze, –n the border
gründen (to) found
der Handel the commerce
herab-sehen (ie), sah herab, herabgesehen (to) look down
der Kaiser, – the emperor
Karl der Große Charles the Great, Charlemagne
das Kloster, ⸚ the cloister
Köln Cologne
die Kultur the culture
der linke the left
Mainzer Mainz, of Mainz
das Mittelalter the Middle Ages
der Name, (–ns), –n the name
die Nord-Süd-Verbindung the north-south connection
pflanzen (to) plant
die Rebe, –n the grape
das Reich the Empire
der Römer, – the Roman
römisch Roman
ruhmreich glorious
die Sage, –n the saying, legend
der Schwarzwald the Black Forest
segnen (to) bless, give a blessing to
der Süden the south
das Tal, ⸚er the valley
der Teil, –e the part
das Tor, –e the gate
überall everywhere
die Überreste the remains, ruins
das Ufer, – the bank
umgeben (i), umgab, umgeben (to) surround
die Verbindung, –en the combination, union
die Vergangenheit the past
der Verkehr the traffic, communication
versteckt concealed, hidden
wählen (to) choose
der Weinberg, –e the vineyard
wurden were (*as in* VIII *of the last lesson*)
das Zeichen, – the sign

Aufgabe Siebzehn

REFLEXIVE PRONOUNS AND VERBS MODALS IN COMPOUND TENSES

I. Reading Selection

Während des ganzen Monats Dezember hatten die Löwenzahns Besuch aus Österreich. Ihre Tochter kam mit ihren zwei kleinen Kindern, einem Jungen von sechs und einem Mädchen von fünf Jahren. Sie hießen Henning und Henriette. Spät in der Nacht kamen sie an.

„Wie geht es euch?" fragte Herr Löwenzahn. „Seid ihr alle gesund?"

„Es geht uns gut", sagte seine Tochter. „Wir sind nur sehr müde, denn wir mußten schon um fünf Uhr aufstehen, und wir haben 14 Stunden im Zug gesessen."

„Wo ist dein Mann?" wollte Frau Löwenzahn wissen. „Warum ist er nicht mitgekommen?"

„Er hat die Reise nicht machen können", antwortete die Tochter, „weil man ihn in seinem Büro braucht. Er wird erst am Tage vor Weihnachten kommen können."

Am nächsten Tage war Nikolaustag. „Henning und Henriette müssen einen Nikolaus haben", sagte Herr Löwenzahn. „Wir haben oben noch den roten Anzug und den weißen Bart. Die Kinder werden viel Spaß haben."

„Soll ich den Nikolaus spielen?" fragte ich.

„Nein, das geht nicht", sagte Herr Löwenzahn. „Die Kinder werden Ihren amerikanischen Akzent erkennen. Ich bin ein guter Nikolaus. Vor vielen Jahren habe ich ihn in einem Kindergarten spielen müssen, und alle Leute waren sehr zufrieden mit mir."

Herr Löwenzahn zog sich oben an. Er trug den roten Anzug, die hohe Mütze und den weißen Bart und ging durch die Hintertür auf die Straße. Es war schon ein wenig dunkel geworden.

Ich sah vom Wohnzimmer durch das Fenster auf die Straße. „Ich glaube, ich habe den Nikolaus jetzt gerade kommen sehen", sagte ich und setzte mich neben die kleine Henriette. „Wirst du ein Gebet sagen können, wenn er kommt?"

Sie war sehr blaß im Gesicht, und ohne zu warten, fing sie sofort an zu beten:

Ich bin klein,
Mein Herz ist rein
Soll niemand drin wohnen
Als Jesus allein.

„Das war zu früh", sagte ich, „ich habe ihn jetzt erst an die Tür klopfen hören."

„Herein!" riefen wir alle.

Jetzt machte Herr Löwenzahn-Nikolaus die Tür auf und kam ins Zimmer. Henriette schrie laut und lief zu ihrer Mutter.

„Schämst du dich nicht?" fragte der Nikolaus mit tiefer Stimme. „Warum schreist du? Warum fürchtest du dich vor mir? Freust du dich nicht, daß der Nikolaus hier ist? Komm, setz dich auf meinen Schoß und sag ein kleines Gebet, dann habe ich ein hübsches Geschenk für dich."

Die kleine Henriette schrie immer lauter. Man konnte sehen, daß sie weder an Gebete noch an Geschenke dachte.

„Nun", meinte der Nikolaus (seine Stimme war jetzt ein wenig leiser geworden), „dann wollen wir sehen, ob dein

Bruder etwas gelernt hat. Kann unser kleiner Freund Henning für den Nikolaus ein Gebet sagen?"

„Großvater, ärgere dich nicht über sie", sagte der kleine Henning freundlich. „Sie ist noch ein Kind."

Wir alle lachten.

Herr Löwenzahn setzte sich auf einen Stuhl und nahm den Bart ab. „Ich verstehe es nicht", sagte er. „Im Kindergarten habe ich ihn so gut gespielt."

II. Vocabulary

der Akzent, –e the accent
***amerikanisch** (*adj.*) American
***sich an-ziehen, zog sich an, hat sich angezogen** (to) dress, get dressed
***der Anzug, ⸗e** the suit
***sich ärgern über** (*with acc.*) (to) be angry with *or* about, be mad at
der Bart, ⸗e the beard
der Besuch, –e the visit
der Besucher, – the visitor
blaß pale
***der Bruder, ⸗** the brother
das Büro, –s the office
***der Dezember** December
drin = darin in it
erkennen, erkannte, erkannt (to) recognize
***erst** (*adv.*) only, not until
***sich freuen über** (*with acc.*) (to) be glad about, to rejoice in
***sich fürchten vor** (*with dat.*) to be afraid of
das Gebet, –e the prayer
***das Gesicht, –er** the face
***gesund** well, healthy
der Großvater, ⸗ the grandfather
***heißen, hieß, geheißen** (to) be called
***Herein!** Come in!
die Hintertür the back door
der Kindergarten, ⸗ the kindergarden
***klopfen** (to) knock
***mit-kommen, kam mit, ist mitgekommen** (to) come along, come too
***müde** tired
die Mütze, –n the cap
***der nächste** the next
***niemand** no one, nobody
der Nikolaus Santa Claus, St. Nick
der Nikolaustag St. Nicholas' Day (Dec. 6)
***oben** upstairs, above
***Österreich** Austria
rein pure
***sich schämen über** (*with acc.*) (to) be ashamed of
***schon** already
der Schoß the lap
***sich setzen** (to) be seated, sit down
***siebzehn** seventeen
der Spaß, ⸗e (the) fun
***spielen** (to) play
***tief** deep
***die Tochter, ⸗** the daughter
***die Tür, –en** the door
***Weihnachten** Christmas

IDIOMS

Besuch haben (to) have a visitor *or* visitors
***das geht nicht** that won't do
jetzt erst only now, just now
nichts als nothing but
niemand als no one but
***Wie heißen Sie?** What is your name?
***Ich heiße Conrad** My name is Conrad

III. Grammar

A. REFLEXIVE PRONOUNS AND REFLEXIVE VERBS

1. If a dative or accusative pronoun refers back to the subject of the sentence or clause, we call it "reflexive." For example: *I seat myself*, where *myself* is reflexive because it is the same individual as *I*. English marks this particular pronoun situation by using distinct reflexive pronouns such as *myself, yourself, himself, ourselves,* etc.

2. **The reflexive pronoun in German is identical with the personal pronoun, except in the third person** (masc., fem. or neut.; sing. or plur.; dat. or acc.), **where it is always** ***sich.***

REFLEXIVE PRONOUNS

	DATIVE	ACCUSATIVE
SINGULAR		
First pers.	mir	mich
Second pers.	dir	dich
Third pers.	**sich**	**sich**
PLURAL		
First pers.	uns	uns
Second pers.	euch	euch
Third pers.	**sich**	**sich**

3. The reflexive pronoun may be used in the accusative or dative. Here an illustration for an accusative reflexive pronoun:

1.	ich setze mich	I sit down
2.	du setzt dich	you sit down
3.	er setzt **sich**	he sits down
	sie setzt **sich**	she sits down
	es setzt **sich**	he *or* she sits down *

1.	wir setzen uns	we sit down
2.	ihr setzt euch	you sit down
3.	sie setzen **sich**	they sit down
	Sie setzen **sich**	you sit down

4. If we take an English colloquialism such as "I'm going to buy me a shirt," we have the case of a reflexive pronoun in the dative, since here the pronoun *me* actually stands for the indirect object *for myself*.

1.	ich kaufe mir ein Hemd	I buy a shirt for myself
2.	du kaufst dir ein Hemd	you buy a shirt for yourself
3.	er kauft **sich** ein Hemd	he buys a shirt for himself
	sie kauft **sich** ein Hemd	she buys a shirt for herself
	es kauft **sich** ein Hemd	he *or* she buys himself *or* herself a shirt *

1.	wir kaufen uns ein Hemd	we buy ourselves a shirt
2.	ihr kauft euch ein Hemd	you buy yourselves a shirt
3.	sie kaufen **sich** ein Hemd	they buy themselves a shirt
	Sie kaufen **sich** ein Hemd	you buy yourselves a shirt

5. Many verbs may be used with an ordinary personal pronoun or a reflexive pronoun as shown in No. 4 above. Here are a few other verbs of the same type: **ich frage mich, er hilft sich, ich bestelle mir, er schneidet sich, er zeigt sich dem Volk,** etc.

* We would have to use the personal pronoun **es** if this pronoun stands for a neuter noun such as **das Kind** or **das Mädchen.**

Also there are some verbs in German which are always used as reflexive verbs, for instance **sich schämen** and **sich freuen über.** Then there is quite a large group of verbs which in German are used as reflexive verbs while in English no pronoun is given, for instance **er fürchtet sich,** *he is afraid;* **er ärgert sich,** *he is angry*; **wir setzen uns,** *we sit down*; **sie ziehen sich an,** *they get dressed.* If a reflexive is required with a verb, this is always indicated in our vocabulary by placing **sich** in front of the infinitive form. Otherwise, however, **sich** follows the rules of word order for pronoun objects: **er freut sich, er freute sich, er wird sich freuen, er hat sich gefreut,** etc. Reflexive verbs normally use **haben** to form the perfect tenses. The reflexive pronoun of the polite forms is not capitalized, e.g., imperative (polite): *Don't be afraid!*—**Fürchten Sie sich nicht!**

B. Impersonal Verbs

Some verbs obviously cannot have a person as the subject either in English or in German: **es geschieht,** *it happens*; **es regnet,** *it rains*; **es schneit,** *it snows.*

Others are used "impersonally" in a special sense: **es gibt,** *there is* or *there are*; **Wie geht es dir?** *How are you?* (literally: *How goes it with you?*); **Es geht mir gut,** *I am fine* (literally: *It goes well with me*).

Still others are used both with personal and impersonal subjects: **Es tut mir leid,** *I am sorry* (about it); **Der arme Mann tut mir leid,** *I am sorry for the poor man*; **Es gefällt mir,** *I like it*; **Sie gefällt mir,** *I like her* or *I find her pleasing.*

Such impersonal expressions which in English are rendered by a personal construction are very frequent in German: **Es ist mir kalt;** *I am cold.* **Es ist ihm warm;** *he is warm.* **Es freut ihn;** *he is pleased.* As you see, the person in these idioms stands in some of these expressions in the dative, in others in the accusative.

C. PERFECT AND FUTURE TENSES OF MODAL AUXILIARIES

1. In Lesson X we learned the present and past tenses of the modal auxiliaries **dürfen, können, mögen, müssen, sollen, wollen.** At that time the important thing about them, aside from their irregular conjugation, was that they take an **infinitive without zu.**

2. **The perfect tenses of these modals, when they have a dependent infinitive, do not use the past participle, but form a "double infinitive."** As we pointed out in Lesson X, some difficulties result from the fact that the English modals are defective in their conjugational forms. For instance, we have a present tense "I can," a past "I could," but this modal does not carry us through the remaining tenses. For the future we have to substitute "I shall be able to . . .", for the present perfect "I have been able to . . ." The German modals have all their conjugational forms, but no matter in what tense we may use them: they always connect the infinitive **without zu.**

Here we show you how the present perfect tense is formed with a modal auxiliary and its dependent infinitive:

PRESENT TENSE	PRESENT PERFECT TENSE
Dort darf man nicht rauchen.	Dort hat man nicht rauchen dürfen.
Ich kann diese Tür zumachen.	Ich habe diese Tür zumachen können.
Er mag nicht in die Stadt gehen.	Er hat nicht in die Stadt gehen mögen.
Ich muß meine Aufgabe lernen.	Ich habe meine Aufgabe lernen müssen.
Ich soll früh zu Bett gehen.	Ich habe früh zu Bett gehen sollen.
Ich will eine Reise machen.	Ich habe eine Reise machen wollen.
Ich lasse mir ein Hemd machen.	Ich habe mir ein Hemd machen lassen.

The past perfect tense of the above verbs is the same as the present perfect tense, except that we use the past tense of **haben** as the auxiliary verb.

3. Needless to say, in the future tense we also have a double infinitive. **Er wird bleiben können;** *he will be able to stay.* **Sie werden dort nicht rauchen dürfen;** *you will not be permitted to smoke there.* **Er wird das Geld zahlen müssen;** *he will have to pay the money.*

4. **This double infinitive must always be placed at the very end of its clause,** even after a subordinating conjunction. Examples: Weil man dort nicht hat rauchen dürfen, ging ich in ein anderes Abteil.—Nachdem ich diese Tür habe zumachen können, kam die Luft nicht mehr hindurch.—Wenn er nicht in die Stadt wird gehen mögen, können wir zu Hause bleiben.

D. Pseudo-Modal Auxiliaries

The verbs **hören, sehen, helfen,** and **lassen** (*to let, allow*) resemble the modal auxiliaries. They connect with another verb without **zu** and produce a double infinitive in the perfect tenses. Examples: **Ich höre sie singen. Ich hatte ihn spielen sehen. Wir haben ihm tragen helfen. Sie wird ihn gehen lassen.**

IV. Grammatical Exercises

A. Run the following through all persons, singular and plural: ich fürchte mich vor diesem Tier; es tat mir leid; es gefällt mir; es ging mir gut; ich habe mir einen Anzug bestellt.

B. Put the following sentences into the present perfect tense:

1. Klaus will uns eines Abends besuchen. 2. Wir hören ihn an die Tür klopfen. 3. Er soll um sechs Uhr da sein. 4. Wir dürfen in diesem Zimmer rauchen. 5. Wir sehen unsern Freund in das Haus kommen. 6. Er mag nicht zu

Hause bleiben. 7. Er muß früh aufstehen. 8. Von uns kann er sehr viel darüber lernen. 9. Das können wir. 10. Er will nicht.

C. Re-do B, putting the sentences into the past perfect tense.

D. Re-do B, putting the sentences into the future tense.

E. Translate the English words and expressions in the following:

1. Sie setzten (*themselves*) auf die Bank. 2. Das kleine Mädchen (*was afraid of*) dem Nikolaus. 3. Ich bestelle (*for myself*) eine Flasche Coca Cola. 4. Herr Löwenzahn sollte (*for himself*) ein Glas Wein bestellen. 5. Es (*happens*) oft, daß kleine Kinder alles über den Nikolaus wissen. 6. Ich muß diese Arbeit (*myself*) machen. 7. (*Even*) mein Vater kann das. 8. Ich frage (*myself*) manchmal, was noch geschehen kann. 9. Du (*are glad*) darüber, daß es im Sommer heiß ist. 10. Ich (*am not angry*) darüber, daß kalte Tage ihm besser (*please*).

V. Translation Exercise

1. In the autumn our students will be able to take a trip to the Rhineland. 2. They have seen the sun burn hot upon the mountains. 3. After Conrad had heard the men sing, he became very thirsty. 4. Her husband had wanted to arrive earlier. 5. Instead of coming along, he had to stay at home in order to work. 6. My brother will be able to come before Christmas. 7. Their daughter was sorry that her husband had not been able to come with them. 8. The man wants to buy himself neither a new suit nor a new shirt. 9. Her pretty little daughter sat down on the chair in the living room. 10. Nobody had been permitted to stand on the platform when the train arrived. 11. Since he had got up so late, he had to get

dressed very quickly. 12. It rained very little during this summer. 13. He will have to take his hat off because it is so hot. 14. The old men had wanted to sing this famous song with a soft voice. 15. His name was Till Eulenspiegel. 16. We are always angry when the meadows of other people are greener than ours.

VI. Fragen

1. Was geschah in der Familie Löwenzahn im Dezember? 2. Wer sind die Besucher gewesen? 3. Wann sind sie angekommen? 4. Um wieviel Uhr haben sie an diesem Morgen aufstehen müssen? 5. Warum hat der Mann nicht mitkommen dürfen? 6. Wann wird er kommen können? 7. Warum hat Conrad den Nikolaus nicht spielen dürfen? 8. Wann und wo hat Herr Löwenzahn ihn früher gespielt? 9. Wo zieht er sich jetzt an? 10. Was tat die kleine Henriette, als der Nikolaus kam? 11. Was sagte der Nikolaus zu ihr? 12. Was hat der Nikolaus den Kindern geben wollen?

VII. Lesestück

Das Ruhrgebiet

Viele Nebenflüsse fließen von rechts und links in den Rhein. Vom Neckar singt man in deutschen Liedern, der Main ist eine *Mason and Dixon Line* in der deutschen Geschichte gewesen, die Mosel kennt man wegen des Weines, der dort wächst. Über keinen der Nebenflüsse haben während der letzten Jahre die Zeitungen der Welt so viel geschrieben wie über die Ruhr.

Seit den Zeiten der Römer hat der Rhein im Mittelpunkt der Geschichte gestanden. Das Ruhrgebiet war noch vor 120 (hundertzwanzig) Jahren ein stilles, freundliches Tal, wo Blumen in den Gärten wuchsen und zufriedene Kühe auf grünen Wiesen standen. Heute ist dieses Land, von Duisburg im Westen bis Dortmund im Osten, eine große Stadt. Sie streckt sich über mehr als 200 (zweihundert) Quadratmeilen, auf denen ungefähr vier Millionen Leute leben. Von Duisburg bis Dortmund ist es nicht mehr als 33 (dreiunddreißig) Meilen, aber dieses kleine Stück Land produziert in einem Jahr mehr als 100 (hundert) Millionen Tonnen Steinkohle, ungefähr 20 (zwanzig) Prozent der gesamteuropäischen Kohleproduktion. Vor dem letzten Weltkrieg produzierte die Ruhr jedes Jahr 13 Millionen Tonnen Eisen und 15 Millionen Tonnen Stahl. Nicht nur über die Quantität, auch über die Qualität müssen wir noch ein Wort sagen: die Steinkohle aus dem Ruhrgebiet ist die beste Kohle Europas.

Für jedes Industriegebiet ist es nicht nur wichtig, daß man produziert, sondern auch, daß man transportiert. Man braucht Grubenholz, Erz und Rohmaterial aus anderen Ländern und man muß das, was man produziert hat, schnell und billig an den Verbraucher schicken. Das Ruhrgebiet hat das dichteste Netz von Eisenbahnen, das es auf der Welt gibt. Außerdem hat man in den letzten 50 (fünfzig) Jahren Kanäle gebaut, die das Ruhrgebiet mit der Nordsee, mit der Elbe und mit dem Rhein verbinden. Erze und Grubenhölzer aus Schweden kommen auf Schiffen, und Kohle, Eisen, Maschinen und andere Produkte gehen auf Schiffen in alle Länder der Welt. Es ist billiger, auf dem Wasser als auf dem Lande zu transportieren.

Wir nannten das Ruhrgebiet e i n e große Stadt, doch wir sollten das nicht zu wörtlich nehmen. Zwischen Duisburg und Dortmund drängen sich viele große und kleine Städte, die dicht zusammen liegen. Wir nennen nur ein paar: Essen, Bochum, Gelsenkirchen, Hagen, Solingen, Wuppertal, Düsseldorf. Niemand wird sagen, daß sie in einer schönen Landschaft liegen. Ruhrgebiet: das sind Fabriken, Fördertürme, Kohlenberge, Schornsteine und Rauch. Doch wir wissen, daß hier zwischen Duisburg und Dortmund das wichtigste Stück Land liegt, das es in Deutschland (wir können sagen: in

Europa) gibt. Die Ruhr braucht Europa für ihre Produkte, und Europa braucht die Produkte der Ruhr.

VIII. Wörterverzeichnis

bauen (to) build
billig cheaply, inexpensively
dicht dense, close
sich drängen (to) be crowded
das Eisen the iron
die Eisenbahn, –en the railroad
die Elbe the Elbe (River)
das Erz, –e the ore
die Fabrik, –en the factory
fließen, floß, ist geflossen to flow
der Förderturm, ⸚e the transport tower, haul tower
gesamteuropäisch total European
das Grubenholz, ⸚er the wood for the mine
das Industriegebiet, –e the industrial region
der Kanal, ⸚e the canal
die Kohle, –n the coal
der Kohlenberg, –e the pile of coal
die Kohleproduktion the coal production
die Kuh, ⸚e the cow
links left (*adverb*)
der Main the Main (River)
die Maschine, –n the machine
die Meile, –n the mile
die Million, –en the million
der Mittelpunkt, –e the center
die Mosel the Mosel (River)
der Nebenfluß, –flüsse the tributary
der Neckar the Neckar (River)
das Netz, –e the network
die Nordsee the North Sea
der Osten the east
das Produkt, –e the product
produzieren (to) produce
das Prozent, –e the percent
die Quadratmeile, –n the square mile
die Qualität the quality
die Quantität the quantity
der Rauch the smoke
rechts right (*adverb*)
das Rohmaterial the raw material
der Römer, – the Roman
die Ruhr the Ruhr (River)
das Ruhrgebiet the Ruhr district
schicken (to) send
der Schornstein, –e the chimney
Schweden Sweden
der Stahl the steel
die Steinkohle, –n hard coal
sich strecken (to) extend
das Stück, –e the piece, bit
das Tal, ⸚er the valley
die Tonne, –n the ton
transportieren (to) transport, ship
ungefähr approximately
verbinden, verband, verbunden (to) connect
der Verbraucher, – the consumer
der Weltkrieg, –e the World War
der Westen the west
wörtlich literally

Aufgabe Achtzehn

NUMERALS, TELLING TIME
DAYS, MONTHS, SEASONS

I. Reading Selection

Zum ersten Mal in meinem Leben bin ich zu Weihnachten nicht zu Hause gewesen und zum ersten Mal, seitdem ich nach Deutschland gekommen bin, habe ich ein wenig Heimweh gehabt. Trotzdem war es auch hier ein sehr schönes Fest.

Die Kinder wurden jeden Tag unruhiger. „Noch sieben Tage . . . noch sechs . . . . noch fünf . . . noch vier", hörte man sie jeden Morgen sagen. „Wann ist der vierundzwanzigste?" fragte die kleine Henriette immer wieder. Dann sagte Herr Löwenzahn: „Der vierundzwanzigste ist am vierundzwanzigsten", und sie schien mit dieser Antwort sehr zufrieden zu sein.

Jeden Abend, ehe sie zu Bett gingen, stellten die Kinder einen Schuh vor das Fenster. Am nächsten Morgen lag dann immer Schokolade oder Weihnachtsgebäck darin.

„Ein Weihnachtsengel muß es in den Schuh gelegt haben", sagten wir dann.

„Es kann auch der Nikolaus gewesen sein", meinte der kleine Henning. Hinter dem Rücken seiner Schwester sah er Herrn Löwenzahn an und lächelte heimlich. Doch die kleine Henriette dachte lieber an den Weihnachtsengel als an den Nikolaus.

In Amerika ist der 25. Dezember der wichtigste Tag des Festes. In Deutschland ist es der 24. Der Tag heißt Heilig Abend. An diesem Tag durften die Kinder nach ein Uhr nicht mehr ins Wohnzimmer gehen, denn die Eltern und Großeltern fingen nun an, den Christbaum zu schmücken und die Geschenke in das Zimmer zu tragen.

„Vielleicht schneit es noch", sagte Frau Löwenzahn. Es war kalt, doch der Himmel war klar und blau.

Um fünf Uhr kamen wir alle ins Eßzimmer. Der kleine Henning wollte sofort ins Wohnzimmer laufen, doch die Tür zum Wohnzimmer war noch geschlossen. Herbert setzte sich ans Klavier, und wir alle sangen das Lied „Stille Nacht, heilige Nacht." Dann nahm Herr Löwenzahn die Bibel und las die Weihnachtsgeschichte in der Übersetzung von Martin Luther. Gerade als er sagte „Friede auf Erden", unterbrach die kleine Henriette und rief: „Großvater, wann fangen wir mit dem vierundzwanzigsten an?" Herr Löwenzahn machte das Buch zu und sagte: „In einer Minute, mein Kind." Er öffnete die Tür: da stand der Christbaum mit vielen brennenden Kerzen, und darunter lagen die Geschenke. Wir alle riefen „Fröhliche Weihnachten!"

Es gab Geschenke für jeden von uns, auch für Herbert und mich. Ich kann nicht alles aufzählen, sonst muß ich mein deutsch-englisches Wörterbuch aufmachen, und ich habe versprochen, diese Geschichten ohne Wörterbuch zu schreiben. Doch da wir alle das deutsche Wort „Schnee" kennen, will ich noch sagen, daß es während der Nacht zu schneien anfing. Am nächsten Morgen war alles weiß. „Wir haben ein Weihnachten wie in der guten alten Zeit", sagten die Löwenzahns sehr zufrieden.

Am Tage nach Neujahr fuhren die Kinder und Enkel der Löwenzahns wieder ab. Herr Löwenzahn, Herbert und ich gingen mit ihnen zum Bahnhof. Der Zug nach Wien sollte um 13 Uhr 31 abfahren, aber wir kamen schon um drei Viertel eins am Bahnhof an. Wir standen länger als eine halbe Stunde auf dem Bahnsteig und niemand wußte, was er sagen sollte.

„Zählen Sie in Amerika die Stunden auch von eins bis vierundzwanzig?" fragte uns Herr Löwenzahn, als wir nach Hause gingen.

„Nein", sagte Herbert. „Unsere Uhren gehen bis zwölf und fangen dann wieder mit eins an."

„Auch wir haben die vierundzwanzig Stunden nur auf dem Fahrplan für die Züge", erklärte uns Herr Löwenzahn. „Interessant wird es dann um Mitternacht. Ein Zug kommt um 24 Uhr an. Ein anderer fährt in dieser Minute ab, aber wir sagen: er fährt um null Uhr null ab. Der ankommende Zug schließt den Tag, der abfahrende fängt ihn an. Sind wir nicht ein poetisches Volk?"

II. Vocabulary

***an-sehen (ie), sah an, angesehen** (to) look at
***die Antwort, –en** the answer
auf-zählen (to) enumerate
die Bibel, –n the Bible
der Christbaum, ⸚e the Christmas tree
der Enkel, – the grandchild
***erst–** (*adj.*) first
***der Fahrplan, ⸚e** the timetable
das Fest the celebration, holiday
Friede auf Erden peace on earth
***die Großeltern** the grandparents
***halb** half
Heilig Abend Christmas Eve
***heimlich** secretly
das Heimweh the homesickness
***der Himmel** the heaven, sky
die Kerze, –n the candle
***klar** clear
das Klavier the piano
***legen** (to) lay, place, put
***das Mal, –e** the time
***die Minute, –n** the minute
die Mitternacht the midnight
***der Morgen, –** the morning
Neujahr New Year's
***null** zero
***öffnen** (to) open
poetisch poetic
***der Rücken, –** the back
***scheinen, schien, geschienen** (to) seem; shine
***schließen, schloß, geschlossen** (to) close, end; shut, lock
schmücken (to) decorate
***der Schnee** the snow
***schneien** (to) snow
die Schokolade the chocolate
***die Schwester, –n** the sister
***seitdem** (*conj.*) since
***trotzdem** in spite of that
***die Uhr, –en** the clock; o'clock
unruhig restless
versprechen (i), versprach, versprochen (to) promise

***das Viertel, –** the quarter
der Weihnachtsengel, – the Christmas angel
das Weihnachtsgebäck the Christmas cookies
die Weihnachtsgeschichte the Christmas story
Wien Vienna
das Wörterbuch, ¨er the dictionary
***zählen** (to) count

IDIOM

Fröhliche Weihnachten! Merry Christmas!

III. Grammar

A. NUMERALS: CARDINAL NUMBERS

We have already used several numerals. Add the new ones to your active vocabulary.

1. We count from 0 to 12: **null, eins, zwei, drei, vier, fünf, sechs, sieben, acht, neun, zehn, elf, zwölf.**

2. We count from 13 to 19: **dreizehn, vierzehn, fünfzehn, sechzehn** (note the loss of the final **s** on **sechs** before we add an ending), **siebzehn, achtzehn, neunzehn.**

3. We count from 10 to 100 by tens: **zehn, zwanzig, dreißig** (note that **dreißig** has an irregular form as compared with the **–zig** that everywhere else corresponds to English **–ty**), **vierzig, fünfzig, sechzig** (again the loss of the final **s** on **sechs** before a following **z**), **siebzig** (**sieben** always loses its final **en** before a **z** ending, just as in **siebzehn** above), **achtzig, neunzig, hundert.**

4. We count within the tens: **zwanzig, einundzwanzig, zweiundzwanzig, dreiundzwanzig, vierundzwanzig, fünfundzwanzig, sechsundzwanzig, siebenundzwanzig, achtundzwanzig, neunundzwanzig; dreißig, einunddreißig, zweiunddreißig, dreiunddreißig,** etc.; **vierzig, einundvierzig, zweiundvierzig,** etc.; **hundert; hundert(und)eins, hundert(und)zwei, hundert(und)drei, hundert(und)zwanzig, hundert(und)einundzwanzig, hundert(und)zweiundzwanzig,** etc.; **zweihundert(und)eins, zweihundert(und)zwei, dreihundert(und)einunddreißig, vierhundert(und)zweiundfünfzig,** etc.; **tausend, tausend(und)eins,**

tausend(und)einundsiebzig, zweitausend(und)vierundachtzig, etc.

5. Note that **hundert** means *one hundred,* and **tausend** means *a thousand*—**ein** is not normally used with either **hundert** or **tausend.**

6. The numeral **eins** is used only in counting. If it stands in front of a noun, it coincides with the indefinite article: Er braucht **einen** Pfennig. Es kostet **eine** Mark zwanzig. **Ein** Jahr hat zwölf Monate. Otherwise cardinal numbers take no endings.

B. NUMERALS: ORDINAL NUMBERS

The numerals that take ordinary adjective endings correspond to English *the first, the second, the third, the fourth,* etc. These are called ordinal numbers.

1. *The first,* **der erste,** and *the third,* **der dritte,** are irregular.

2. Otherwise **to form the ordinals from** *the 2nd* **to** *the 19th* **add –t** to the numerals in A above **and** also add the proper **adjective ending: der zweite, vierte, fünfte, sechste, sieb(en)te, achte, neunte, zehnte, elfte, zwölfte, dreizehnte, vierzehnte, fünfzehnte, sechzehnte, siebzehnte, achtzehnte, neunzehnte.**

3. **To form the ordinals from** *the 20th* **on, add –st** to the numerals in A above **and** also add the proper **adjective ending: der zwanzigste, dreißigste, vierzigste, fünfzigste, sechzigste, siebzigste, achtzigste, neunzigste, hundertste, tausendste.** Also **der einundzwanzigste, zweiunddreißigste, dreiundvierzigste, vierundfünfzigste,** etc.; **der hundertunderste, hundertundzweite, zweihundertundzehnte, zweihundertundelfte, dreihundertzwanzigste, vierhundertvierundvierzigste,** etc.

4. Note that **das Mal** means *time* only in the sense of *occasion.* It combines with numerals as follows: **einmal,** *once;* **zweimal,** *twice;* **dreimal,** *three times;* **zehnmal,** *ten times;* **hundertmal,** *a hundred times;* **tausendmal,** *a thousand times,* etc.

It also combines with certain adjectives, e.g., **manchmal,** *sometimes;* **jedesmal,** *every time;* **diesmal,** *this time,* etc.

5. **erst–,** with an ending on it, it is an adjective, e.g., **das erste Mal,** *the first time.* We have previously had the adverb **erst** which means *only* in the sense of *not until:* **Er ist erst gestern angekommen,** *He arrived only yesterday,* or *He didn't arrive until yesterday.*

6. A period after a numeral indicates that it is to be read as an ordinal and given proper declensional endings, e.g., Heute ist der 17. Februar (der siebzehnte Februar).—Dort stand das Heer Friedrichs II. (Friedrichs des Zweiten).—Mein Freund ist am 29. Oktober (am neunundzwanzigsten Oktober) angekommen.—Er sprach über Friedrich III. (Friedrich den Dritten).

C. TELLING TIME

1. Remember the expressions we have already used: **Wie spät ist es?** or **Wieviel Uhr ist es?** *What time is it?*—**Es ist drei Uhr,** *It is three o'clock;* **Es ist sechsundzwanzig Minuten nach drei,** *It is twenty-six minutes after three;* **Es ist sechzehn Minuten vor vier,** *It is sixteen minutes to four;* **Der Zug kommt um vier Uhr an,** *The train arrives at four o'clock.*—Note especially the use of **nach, vor,** and **um** with expressions relating to the time of day.

2. German counts the quarter hours in an entirely different manner from English. Starting with 7:00 o'clock to count the next three quarter hours, the German would be equivalent to the following: 7:15 one quarter on the way to eight; 7:30 one half on the way to eight; 7:45 three quarters on the way to eight. Thus the German would be as follows: 7:00 **sieben Uhr;** 7:15 **(ein) Viertel acht;** 7:30 **halb acht;** 7:45 **drei Viertel acht,** frequently spelled **dreiviertel acht;** 8:00 **acht Uhr.**

3. In railroad, bus, and plane timetables, as with the American armed forces, the hours from midnight to noon are 0 to 12, while the p.m. hours are 13 to 24.

Thus, a train leaving at 6:25 p.m., would leave, for the American armed forces, at "eighteen hundred twenty-five hours," or in German at **achtzehn Uhr fünfundzwanzig.** Note: *Are you taking the 6:25 p.m. train?* **Fahren Sie mit dem achtzehn Uhr fünfundzwanzig Zug ab?**

D. Names of Days, Months, and Seasons

Here are complete lists of the names of the days, months, and seasons. **All of them are masculine.** *All are now to be considered as active vocabulary.*

The days of the week are **Sonntag, Montag, Dienstag, Mittwoch, Donnerstag, Freitag, Samstag** or **Sonnabend.**

The months are **Januar, Februar, März, April, Mai, Juni, Juli, August, September, Oktober, November, Dezember.**

The seasons are **Frühling, Sommer, Herbst, Winter.**

E. Participles as Adjectives

The **past participle,** e.g., in **Die Tür ist geschlossen,** *The door is closed,* can also be used **as an adjective** in front of a noun: **Das ist eine geschlossene Tür,** *That is a closed door.*

The **present participle** is formed by adding **-d** to the infinitive, e.g., **ankommend, abfahrend, brennend.** It too may be used as an ordinary adjective in front of a noun: **der ankommende Zug, die abfahrende Familie, die brennenden Kerzen.**

IV. Grammatical Exercises

A. Count in German from 1 to 12; from 13 to 20; from 21 to 29; from 30 to 39; from 60 to 69; from 70 to 79; from 100 to 112; from 120 to 129; from 230 to 239; from 450 to 459; from 890 to 899; from 1000 to 1012; from 5340 to 5349; from 7560 to 7569; from 9780 to 9789.

B. Tell the following time of day in German: 6:00; 7:02; 8:05; 9:15; 10:22; 11:30; 12:40; 1:43; 2:52; 5:15; 6:30; 7:45.

C. Use the above as in a timetable, using the first six as a.m. hours, and the rest as p.m.

D. Re-do C, so that in each instance you will have a sentence which means "My train arrives at ____ o'clock."

E. Re-do some of the figures in A, using ordinals, e.g. *the first time, the second time, the third time,* etc.

V. Translation Exercise

1. On the day before Christmas the children got up at a quarter to seven. 2. On the twenty-fifth of December they slept until a quarter after eight. 3. He and his brother had vacation and could therefore sleep until half past nine every morning. 4. It was the first time that they had not been at home on this day. 5. I am speaking of the fifty-second week of the year 1918. 6. During the day it was very cold and on the next morning it snowed. 7. His little sister did not go to bed until after half past ten. 8. On the second of January the children and grandchildren had to go home again. 9. They got up early and rode to the station by (the) street car. 10. They stood at the station (*dat.*) half an hour before their train was to leave. 11. The train had arrived only a few minutes ago. 12. They are traveling to Hamburg on the 11:48 train. 13. Come, Conrad, we must not arrive late, otherwise we will not be able to say good-bye to them. 14. Herbert, when you go to bed, do not forget to put your shoes in front of your door. 15. One always does that in Germany.

VI. Fragen

1. Wo sind Conrad und Herbert in diesem Jahre zu Weihnachten? 2. Wo ist Conrad in früheren Jahren zu

Weihnachten gewesen? 3. Wie wurden die Kinder zu dieser Zeit? 4. Was haben sie jeden Morgen gefragt? 5. Was machen sie dann am Abend? 6. Was lag am nächsten Morgen in dem Schuh? 7. Wer muß Schokolade in die Schuhe gelegt haben? 8. Warum hat Hennings Schwester geschrieen, als der Nikolaus kam? 9. Welches ist der wichtigste Tag des Weihnachtsfestes in Deutschland? 10. Wohin haben die Kinder nach ein Uhr nicht gehen dürfen? 11. Was machten die Eltern und Großeltern um diese Zeit? 12. Um wieviel Uhr sind sie alle ins Eßzimmer gekommen? 13. Warum konnte Henning nicht ins Wohnzimmer hinein? 15. Was lag unterm Christbaum? 16. Wie wurde das Wetter während der Nacht? 17. Wann sind die Besucher abgefahren? 18. Wann sollte der Zug nach Wien abfahren?

VII. Lesestück

Der Freiherr vom Stein

In vielen großen deutschen Städten sieht man in der Eingangshalle des Rathauses das Bild eines Mannes im Kostüm des frühen 19. Jahrhunderts. Darunter steht „Karl vom Stein, 1757–1831." Wer war der Freiherr vom Stein, und warum hängt sein Bild so oft in deutschen Rathäusern?

Stein wurde am 26. Oktober 1757 in Nassau geboren. Er studierte in Göttingen und trat, als er 32 Jahre alt war, in den preußischen Staatsdienst ein. Er hatte, als er ein junger Mann war, viele Bücher über englische Geschichte und englische Politik gelesen. „Worin unterscheidet sich das englische Volk von dem deutschen?" fragte er sich. Die Antwort war: „In Deutschland regieren absolute Fürsten. In England interessieren sich die Leute für Politik, sie haben ein Parlament und Gesetze, und darum kann der König nicht immer tun, was er will. Wenn Deutschland nicht hinter den anderen Ländern zurückbleiben will, müssen wir unter den Deutschen das Interesse für Politik wecken."

Im Jahre 1806 wurde Preußen von Napoleon besiegt. Ein Jahr später ernannte der preußische König den Freiherrn vom Stein zum Ministerpräsidenten. Nun begann Stein mit den Reformen, auf die er so lange gewartet hatte. Unter den vielen Reformen, durch die Stein berühmt wurde, nennen wir hier nur die zwei wichtigsten: das Befreiungsgesetz und die Städteordnung. Bis zu dieser Zeit gab es noch viele Leute, besonders auf dem Lande, die nicht frei waren. Das Volk war in soziale Kasten eingeteilt, die man nie verlassen konnte. Ein Bauer mußte immer ein Bauer bleiben, ein Adeliger konnte nicht ein Arzt werden oder ein Geschäft aufmachen. Steins Befreiungsgesetz hob alle diese alten Beschränkungen auf. „Nach dem Martinitag 1810", sagte das Gesetz, „wird es im Lande nur freie Leute geben."

Nicht weniger wichtig war die Städteordnung. Dieses Gesetz gab den Städten Selbstverwaltung. Die Bürger durften sich nun selbst regieren, d.h. sie durften einen Bürgermeister und ein Stadtparlament wählen. Die Städteordnung gab den Bürgern der Städte die Verantwortung für die Geschäfte der Stadt. So war es in Deutschland schon im Mittelalter gewesen, doch in der Zeit des Absolutismus, d.h. im 17. und 18. Jahrhundert, hatten die Fürsten den alten Städten ihre Selbstverwaltung genommen. Die neuen jüngeren Städte hatten Selbstverwaltung nie gekannt. Wir verstehen jetzt, warum Steins Bild noch heute in den Rathäusern der deutschen Städte hängt.

Niemand hat mehr getan als er, aus dem preußischen Untertan einen deutschen Bürger zu machen.

VIII. Wörterverzeichnis

absolut absolute
der Absolutismus the absolutism
der Ad(e)lige, (–n), –n the nobleman
auf-heben, hob auf, aufgehoben (to) remove
der Bauer, –n the peasant
das Befreiungsgesetz the Liberation Edict
die Beschränkung, –en the limitation
besiegt conquered

besonders especially
das Bild, –er the picture, portrait
der Bürger, – the citizen
der Bürgermeister, – the mayor
die Eingangshalle, –n the entrance hall
ein-teilen (to) divide
ein-treten (tritt ein), trat ein, ist eingetreten (to) enter
ernennen, ernannte, ernannt (to) name, appoint
der Freiherr, (–n), –en the baron
der Fürst, (–en), –en the (ruling) prince
geboren born
das Geschäft, –e the business, affairs
das Gesetz, –e the law
hängen, hing, gehangen (to) hang
sich interessieren für (to) be interested in
die Kaste, –n the caste
der König, –e the king
das Kostüm, –e the costume
auf dem Lande in the country
der Martinitag St. Martin's Day (Nov. 11)
der Ministerpräsident, (–en), –en the prime minister
das Mittelalter the Middle Ages
das Parlament, –e the parliament
die Politik politics
Preußen Prussia
preußisch Prussian
die Reform, –en the reform
die Selbstverwaltung the self-government
sozial social
der Staatsdienst the state service
die Städteordnung the Municipal Autonomy Statute
das Stadtparlament, –e the city council
sich unterscheiden von, unterschied, unterschieden (to) be different from
der Untertan, –en the subject
die Verantwortung the responsibility
verlassen (ä), verließ, verlassen (to) leave
wählen (to) choose
wecken (to) awaken
weniger less
zurück-bleiben, blieb zurück, ist zurückgeblieben (to) remain behind

Aufgabe Neunzehn

THE PASSIVE VOICE

I. Reading Selection

Gestern abend waren wir im Theater. Da Schillers „Wallenstein“ zum 1. Mal gespielt wurde, war das ganze Theater ausverkauft. Wir kamen viel zu früh. Als wir am Theater ankamen, waren die Türen noch geschlossen. Wir mußten fünf Minuten warten, und während wir warteten, sprachen wir mit einem alten Herrn. „Ich war ein Junge von zehn Jahren“, erzählte er uns, „als dieses Theater gebaut wurde. Und ich erinnere mich noch an den 3. September 1901, als diese Türen zum ersten Mal aufgemacht wurden.“ Während wir sprachen, wurden die Türen geöffnet, und wir gingen hinein.

Im Theater wurden Programme verkauft, worin ein wenig über das Leben des Dichters berichtet wurde, dessen Werk heute abend gespielt wurde. Wir lasen, daß Friedrich Schiller am 10. November 1759 geboren wurde und am 9. Mai 1805 starb, und daß sein größtes Drama, der Wallenstein, zwischen Oktober 1796 und März 1799 geschrieben wurde. Das Drama erzählt die Geschichte eines großen Generals aus dem Dreißigjährigen Krieg. Wallenstein war von dem Kaiser an die Spitze des Heeres gestellt worden, er wurde von den Soldaten verehrt und geliebt, und seine Stellung im Reich wurde immer größer und stärker. Als er dann so mächtig wurde, daß der Kaiser anfing, sich vor ihm zu fürchten, wurde Wallenstein entlassen. Bald danach wurde das Heer des Kaisers von den Schweden besiegt. „Das Reich wird nur gerettet werden, wenn Wallenstein zurückgerufen wird“, sagte der Kaiser nun. Zum zweiten Mal wurde jetzt das Heer von Wallenstein geführt, und wieder wurde der General zu mächtig. Er wußte, daß er zum zweiten Mal entlassen werden sollte, und er dachte nun sogar daran, das Heer des Kaisers gegen den Kaiser zu führen. Doch ehe er das noch tun konnte, wurde er von einem Offizier, der von ihm schlecht behandelt worden war, in der Stadt Eger ermordet. Das geschah im Jahre 1634.

In der Pause trafen wir unsern Lehrer. „Es wird gut gespielt, nicht wahr?“ fragte er. „Schillers Wallenstein ist nicht nur ein großes, sondern auch ein langes Drama. Bis jetzt wurde es immer an zwei Abenden gespielt. Es ist das erste Mal, daß ich das ganze Drama in e i n e r Vorstellung gesehen habe. Es ist gekürzt worden, so daß es an einem Abend gespielt werden kann. Ich freue mich, daß Sie heute abend hier sind. Können Sie alles verstehen?“

„Alles“, antwortete ich. „Ich verstehe jedes Wort.“

„Conrad“, sagte Herbert, als wir wieder allein waren, „ich verstehe nicht alles. Entweder ist dein Deutsch besser, oder du hast gelogen.“

Ich wurde ein wenig rot. „Das zweite. Ich wollte ihn nicht traurig machen. Ich verstehe vielleicht 70 Prozent. Schillers Sprache ist gewiß schöner, aber auch schwerer zu verstehen als Herrn Löwenzahns Deutsch.“

Die Vorstellung dauerte bis halb zwölf. Alle Leute im Theater waren sehr begeistert. Die Schauspieler kamen immer wieder vor den Vorhang, auch der Schauspieler, der den Wallenstein gespielt hatte, obwohl er gerade ermordet worden war. Schließlich wurde der eiserne Vorhang herabgelassen.

„Auch dies ist etwas Neues für mich“, meinte Herbert. „Wie oft haben wir in der Zeitung vom eisernen Vorhang gelesen. Dies ist der erste, den ich gesehen habe.“

II. Vocabulary

ausverkauft sold out
***bauen** (to) build
begeistert enthused, enthusiastic
behandeln (to) treat
besiegen (to) vanquish, conquer
***dauern** (to) last
***der Dichter, –** the poet, author
das Drama, Dramen the drama
der Dreißigjährige Krieg the Thirty Years' War
eisern iron
entlassen (ä), entließ, entlassen (to) remove, discharge
***entweder . . . oder** either . . . or
***sich erinnern an** (*with acc.*) (to) remember
ermorden (to) murder
***führen** (to) lead, conduct
***geboren** born
der General, ⸚e the general
***das Heer, –e** the army
herab-lassen (ä), ließ herab, herabgelassen (to) let down, lower
***der Herr, (–n), –en** the man, Mr.
hinein-gehen, ging hinein, ist hineingegangen (to) go in
der Kaiser, – the emperor
kürzen (to) shorten
***lieben** (to) love
***lügen, log, gelogen** (to) lie, tell a lie
***mächtig** mighty, powerful
der Offizier, –e the officer
die Pause, –n the intermission
das Programm, –e the program
Prozent percent
das Reich the empire
***retten** (to) save
der Schauspieler, – the actor
Schiller Schiller (*German poet*)
***schlecht** bad
***schließlich** finally
der Schwede, –n the Swede
***der Soldat, (–en), –en** the soldier
die Spitze, –n the top, head
die Stellung, –en the position
das Theater, – the theater
verehren (to) honor, respect
***von** by
***der Vorhang, ⸚e** the curtain
die Vorstellung, –en the performance
***während** (*conj.*) while
***das Werk, –e** the (creative) work
zurück-rufen, rief zurück, zurückgerufen (to) call back

IDIOMS

***gestern abend** last evening, yesterday evening
***nicht nur . . . sondern auch** not only . . . but also

III. Grammar

A. THE PASSIVE VOICE

There are very few facts that you need to know in order to understand the above Reading Selection:

1. While English forms the passive by using forms of (*to*) *be* + *the past participle,* **German uses forms of werden + the past participle.**
2. The form **geworden** is not used after another past participle. So, in the perfect tenses of the passive voice, **geworden** is always shortened to **worden.**
3. In an independent passive clause the past participle stands at the end of the clause if the verb is in the present or past tenses; if the verb is in the future or perfect tenses the past participle precedes the forms **werden** and **worden** respectively. In a dependent clause, here as always, the finite verb goes to the very end.

To use a few illustrations from our Reading: **Es wird gespielt** (present) means *It is played;* **Wallenstein wurde gespielt** (past) means *Wallenstein was played;* **Das Reich wird gerettet werden** (future) means *The empire will be saved;* **Es ist gekürzt worden** (present perfect) means *It has been shortened;* **Wallenstein war an die Spitze des Heeres gestellt worden** (past perfect) means *Wallenstein had been placed at the head of the army.*

Note how the various tenses of the passive voice are formed, starting with the example "The letter is written to my mother by him."

PRES.	Der Brief **wird** meiner Mutter von ihm **geschrieben**
PAST	Der Brief **wurde** meiner Mutter von ihm **geschrieben**
FUT.	Der Brief **wird** meiner Mutter von ihm **geschrieben werden**
PRES. PERF.	Der Brief **ist** meiner Mutter von ihm **geschrieben worden**
PAST PERF.	Der Brief **war** meiner Mutter von ihm **geschrieben worden**

The "agent" appearing in so many passive voice sentences, i.e., the one who performs the action ("something was done *by* . . .") is indicated in German by the preposition **von + dative.**

In the passive voice, the subject is not performing the action; it is merely "passive" and is letting the action be performed on it. Let's take the active voice sentence **Er schreibt meiner Mutter einen Brief.** If we change this into a passive voice sentence, the various grammatical elements change their functions and places. The direct object becomes subject; the subject is placed after a preposition, in English *by,* in German **von**; the finite verb becomes a past participle and is replaced by an auxiliary, in English a form of (*to*) *be,* in German a corresponding form of **werden**; only the dative object remains unchanged. Thus, we would get the passive voice sentence **Ein Brief wird meiner Mutter von ihm geschrieben.**

Verbs that take only a dative object appear with no apparent subject in the passive: **Meine Freunde helfen mir** becomes in the passive **Mir wird von meinen Freunden geholfen.**

B. Substitutes for the Passive Voice

German usage frequently avoids the passive voice. So, instead of saying **Die Tür wird geöffnet,** German may resort to a reflexive construction **Die Tür öffnet sich.** Often an artificial, impersonal subject **man** is used as a device for channeling a passive voice into an active voice sentence. Instead of saying *Many gay songs were sung,* we would say in idiomatic German **Man sang viele lustige Lieder.**

C. The Static Passive

1. Despite the term "passive," action is always going on in a true passive with *werden*: **Das Haus wird verkauft** means *The house is being sold,* i.e., someone is selling it now; **Die Tür wurde geschlossen** means *The door was being closed,* i.e., someone was closing it then; **Das Reich wird gerettet werden** means *The empire will be saved* and some person will be saving it.

2. A past participle with the subject not the recipient of any action and with no person (after *by* or **von**) as the doer of

the action is merely static, i.e., it denotes only the state or condition of the subject of the clause.

We say **Das Haus wird verkauft** only if it is in the process of being sold. After the purchase is completed and the real estate agent puts his SOLD sign on the front lawn, he would say **Das Haus ist verkauft.** The first sentence describes a dynamic process: the selling is going on. The second sentence describes a status. **Verkauft** could now be treated as a descriptive adjective used predicatively; it describes a status but does not express action. **Die Tür war geschlossen, als ich ankam** means *The door was (already) closed when I arrived,* i.e., *It was a closed door,* **Es war eine geschlossene Tür.** The static passive does not show any doer or agent indicated by the prepositions *by* or **von.**

D. GEBOREN

Geboren (born), when referring to historical personalities of the past, uses the auxiliary **werden**; when I refer to myself, to conversational partners, or to other contemporaries, **geboren** takes the present tense forms of **sein.**

Schiller wurde 1759 geboren.
Wann wurde Mozart geboren?
Wann sind Sie geboren?
Ich bin im August geboren.

IV. Grammatical Exercises

A. Change the following sentences into the passive:

1. Die Enkel stellen einen Schuh vor das Fenster. 2. Henning sieht den Großvater hinter dem Rücken seiner Schwester an. 3. Herr Löwenzahn zieht den roten Anzug an. 4. Die Männer singen ein trauriges Lied mit leiser Stimme. 5. Annas Vater erzählt mir vieles aus der Geschichte Bremens. 6. Der Student hilft dem Mädchen bei der Arbeit. 7. Die Freunde machen eine Reise am Sonntag. 8. Er macht alle Fenster

abends zu. 9. Das deutsche Volk nennt diesen Fluß den Rhein. 10. Die Loreley bringt diese Männer in Gefahr. 11. Spät abends singt sie ein schönes Lied. 12. Herr Löwenzahn trägt eine Flasche Wein auf den Balkon. 13. Er gießt Wein in das Glas. 14. Ihr erzählt mir viel über Europa. 15. Der kleine Junge wirft einen Stein nach dem Tier.

B. Re-do A in the past tense of the passive.

C. Re-do A in the future tense of the passive.

D. Re-do A in the present perfect tense of the passive.

V. Translation Exercise

1. The cake which stood on the table was eaten either by my little brother or by my little sister. 2. A strawberry punch was made by Mr. Löwenzahn. 3. The story of this river will be explained to the girls by the student. 4. Something had been thrown by the boy through the window. 5. Yesterday Monika and her friend Vera were driven downtown by the two friends. 6. The door is being opened. 7. After the windows had been opened, cold air came into the room. 8. He remembered the day when the great poet died. 9. I was born before the new railroad station was built. 10. This story has often been told by the most famous physician of our time. 11. Wallenstein was played for the (*zum*) first time in Weimar in April 1799. 12. The woman has been helped by Herbert in the garden. 13. Their army is being led by the greatest soldier in their country. 14. A present has been given to Mr. Löwenzahn for his sixtieth birthday. 15. When we arrived, the house was already sold. 16. Only German is spoken here!

VI. Fragen

1. Wo sind die Studenten gestern gewesen? 2. Konnten sie sofort ins Theater gehen, als sie ankamen? 3. Warum

nicht? 4. Wie lange haben sie warten müssen, ehe sie hineingehen konnten? 5. Was wurde im Theater verkauft? 6. Was wurde an diesem Abend gespielt? 7. Von wem war dieses Drama? 8. In welchem Jahrhundert hat der Dichter gelebt? 9. Wer war Wallenstein? 10. Warum hat ihn der Kaiser an die Spitze des Heeres gestellt? 11. In welchem Jahre ist der General ermordet worden? 12. Was hat man getan, sodaß man den „Wallenstein" an einem Abend spielen kann? 13. Wen haben Conrad und Herbert im Theater getroffen? 14. Versteht Conrad Schillers Deutsch ganz? 15. Warum hat er gelogen? 16. Wie lange hat die Vorstellung gedauert? 17. Was ist schließlich herabgelassen worden?

VII. Lesestück

Salzburg und Bayreuth

Man hat die Deutschen oft das Volk der Dichter und Denker genannt. Man kann sie auch das Volk der Komponisten und Musiker nennen. Ob man ein Konzertprogramm in Hamburg oder Cleveland, in Stockholm oder San Francisco öffnet: immer wieder sehen wir darin Namen wie Bach, Beethoven, Schumann, Brahms. Zu den berühmtesten deutschen Komponisten zählt man Wolfgang Amadeus Mozart (1756–1791) und Richard Wagner (1813–1883).

Auch ihre Musik wird in der ganzen Welt gespielt. Doch in zwei Städten wird das Werk dieser beiden Komponisten besonders geehrt: Mozart in Salzburg und Wagner in Bayreuth.

Mozart war kein Deutscher, er war Österreicher. Er wurde am 27. Januar 1756 in Salzburg geboren, er starb am 5. Dezember 1791 in Wien, und er verbrachte den größten Teil seines Lebens in Österreich. Er war, als er starb, nur 35 Jahre alt, doch es gibt kaum einen zweiten Komponisten, der in solch kurzer Zeit so viele große Werke geschrieben hat wie er: Sonaten, Symphonien und Opern. Seine berühmtesten Opern sind „Die Hochzeit des Figaro", „Don Giovanni" und „Die

Zauberflöte." Die österreichische Stadt Salzburg ehrt ihren größten Sohn jedes Jahr durch die Mozart-Festspiele. Dann kommen die besten Musiker nach Salzburg, um hier seine Werke zu spielen. Auch die Zuhörer kommen aus allen Ländern der Welt. In den Wochen der Mozart-Festspiele kann man auf den Straßen von Salzburg die Sprachen vieler Völker hören. Sehr oft geschieht es, daß ein Zuhörer nicht die Sprache des Mannes versteht, der neben ihm oder hinter ihm sitzt, aber sie alle verstehen die Sprache Mozarts.

Wagner ist der größte deutsche Opernkomponist des 19. Jahrhunderts. Er schrieb nicht nur die Musik, sondern auch den Text seiner Opern. Sehr oft hat er für seine Opern Sagen aus der alten deutschen Literatur oder der germanischen Mythologie gebraucht, so z.B. in „Lohengrin", „Tannhäuser", „Tristan und Isolde", „Parsifal" und im „Ring des Nibelungen." „Die Meistersinger von Nürnberg", vielleicht Richard Wagners schönste Oper, zeigt das Problem jedes echten Künstlers in seiner Stellung zwischen Intuition und Tradition. Wagners Werk ist besonders eng verbunden mit dem Namen der Stadt Bayreuth in Bayern. Hier hat er im Jahre 1876 ein Theater gebaut, in dem nur seine eigenen Opern gespielt werden sollten. So geschah es, und so geschieht es noch in unserer Zeit. Die Wagner-Festspiele in Bayreuth locken in jedem Sommer eine große, internationale Menge in die kleine Stadt in Bayern. Die Festspiele sind noch heute in den Händen der Familie. Richard Wagners Enkel, Wieland und Wolfgang, führen die Tradition ihres Großvaters weiter.

Salzburg und Bayreuth sind zwei große Namen unter den musikalischen Hauptstädten der Welt.

VIII. Wörterverzeichnis

Bayern Bavaria
besonders especially
der Denker, – the thinker
echt true, genuine
ehren (to) honor
eigen own
eng closely
das Festspiel, –e the festival

germanisch Germanic
der Großvater, ⸚ the grandfather
die Hauptstadt, ⸚e the capital
die Hochzeit, –en the marriage
der Komponist, (–en), –en the composer
das Konzertprogramm, –e the concert program
der Künstler, – the artist
kurz short
die Literatur, –en the literature
locken (to) lure
die Meistersinger the master-singers
die Menge, –n the throng, crowd
die Musik the music
musikalisch musical
der Musiker, – the musician
die Mythologie the mythology
der Name, (–ns), –n the name
die Oper, –n the opera
der Opernkomponist, (–en), –en the composer of operas
der Österreicher, – the Austrian
österreichisch Austrian
das Problem, –e the problem
der Ring des Nibelungen the Ring of the Nibelung
die Sage, –n the saying, legend
die Sonate, –n the sonata
die Stellung, –en the position
die Symphonie, –n the symphony
der Teil, –e the part
der Text, –e the text, libretto
verbringen, verbrachte, verbracht (to) spend
verbunden connected
weiter-führen, führte weiter, weitergeführt (to) carry on
Wien Vienna
zählen zu (to) count among
die Zauberflöte the Magic Flute
der Zuhörer, – the listener; *plur.* audience
z.B.; zum Beispiel e.g.; for example

Aufgabe Zwanzig

THE SUBJUNCTIVE: UNREAL CONDITIONS

I. Reading Selection

Auf einem kleinen Berg über unserer Stadt ist ein Restaurant. Man sitzt an Tischen unter großen Bäumen und kann von hier die ganze Stadt sehen, die Häuser, die Kirchen, das Rathaus und die Berge auf der anderen Seite des Tales.

Es ist Frühling. Wir haben an einem schönen Nachmittag mit den Löwenzahns einen Spaziergang auf den Berg gemacht und sitzen nun an einem Tisch unter den Bäumen. Im Radio singt eine laute Stimme deutsche Volkslieder. Gerade jetzt fängt ein neues Lied an:

Wenn ich ein Vöglein wär'
Und auch zwei Flügel hätt',
Flög' ich zu dir . . .

„Wenn es etwas klarer wäre, könntest du von hier den Rhein sehen", sagt am nächsten Tisch ein Mann zu seinem kleinen Sohn.

Der Kellner hat Kaffee und Kuchen gebracht, Herr Löwenzahn raucht seine Pfeife, der Himmel ist blau, die Bäume sind grün, und alle Leute scheinen sehr zufrieden zu sein.

„Sprich nicht davon, Heinrich", sagt Frau Löwenzahn.

„Wenn ich hier sitze, Lisette, muß ich daran denken", antwortet Herr Löwenzahn.

Weder Herbert noch ich verstehen, wovon sie sprechen. „Sie machen uns neugierig", sage ich schließlich.

„Dort unten", Herr Löwenzahn zeigt nach der Stadt, „sehen Sie vier oder fünf Straßen mit neuen, modernen Häusern. Vor 30 Jahren war dort noch ein großes, leeres Feld. Wenn ich damals das Feld gekauft hätte, hätte ich es für 1 000 Mark haben können. Ich habe es nicht getan. Vor fünf Jahren wurde das Feld verkauft. Auf dem Feld waren 28 Bauplätze, und jeder kostete 2 000 Mark. Wenn ich damals schneller gewesen wäre, wäre ich heute ein reicher Mann."

„Haben Sie damals, ich meine vor 30 Jahren, gewußt, daß das Feld verkauft werden sollte?" fragt Herbert.

„Habe ich es gewußt!", ruft Herr Löwenzahn. „Das Feld gehörte meinem besten Freund. Er wollte nach Amerika auswandern und darum das Feld schnell verkaufen. Er hatte mich gebeten, es zu kaufen. Zuerst wollte er 2 200 Mark dafür haben, dann 1 500, schließlich 1 000. Er brauchte Geld. Hätte ich damals nur mehr Mut gehabt! Außerdem wollte es meine Frau nicht. Wäre sie nicht gewesen, hätte ich es gekauft."

„Wenn meine Frau nicht gewesen wäre", wiederholt Frau Löwenzahn. „Da muß ich lachen. Heinrich, du hättest es vielleicht gekauft, wenn du damals mehr Geld gehabt hättest."

„Vielleicht hat sie recht", meint Herr Löwenzahn. „Wer hätte auch damals geglaubt, daß so viele Häuser gebaut werden würden. Wenn die Stadt nicht so schnell gewachsen wäre, wäre das Feld nicht so wertvoll geworden. Sie werden verstehen, daß ich mich immer wieder ärgere, wenn ich hier sitze und dort unten die neuen Häuser sehe."

„Er kann es nicht vergessen", sagt Frau Löwenzahn. „Wenn du viel Geld hättest, würdest du Angst haben, es zu verlieren. Du würdest schlecht schlafen und müßtest höhere Steuern zahlen. Du hast alles, was du zum Leben brauchst.

Denk' nicht immer, was wäre geschehen, wenn . . . Freu' dich über den warmen Tag und die schöne Landschaft."

Herr Löwenzahn lächelt. „Du sprichst wie eine Frau."

„Wie eine kluge Frau", sagt sie. „Wenn du nicht so viel an das wertvolle Feld dächtest, würdest du hören, was der Mann im Radio jetzt singt."

Wir alle werden still. Die laute Stimme im Radio fängt ein neues Lied an:

Was frag' ich viel nach Geld und Gut,
Wenn ich zufrieden bin.
Gibt Gott mir nur gesunden Mut,
So hab' ich frohen Sinn. . . .*

II. Vocabulary

aus-wandern (to) emigrate
***der Baum** ⸗e the tree
der Bauplatz, ⸗e the building lot
***bitten, bat, gebeten** (to) ask (*a favor*)
***damals** then, at that time
dort unten down there
***fliegen, flog, ist geflogen** (to) fly
der Flügel, – the wing
***der Frühling,** –e the spring
***gehören** (*with dat.*) (to) belong to
***klug** clever
***leer** empty, vacant
modern modern
***der Mut** the courage
***neugierig** curious
das Radio, –s the radio
***reich** rich
***die Seite,** –n the side, page
die Steuer, –n the tax
***das Tal,** ⸗er the valley
***verlieren, verlor, verloren** (to) lose
das Vöglein, – the little bird
das Volkslied, –er the folksong
***wertvoll** valuable
***wiederholen, wiederholte, wiederholt** (to) repeat

IDIOMS

***bitten um** (to) ask for
***recht haben** (to) be right

* What do I care for might and wealth
If only I'm content.
If God lets live me in good health
I live in merriment. . . .

III. Grammar

Every verb can appear in two different "moods," the indicative and the subjunctive. You will find out later in what situations the subjunctive mood is used. First you have to learn the set of endings used to produce the different tenses of the subjunctive mood.

A. THE SUBJUNCTIVE FORMS

1. The subjunctive endings are the following:

	SINGULAR	PLURAL
1.	**—e**	**—en**
2.	**—est**	**—et**
3.	**—e**	**—en**

While the indicative mood has six tenses, the subjunctive furnishes four time relationships: **present, past, future,** and **future perfect.** However, each of these "tenses" has two distinct forms which we shall call **Form I** and **Form II.**

2 a. *Present Subjunctive I.* Add the subjunctive endings to the stem of the verb; there are no vowel changes to worry about:

1. ich	habe	liebe	sei	werde	gebe	schlafe	müsse
2. du	habest	liebest	sei(e)st	werdest	gebest	schlafest	müssest
3. er	habe	liebe	sei	werde	gebe	schlafe	müsse
1. wir	haben	lieben	seien	werden	geben	schlafen	müssen
2. ihr	habet	liebet	seiet	werdet	gebet	schlafet	müsset
3. sie	haben	lieben	seien	werden	geben	schlafen	müssen

[You will notice that **sein,** as so often before, is irregular.]

2 b. *Present Subjunctive II.* This form (although it expresses a present time, as in English) is, also as in English, derived from the simple past tense of the indicative. The present subjunctive II of weak verbs is identical with the past tense of the indicative. The present subjunctive II of strong

(or vowel-changing) verbs adds the above subjunctive endings to the second principal part of the verb and umlauts its vowel whenever possible:

1. ich	hätte	liebte	wäre	würde	gäbe	schliefe	müßte
2. du	hättest	liebtest	wärest	würdest	gäbest	schliefest	müßtest
3. er	hätte	liebte	wäre	würde	gäbe	schliefe	müßte
1. wir	hätten	liebten	wären	würden	gäben	schliefen	müßten
2. ihr	hättet	liebtet	wäret	würdet	gäbet	schliefet	müßtet
3. sie	hätten	liebten	wären	würden	gäben	schliefen	müßten

NOTE: a) **hätte** is slightly irregular; although a weak verb it does take an umlaut;
b) all modal auxiliaries which have an umlaut in their infinitive also have umlaut here, as does **wissen: dürfte, müßte, könnte, möchte, wüßte;**
c) **denken** and **bringen** also add umlaut: **dächte, brächte.**
d) the remaining irregular weak verbs have the following forms: **brennte, kennte, nennte.**

3 a. *Past Subjunctive I.* This form parallels the perfect tense by using the present subjunctive I of the auxiliaries **haben** or **sein:**

1. ich habe ihn gesehen
2. du habest ihn gesehen, etc.

1. ich sei nach Hause gegangen
2. du sei(e)st nach Hause gegangen, etc.

3 b. *Past Subjunctive II.* This form parallels the past perfect tense by using the present subjunctive II of the auxiliaries **haben** or **sein:**

1. ich hätte ihn gesehen
2. du hättest ihn gesehen, etc.

1. ich wäre nach Hause gegangen
2. du wärest nach Hause gegangen, etc.

4 a. *Future Subjunctive I.* It uses the present subjunctive I of the auxiliary **werden**:

1. ich werde nach Hause gehen
2. du werdest nach Hause gehen, etc.

4 b. *Future Subjunctive II.* It uses the present subjunctive II of the auxiliary **werden**:

1. ich würde nach Hause gehen
2. du würdest nach Hause gehen, etc.

5 a. *Future Perfect Subjunctive I.* This form parallels the future perfect tense by using the present subjunctive I of the auxiliary **werden**:

1. ich werde es gesehen haben
2. du werdest es gesehen haben, etc.

1. ich werde in die Stadt gegangen sein
2. du werdest in die Stadt gegangen sein, etc.

5 b. *Future Perfect Subjunctive II.* It is the same as above, but uses the present subjunctive II of the auxiliary **werden**:

1. ich würde es gesehen haben
2. du würdest es gesehen haben, etc.

1. ich würde in die Stadt gegangen sein
2. du würdest in die Stadt gegangen sein, etc.

The future subjunctive II (4 b) and the future perfect subjunctive II (5 b) are often called the *present* and *perfect conditional moods* respectively. They correspond to the *would*-forms in English. (*I would write,* **ich würde schreiben.** *I would have written,* **ich würde geschrieben haben.**) They are called *conditionals* because they appear in the conclusion of a conditional sentence: If my friend had time, he would go downtown; or: If my friend had had time, he would have gone downtown.

B. The Use of the Subjunctive

In contrast to the indicative, the subjunctive mood expresses something merely hypothetical, something which is not "real"; it only indicates an eventuality, a possibility, a wish. The subjunctive is most frequently used in conditional statements of a hypothetical character, something we may call "statements contrary to fact."

1. If a "real" condition is expressed, we use the indicative in English and in German: *If he is well, he will come;* **Wenn er gesund ist, wird er kommen.**

2. However, if an "unreal" condition is expressed, we use the subjunctive in English and in German: *If he were well, he would come;* **Wenn er gesund wäre, würde er kommen.**

NOTICE: *in these unreal conditions only subjunctives II can be used* (2 b, 3 b, 4 b, 5 b). German differs from English in that it may use in the conclusion the present subjunctive II (2 b) instead of the conditional (4 b).

Wenn er gesund wäre, { **würde er kommen.** / **käme er.** }

To express it in a formula: the **wenn**-clause has the present subjunctive II **(wäre)**, the conclusion has either the future subjunctive II, also called *conditional* **(würde . . . kommen)**, or it has the present subjunctive II **(käme)**.

3. If we transpose the whole idea into the past, we then get: *If he had been well, he would have come.* Again, expressed in a formula, you need in German the past subjunctive II (3 b) in the **wenn**-clause, and in the conclusion either the future perfect subjunctive II (perfect conditional, 5 b) or the past subjunctive II (3 b). So, we would have the sentence:

Wenn er gesund gewesen wäre, { **würde er gekommen sein.** / **wäre er gekommen.** }

A few other examples are the following:

With the "present" idea:

If he were here, he would see it. { **Wenn er hier wäre, würde er es sehen.** / **Wenn er hier wäre, sähe er es.** }

With the "past" idea:

If he had been here, he would have seen it.	**Wenn er hier gewesen wäre, würde er es gesehen haben.** **Wenn er hier gewesen wäre, hätte er es gesehen.**

With the "past" and "present" ideas mixed:

If he had bought the field, he would be rich now.	**Wenn er das Feld gekauft hätte, würde er jetzt reich sein.** **Wenn er das Feld gekauft hätte, wäre er jetzt reich.**

C. Contrary-to-Fact Wishes

The "if clause" of a contrary-to-fact condition is used frequently without any conclusion expressed. This results in a contrary-to-fact wish that has only an implied conclusion. Here a few examples: **doch** or **nur** stand in this idiomatic expression for *only.*

If only he were well!	**Wenn er nur gesund wäre!**
If only he had been well!	**Wenn er nur gesund gewesen wäre!**

D. Details Concerning Conditions

1. In conditional clauses, especially in contrary-to-fact clauses, German may omit the conjunction **wenn**, in which case the finite verb opens the conditional clause. In such cases, the conclusion is often introduced by **so** or **dann.** *If he had time, he would write to me;* **Hätte er Zeit, so würde er mir schreiben.**—*If he wrote me, I would answer;* **Schriebe er mir, dann würde ich antworten.** Even if the conjunction **wenn** is not omitted, the two parts of the sentences are often connected by **so** or **dann** (*then*). *If he had been here, he would have seen it;* **Wenn er hier gewesen wäre, so würde er es gesehen haben.**

2. The clauses in conditional sentences may readily be switched around so that the conclusion comes ahead of the

condition: *My friend would have gone downtown, if he had had time;* **Mein Freund würde in die Stadt gegangen sein, wenn er Zeit gehabt hätte.**

3. Certain modal auxiliaries are often used in the past subjunctive. **Hätte + infinitive + sollen** means *should + have + past participle. I ought to* (or *should*) *have gone home;* **ich hätte nach Hause gehen sollen. Hätte + infinitive + können** means *could + have + past participle. He could have done that himself;* **er hätte das selbst tun können.**

IV. Grammatical Exercises

A. Make the following into present contrary-to-fact conditions:

1. Wenn es regnet, werde ich zu Hause bleiben. 2. Wenn es schneit, ist es sehr kalt. 3. Wenn mehr Studenten hier sind, arbeiten wir schneller. 4. Wenn ich Zeit habe, werde ich die Aufgabe wiederholen. 5. Wenn er mich darum bittet, werde ich es ihm gerne geben. 6. Wenn er keine Tasche hat, wird er sein Geld verlieren. 7. Wenn er in diesem Restaurant sitzt, kann er das ganze Tal sehen. 8. Wenn ein kluger Mann dieses große Feld kauft, wird er später reich werden. 9. Wenn er das weiß, so kauft er es gewiß. 10. Wenn meine Frau recht hat, werde ich es gerne tun. 11. Wenn sie neugierig ist, wird sie Sie fragen. 12. Wenn er nicht daran denkt, kann er sich über den schönen Tag freuen. 13. Wenn der Frühling da ist, sind alle Bäume grün. 14. Wir können dieses Drama sehen, wenn wir ins Theater gehen. 15. Wenn wir alles sehen wollen, müssen wir früh ankommen. 16. Wenn man im Theater Programme verkauft, können wir etwas über den Dichter lesen.

B. Make the sentences in A into past contrary-to-fact conditions.

C. Re-do some sentences of A and B omitting **wenn.**

D. Re-do some sentences of A using the conditional clauses only as present contrary-to-fact wishes. (Wenn es doch regnete!, etc.)

E. Re-do some sentences of A changing the conditional clauses into past contrary-to-fact wishes. (Wenn es doch geschneit hätte!, etc.)

V. Translation Exercise

1. If Conrad is in Germany at Christmas, then he cannot be with (*bei*) his parents. 2. If there were beautiful presents for him, he would perhaps not be so sad. 3. If the clever children had asked their grandparents, they would have been very pleased with the answer. 4. Conrad ought to have placed his shoe in front of the window too. 5. If it had snowed yesterday, the whole valley would be white. 6. If he were only more curious! 7. If the children had come into the dining room before five o'clock, they would have seen all the presents under the tree. 8. If they sang a song, they would not think of their presents. 9. If Mr. Löwenzahn tells a story, nobody will interrupt him. 10. If they had left after January 1st, we would have gone to the station with them. 11. We could see them leave if we stayed on the platform. 12. It would be hard if we counted the hours from zero to twenty-four every day. 13. If his brother had only been right! 14. If we had repeated our words, we would know the German word for "snow." 15. If it rained in the Rhineland in the late summer, the wine would not be so good.

VI. Fragen

1. Wo liegt dieses Restaurant, von dem wir lesen? 2. Was sieht man auf der anderen Seite des Tales? 3. Worunter sitzen die Studenten nun? 4. Was hat der Kellner gebracht?

5. Was macht Herr Löwenzahn? 6. Wie scheinen alle Leute zu sein? 7. Woran muß Herr Löwenzahn denken? 8. Was zeigt er den Studenten? 9. Wem gehörte damals das Feld? 10. Warum wollte der Freund das Feld so schnell verkaufen? 11. Was hätte Herr Löwenzahn tun können, wenn er damals Geld gehabt hätte? 12. Wieviel hätte er vor dreißig Jahren für das Feld gezahlt? 13. Warum konnte er es nicht kaufen? 14. Was ist später auf dem Feld gebaut worden? 15. Ärgert sich Frau Löwenzahn, weil sie nicht reich geworden ist? 16. Worüber freut sich Frau Löwenzahn an diesem Nachmittag?

VII. Lesestück

Potsdam und Weimar

Potsdam und Weimar sind zwei deutsche Städte, Weimar, klein und schläfrig, im Herzen Deutschlands, Potsdam, mittelgroß und schläfrig, sechzehn Meilen südwestlich von Berlin. Weder die eine noch die andere ist oder war wichtig als Stadt, aber beide waren in der deutschen Geschichte wichtig als Symbole.

Potsdam wurde im 17. Jahrhundert die Residenz der preußischen Könige. Im Potsdamer Schloß wohnte der König Friedrich Wilhelm I., den die deutsche Geschichte den „Soldatenkönig" genannt hat. In seiner Zeit wuchs das preußische Heer von 38 000 auf 83 000 Soldaten. Unter ihm wurde es das disziplinierteste Heer Europas, mit dem dann sein Sohn Friedrich der Große Kriege führte und Eroberungen machte. Durch Friedrich den Großen wurde Preußen mächtig, und durch ihn wurde Potsdam berühmt. Hier baute er ein neues Schloß, das er Sanssouci nannte. Friedrich Wilhelm I. und Friedrich der Große wurden in Potsdam begraben. Alle späteren preußischen Könige haben oft in den Schlössern von Potsdam gewohnt. Hier lebt der Geist der alten preußischen

Könige. In Deutschland, in Europa, in der Welt hat man mehr und mehr Potsdam mit dem preußischen Charakter identifiziert. Potsdam, das war eine Stadt mit Schlössern, Garnisonen, Kadettenanstalten, Soldaten, Generälen und Königen. Der Geist von Potsdam bedeutete Sparsamkeit, Disziplin, Uniform, Unterordnung, Eroberung. Als im Jahre 1933 Adolf Hitler sein erstes Parlament versammelte, rief er es in Potsdam zusammen. Er hat sich, mit Recht oder Unrecht, mit der preußischen Tradition identifiziert. Mit dem Wort Potsdam wollte er der Welt zeigen, daß mit ihm eine Zeit von Unterordnung, von Uniformen und Eroberungen angefangen hatte.

Mit Hitler endete ein Kapitel deutscher Geschichte, das im Jahre 1919 begonnen hatte. Damals versuchte das deutsche Volk, eine republikanische Staatsform zu finden. Als im Sommer 1919 die Vertreter des Volkes zusammenkommen wollten, um eine neue Verfassung zu schreiben, wählten sie die kleine Stadt Weimar für ihre erste Versammlung. Wir sprechen darum von der Weimarer Verfassung, und wir nennen die Jahre von 1919 bis 1933 die Zeit der Weimarer Republik. Auch die Männer von 1919 nahmen eine Stadt als Symbol. Sie wollten der Welt zeigen, daß sie sich mit dem Geist von Weimar identifizierten. Was bedeutet das Wort Weimar in der deutschen Geschichte? Weimar wurde am Ende des 18. Jahrhunderts das größte Kulturzentrum in Deutschland. Viele berühmte Dichter und Denker lebten hier, Wieland, Herder, Schiller und der größte unter ihnen, Johann Wolfgang von Goethe (1749–1832). Ihre Sorge war nicht ein mächtiger, starker Staat, sondern ein freies, glückliches Individuum. Sie dachten nicht an Unterordnung und Eroberung, sie glaubten an Freiheit und Menschlichkeit.

An allen großen Kreuzwegen in der deutschen Geschichte werden immer die Zeichen „Nach Potsdam“ oder „Nach Weimar“ stehen.

VIII. Wörterverzeichnis

bedeuten (to) mean, signify
beginnen, begann, begonnen (to) begin
begraben, (ä), begrub, begraben (to) bury
der Denker, – the thinker
die Disziplin the discipline
diszipliniert disciplined, trained
enden (to) end
die Eroberung, –en the conquest
finden, fand, gefunden (to) find
die Freiheit the freedom
Friedrich der Große Frederick the Great
Friedrich Wilhelm I. Frederick William I
die Garnison, –en the garrison
der Geist the spirit
der General, ⸚e the general
glücklich happy
identifizieren (to) identify
das Individuum the individual
die Kadettenanstalt, –en the military college
das Kapitel, – the chapter
der König, –e the king
der Kreuzweg, –e the crossroad
der Krieg, –e the war
das Kulturzentrum the cultural center
die Menschlichkeit the humaneness
mittelgroß medium-sized
das Parlament, –e the parliament
preußisch Prussian
mit Recht rightly
republikanisch republican
die Residenz, –en the residence, seat
schläfrig sleepy
das Schloß, Schlösser the castle
der Soldatenkönig the soldier-king
die Sorge, –n the worry, concern
die Sparsamkeit the thrift, economy
die Staatsform, –en the form of government
südwestlich von southwest of
mit Unrecht wrongly
die Unterordnung the subordination
die Verfassung, –en the constitution
versammeln (to) call together, assemble
die Versammlung, –en the meeting
versuchen (to) try, attempt
der Vertreter, – the representative
wählen (to) choose
das Zeichen, – sign-post
zusammen-kommen, kam zusammen, ist zusammengekommen (to) meet, come together

Aufgabe Einundzwanzig

THE SUBJUNCTIVE: INDIRECT DISCOURSE

I. Reading Selection

Herbert und ich wollen so viel wie möglich Deutsch sprechen und Deutsch hören. Darum gehen wir zu deutschen Vorträgen, die später auf deutsch diskutiert werden, in die Kirchen, wo auf deutsch gepredigt wird und in die Kinos, in denen deutsche Filme laufen. Wir möchten auch so viel wie möglich von dem Leben der Deutschen sehen. Darum haben wir gestern ein deutsches Gericht besucht.

Es war kein wichtiger Fall. Jemand war betrogen worden. Dieser „jemand" war ein junger Mann, der Kurt Möller hieß. Er hatte hellblondes Haar und trug einen dunkelblauen Anzug. Jetzt stand er vor dem Richter und berichtete seine Geschichte.

Er habe in der Zeitung gelesen, daß ein reicher Mann seine Brieftasche mit Geld verloren hätte. In der Zeitung versprach der Mann, er werde dem Finder eine Belohnung von 100 Mark zahlen, wenn er ihm die Brieftasche zurückbringe. Zwei Tage später habe er, Kurt Möller, wirklich die Brieftasche gefunden; sie habe unter einer Bank im Park gelegen. Er habe sie mit nach Hause genommen, ohne sie zu öffnen. Da sei noch die Zeitung gewesen, in der der Mann 100 Mark Belohnung versprochen habe. Er hätte den Mann angerufen und ihm dann die Brieftasche gebracht. Als er dann zu ihm gekommen sei, habe der Mann gefragt, ob auch noch 700 Mark darin seien.

Möller habe gesagt, er wisse nicht, wieviel Geld darin sei, denn er habe die Brieftasche nicht aufgemacht. Der Mann habe dann das Geld gezählt, aber es seien nur 600 Mark darin gewesen. Aha, hätte der Mann gesagt, es seien 700 Mark darin gewesen. Da er 700 Mark verloren hätte und Möller nur 600 Mark zurückbringe, so wäre es klar, daß Möller sich schon 100 Mark als Belohnung herausgenommen habe, und darum brauche er nun keine Belohnung mehr zu zahlen.

Bis jetzt hatte der junge Kurt Möller sehr ruhig gesprochen. Jetzt aber wurde seine Stimme laut und er rief, er hätte nie viel Geld gehabt, das sei wahr, aber er wäre immer ehrlich gewesen, und niemand könne sagen, daß er anderer Leute Geld genommen hätte.

Der dicke Mann, der seine Brieftasche verloren hatte, sagte nicht viel. Er saß auf einem Stuhl, rauchte eine Zigarre und wiederholte immer wieder, er hätte 700 Mark verloren. Ob er schwören könne, daß dies die Wahrheit sei, wurde er von dem Richter gefragt. Gewiß, sagte der dicke Mann mit der dicken Zigarre, er könne schwören, daß 700 Mark in der Brieftasche gewesen wären.

Der Richter stand auf und verkündete das Urteil. Wenn der Mann eine Brieftasche mit 700 Mark verloren habe, dann sei dieses nicht seine Brieftasche. Er müsse warten, bis jemand komme und ihm eine Brieftasche mit 700 Mark bringe. Die Brieftasche mit 600 Mark müsse an Kurt Möller zurückgegeben werden, und Möller müsse warten, ob nicht jemand komme, der sie verloren habe. Wenn er drei Jahre gewartet habe und niemand gekommen sei, dann solle ihm das ganze Geld gehören.

Die Brieftasche mit dem Geld hatte bis jetzt vor dem Richter auf dem Tisch gelegen. Jetzt nahm er sie in die Hand und gab sie Kurt Möller. Der reiche Mann wurde rot im Gesicht, er warf ärgerlich seine Zigarre auf den Boden und lief hinaus. „Das ist noch nicht das letzte Wort“, hörte man ihn rufen.

„Ich glaube nicht, daß Sie gestohlen haben“, sagte der Richter zu Kurt Möller. „Warten Sie drei Jahre; wahrscheinlich gehört Ihnen dann das Geld.“

Als wir am Abend wieder zu Hause waren, berichteten wir Herrn Löwenzahn über unseren Tag im Gericht. „Das ist eine schöne Geschichte“, sagte er. „Ich wünschte, ich wäre mit Ihnen gegangen. Und ich freue mich, daß es noch kluge Richter in Deutschland gibt.“

. . .

Dies war nun die letzte Geschichte, die ich aus Deutschland schreibe. Bald fahren wir nach Amerika zurück. Aber ich wünschte, wir hätten noch ein zweites Jahr bleiben können. Als wir hier ankamen, schien alles so schwer. Heute weiß ich, daß Deutsch eine sehr leichte Sprache ist. Man muß nur ein wenig dafür arbeiten!

II. Vocabulary

*__an-rufen, rief an, angerufen__ (to) call up, telephone
*__ärgerlich__ angry
__die Belohnung, –en__ the reward
*__betrügen, betrog, betrogen__ (to) deceive, cheat
*__der Boden, ⸚__ the floor, ground
__die Brieftasche, –n__ pocketbook
*__dick__ thick, fat
__diskutieren__ (to) discuss
*__ehrlich__ honest
__der Fall, ⸚e__ the case
*__der Film, –e__ the film
*__finden, fand, gefunden__ (to) find
__der Finder, –__ the finder
*__das Gericht, –e__ the (law) court
*__hell__ bright
*__heraus-nehmen (nimmt heraus), nahm heraus, herausgenommen__ (to) take out
__hinaus-laufen (ä), lief hinaus, ist hinausgelaufen__ (to) run out
*__jemand__ someone
*__das Kino, –s__ the movie house
*__leicht__ easy
*__möglich__ possible
__predigen__ (to) preach
*__der Richter, –__ the judge
*__ruhig__ quiet
__schwören, schwur, geschworen__ (to) swear, take an oath
*__stehlen (ie), stahl, gestohlen__ (to) steal
*__das Urteil, –e__ the verdict, judgment
__verkünden__ (to) announce
*__versprechen (i), versprach, versprochen__ (to) promise
*__der Vortrag, ⸚e__ the lecture
*__wahr__ true

***die Wahrheit, –en** the truth
***wahrscheinlich** probably
***wirklich** actually, really
***wünschen** (to) wish
***zurück-bringen, brachte zurück, zurückgebracht** (to) bring back
***zurück-geben (i), gab zurück, zurückgegeben** (to) give back, return

IDIOMS

ins Kino gehen (to) go to the movies

III. Grammar

A. INDIRECT DISCOURSE

1. One of the primary functions of the subjunctive in German is to express indirect discourse, i.e., a statement which is not made by the speaker directly, but given through indirect report. As an example:

Direct discourse: Conrad said: "The film is bad."
Indirect discourse: Conrad said that the film was bad.

Besides *to say,* other verbs expressing mental action, such as *to think, write, tell, believe, feel,* etc. are likely to introduce indirect-discourse statements. In general, German uses the subjunctive in indirect discourse, but there is a tendency to preserve the indicative if the leading verb [i.e., the one on which the *that*-clause depends] appears a) in the present tense, b) in the *ich*-form. However, even in these cases the subjunctive is possible.

2. When switching from direct to indirect discourse, you have to watch the time relationship between the leading verb and the depending sentence, and use the proper tense of the subjunctive, of which, as you remember, there are four: present, past, future, and future perfect. Each of these tenses has two forms, I and II (look up again the previous lesson, A, 2 a through 5 b), and both these forms can be used interchangeably. When making your choice between these two forms, always give preference to the one which clearly shows its character as a subjunctive. So, **ich hätte** (present subjunctive II)

is preferable to **ich habe** (present subjunctive I); **er liebe** (present subjunctive I) is preferable to **er liebte** (present subjunctive II).

Examples:

DIRECT: Conrad sagt (sagte, hat gesagt, hatte gesagt, wird sagen):
„Ich gehe nach Hause."

As you see, the verb in the direct discourse is in the *present* tense. German always tries to retain the same time or tense in the indirect discourse, therefore we get the indirect statement:

INDIRECT: Conrad sagt (sagte, hat gesagt, hatte gesagt, wird sagen):
{daß er nach Hause **gehe** (*Present* subjunctive I).
{daß er nach Hause **ginge** (*Present* subjunctive II).

DIRECT: Conrad sagt (sagte, hat gesagt, hatte gesagt, wird sagen):
„Ich ging nach Hause."
„Ich bin nach Hause gegangen."
„Ich war nach Hause gegangen."

As you see, the verb in the direct discourse is in one of the three possible tenses indicating "pastness," therefore we change as follows:

INDIRECT: Conrad sagt (sagte, hat gesagt, hatte gesagt, wird sagen):
{daß er nach Hause **gegangen sei** (*Past* subjunctive I).
{daß er nach Hause **gegangen wäre** (*Past* subjunctive II).

DIRECT: Conrad sagt (sagte, hat gesagt, hatte gesagt, wird sagen):
„Ich werde nach Hause gehen."

As you see, the verb in the direct discourse is in the future, therefore the indirect statement will be:

INDIRECT: Conrad sagt (sagte, hat gesagt, hatte gesagt, wird sagen):
{daß er nach Hause **gehen werde** (*Future* subjunctive I).
{daß er nach Hause **gehen würde** (*Future* subjunctive II).

The future perfect is used so seldom that we shall omit it here. The principle would be exactly the same.

3. Omission of **daß.** As in English, the conjunction *that* **(daß)** can be omitted, but in this case the word order in the

indirect discourse is that of an independent clause (finite verb: second grammatical unit): **Er sagte, er sei (wäre) nach Hause gegangen.**

4. Since by the use of the subjunctive it is indicated that we are dealing with an indirect discourse statement, German has the advantage of omitting the introductory clause such as "he said," "he reported," "he continued," etc., when rendering indirectly (through the mouth of a reporter) what someone else has said. (See as an example the third paragraph of the above Reading Selection.)

5. If the direct statement is a command, the German indirect statement uses the proper form of **sollen,** just as in English we would use *should, ought to, am to.*

DIRECT: Er sagte zu ihr: „Sprich nicht so laut!"
INDIRECT: Er sagte ihr, sie **solle (sollte)** nicht so laut **sprechen.**

(Note that in direct discourse **sagen** generally takes the preposition **zu** (*dat.*), in indirect discourse generally not.)

6. Indirect questions after **ob**, or such interrogatives as **wann, warum, wie, wer, was, wo,** etc., belong, of course, under the general heading "Indirect Discourse" and follow the same rules.

DIRECT: Conrad fragte mich: „Studiert dein Freund in Heidelberg?"
INDIRECT: Conrad fragte mich, **ob** mein Freund in Heidelberg **studiere.**

(Only Form I should be used, since Form II **studierte** coincides with the past indicative.)

DIRECT: Conrad fragte mich: „Wo sahst du ihn?"
INDIRECT: Conrad fragte mich, **wo** ich ihn **gesehen hätte.**

(Only Form II should be used, since Form I **habe** coincides with the present indicative.)

DIRECT: Conrad fragte mich: „Wann wird er ankommen?"
INDIRECT: Conrad fragte mich, **wann** er **ankommen werde (würde).**

(Both forms are good, since each clearly indicates the subjunctive.)

B. OTHER USES OF THE SUBJUNCTIVE

1. **Als ob, als wenn.** Always introducing a statement whose veracity is in doubt or at least undecided, **als ob** (or its synonym **als wenn**) is followed by the subjunctive, either Form I or II. **Es schien, als ob er die Antwort nicht wisse** (or **wüßte**); *it seemed as if he did not know the answer.* Very often the **ob** or **wenn** is left out, in which case the finite verb follows **als** immediately. **Es schien, als wisse (wüßte) er die Antwort nicht.**

2. *Hopes and wishes.* If an exclamation expresses a hope or a wish the subjunctive is indicated. **Lang lebe der Kaiser!** *Long live the emperor!*—**So sei es!** *So be it!*

Also, in statements expressing a wish the subjunctive is very common: **Ich wünschte, ihr kämet alle mit mir!** Likewise in statements expressing hope the subjunctive is frequently used, if the hope proves unfulfilled: **Ich hatte gehofft, er würde mit mir kommen.**

3. *The polite subjunctive.* To stress politeness in a request is also one of the functions of the subjunctive. **Könnten Sie mir sagen, wie ich zum Bahnhof komme?** *Could you please tell me how to get to the station?*

4. *The potential subjunctive.* The subjunctive in general expresses possibility or potentiality. **Das wäre wirklich schön!** *That would really be nice!*—**Daran hätte ich auch denken können!** *I also could (should, might) have thought of that!*—**Ich könnte mich nicht daran erinnern.** *I wouldn't be able to remember that.*

IV. Grammatical Exercises

A. Make the following statements into indirect discourse after **Conrad sagte:**

1. Ein Restaurant ist auf dem Berg über dieser Stadt. 2. Man wird an Tischen unter großen Bäumen sitzen. 3. Wir können

von hier die Berge auf der anderen Seite des Tales sehen. 4. Frau Löwenzahn machte einen Spaziergang. 5. Die Männer haben deutsche Lieder gesungen. 6. Jemand fängt gerade jetzt ein neues Lied an. 7. Der Kellner hat Kaffee und Kuchen gebracht. 8. Herr Löwenzahn raucht seine Pfeife. 9. Alle Leute scheinen sehr zufrieden zu sein. 10. Sprich nicht davon! 11. Er sieht dort unten ein großes, leeres Feld. 12. Er ist damals nicht schnell genug gewesen. 13. Das Feld wurde an einen anderen verkauft. 14. Er ist nicht reich geworden. 15. Das Feld gehörte einem seiner Freunde. 16. Dieser Mann wollte nach Amerika auswandern. 17. Er hat mich gebeten, das Feld zu kaufen. 18. Er will zu viel Geld dafür haben. 19. Haben Sie mehr Mut! 20. Frau Löwenzahn hat es nicht gewollt. 21. Er wird schlecht schlafen, wenn er viel Geld hat. 22. Er hatte damals alles, was er zum Leben brauchte. 23. Freut euch über die schöne Landschaft! 24. Frau Löwenzahn ist eine sehr kluge Frau.

B. Make the following into indirect questions after **Herbert fragte:**

1. Mußt du immer daran denken? 2. Versteht er das nicht? 3. Haben Sie dieses Feld vor 30 Jahren kaufen können? 4. Wird Herr Löwenzahn reich werden? 5. Können wir es nicht vergessen? 6. Wer hat so viel Geld gehabt? 7. Warum hatte er es nicht gekauft? 8. Wo wächst der beste Wein in Deutschland? 9. Woran denkt er? 10. Was ist geschehen? 11. Welches Lied hat man gesungen? 12. Wann werden wir ins Theater gehen? 13. Welcher Film läuft jetzt im Kino? 14. Wie hieß dieser junge Mann? 15. Was hatte der reiche Mann verloren?

C. In the Reading Selection above change all indirect discourse into direct discourse.

V. Translation Exercise

Translate the following, changing all direct discourse in quotation marks into indirect discourse:

1. I wished he had not been so curious. 2. Herbert asked me: "Can we talk German with his sister?" 3. He said to me: "We went to this church on Sunday." 4. Conrad wrote to his mother: "We were in a German court yesterday." 5. "Someone had been cheated." 6. Conrad tells us: "First the young man had spoken very quietly." 7. "But now his voice became loud and he began to shout." 8. He said: "I will never take other people's money, and I will always be honest." 9. Herbert tells us: "The fat man who had lost the money didn't say much." 10. "He sat on a chair, smoked a cigar, and repeated one sentence again and again." 11. The judge said to him: "Tell the truth!" 12. Herbert told us later: "Finally the judge stood up, and the fat man became angry." 13. The judge told the young man: "Wait three years!" 14. He said: "I do not believe that he really stole the money." 15. Your friend called me up yesterday and asked me why I had been so angry. 16. My brother said that our last lesson had been very easy. 17. I do not believe that he is right. 18. But I wish it were true!

VI. Fragen

1. Warum sind Conrad und Herbert nach Deutschland gekommen? 2. Wohin gehen sie oft, wenn sie Deutsch hören wollen? 3. Wo sind sie gestern gewesen? 4. Wer stand vor dem Richter? 5. Was hatte er in der Zeitung gelesen? 6. Was hatte ihm der reiche Mann versprochen? 7. Wo hat der junge Mann die Brieftasche gefunden? 8. Warum wollte ihm der reiche Mann die Belohnung nicht geben? 9. Was wiederholt der reiche Mann immer wieder? 10. Glauben Sie, daß er die

Wahrheit sagte? 11. Was war das Urteil des Richters? 12. Wie lange muß Kurt Möller warten, ehe ihm die Brieftasche gehört? 13. Wo hat die Brieftasche bis jetzt gelegen? 14. Was glaubt der Richter nicht? 15. Was tun die beiden Jungens, als sie an diesem Tag nach Hause kommen? 16. Worüber freut sich Herr Löwenzahn?

VII. Lesestück

Eine Legende

Es war ein schöner, blauer Tag im Sommer, als sie durch's Heilige Land gingen. Christus und Petrus gingen voran und die anderen Jünger folgten. Da lag auf dem Weg ein altes Hufeisen. Der Herr zeigte es Petrus und fragte ihn, ob er es nicht aufheben wolle. Man würde es später vielleicht brauchen können. Petrus bückte sich nicht gern. Er schüttelte den Kopf und ging weiter, aber hinter ihm hob Christus das Hufeisen auf und nahm es mit.

Sie kamen bald in eine kleine Stadt, wo gerade an diesem Tage Markt war. Ehe sie über den Marktplatz gingen, sah der Herr einen Hufschmied, der vor seinem Haus arbeitete. Christus fragte ihn, wieviel er ihm für das Hufeisen geben könne. Der Hufschmied antwortete, es sei ein altes Hufeisen und es sei nicht sehr wertvoll, doch er könne ihm zwölf Pfennig dafür geben. Der Herr war damit zufrieden, ging zum Marktplatz und kaufte mit dem Geld ein halbes Pfund Kirschen, die er dann in seiner Tasche versteckte. Petrus hatte nichts gesehen. Er sprach gerade mit einem alten Mann, der Fische verkaufte, und er sagte dem Alten, daß er selbst früher ein Fischer gewesen wäre. Und dann erzählte er eine Geschichte von einem sehr großen und schweren Fisch, den er gefangen hätte, und der alte Mann hörte ruhig zu, obwohl er die Geschichte nicht ganz glaubte.

Sie gingen nun auf der anderen Seite der Stadt zum Tor hinaus, über einen kleinen Berg, durch Wiesen und Felder, auf denen kein Baum stand. Sie alle wurden durstig. Die Sonne brannte heiß vom Himmel, die Luft war trocken und der Weg staubig, doch da war weder Baum noch Wald, weder Bach noch Quelle.

Petrus, der hinter dem Herrn ging, dachte gerade an das klare, kalte Wasser, in dem die Fische schwammen, als er eine schöne, rote Kirsche auf dem Weg liegen sah. Sofort bückte er sich, hob sie auf und aß sie. Leider nur eine, sagte er still zu sich selbst, warum konnten es nicht vier oder fünf sein? Doch sieh, da war eine zweite, nach wenigen Minuten eine dritte . . . eine vierte . . . eine fünfte . . . mehr und mehr. Petrus bückte sich nicht gern, aber wer würde an einem heißen Tag durch ein trockenes, staubiges Feld gehen und die schönen Kirschen, die jemand verloren hatte, nicht aufheben?

Sechsundzwanzig Kirschen machen ein halbes Pfund. Sechsundzwanzig Mal bückte sich Petrus, der sich nicht gerne bückte, an diesem heißen Tag im Sommer. Nachdem er sich zum letzten Mal gebückt hatte, stand der Herr vor ihm und lächelte.

„Erinnerst du dich an das Hufeisen, Petrus?" fragte er ihn. Und dann erzählte er, wie er das Hufeisen gefunden und die Kirschen gekauft hätte.

„Wieviel leichter wäre es gewesen, das Hufeisen aufzuheben!—

Wer geringe Dinge wenig acht,
sich um geringere Mühe macht." *

. . .

Sie werden unsere Geschichte von Christus, dem Hufeisen und den Kirschen nicht in der Bibel finden. Es ist eine Legende. Dem deutschen Volk ist sie in einem Gedicht erzählt worden, geschrieben von dem größten deutschen Dichter, Johann Wolfgang von Goethe.

* Free translation: Who's scornful of a thing that's small
Will have to labor for nothing at all.

VIII. Wörterverzeichnis

auf-heben, hob auf, aufgehoben (to) pick up
der Bach, ⸚e the brook
die Bibel the Bible
sich bücken (to) bend down
Christus Christ
fangen (ä), fing, gefangen (to) catch
der Fisch, –e the fish
der Fischer, – the fisher, fisherman
folgen (*with dat.*) (to) follow
der Herr (*here*) the Lord
hinaus-gehen, ging hinaus, ist hinausgegangen (to) go out
das Hufeisen, – the horse shoe
der Hufschmied, –e the blacksmith
der Jünger, – the apostle, disciple
die Kirsche, –n the cherry
die Legende, –n the legend
der Markt, ⸚e the market, fair
der Marktplatz, ⸚e the market place
mit-nehmen (nimmt mit) nahm mit, mitgenommen (to) take along
Petrus Peter
das Pfund, –e the pound
die Quelle, –n the spring
schütteln (to) shake
staubig dusty
das Tor, –e the gate
trocken dry
verstecken (to) hide, conceal
voran-gehen, ging voran, ist vorangegangen (to) go ahead
weiter-gehen, ging weiter, ist weitergegangen (to) go on
zu-hören (to) listen

Appendix

ZWEI MÄRCHEN DER BRÜDER GRIMM[1]

Rumpelstilzchen

Es war einmal[2] ein Müller,[3] der sehr arm[4] war, aber eine schöne Tochter hatte. Es geschah einmal, daß er mit dem König sprach, und, um sich wichtig zu machen, sagte er zum König, er habe eine Tochter, die Stroh[5] zu Gold[6] spinnen[7] könne. „Das ist eine Kunst,[8] die mir gefällt", sagte der König. „Wenn deine Tochter so geschickt[9] ist, wie du sagst, so bring sie morgen in mein Schloß. Dort soll sie ihre Kunst zeigen." Als am nächsten Tage das Mädchen zu ihm gebracht wurde, führte der König es in eine Kammer,[10] die ganz mit Stroh gefüllt[11] war, gab ihm ein Spinnrad[12] und sprach: „Jetzt fang mit der Arbeit an, und wenn du bis morgen früh dieses Stroh nicht zu Gold gesponnen hast, mußt du sterben." Damit schloß er die Kammer, und sie blieb allein.

Da saß nun die arme Müllerstochter und wußte nicht, was

[1] The brothers Jacob and Wilhelm Grimm, two eminent German philologists and folklorists, collected and published their famous fairy tales (*Märchen*) in the beginning of the nineteenth century.

[2] once upon a time
[3] miller
[4] poor
[5] straw
[6] gold
[7] **spinnen, spann, gesponnen** (to) spin
[8] art
[9] skillful
[10] chamber
[11] filled
[12] spinning wheel

sie tun sollte. Sie wußte nicht, wie man Stroh zu Gold spinnt, und ihre Angst wurde immer größer, so daß sie schließlich zu weinen [13] anfing. Plötzlich öffnete sich die Tür, und ein kleines Männchen [14] kam herein [15] und sagte „Guten Abend, warum weinst du so sehr?“ „Ach“, antwortete sie, „ich soll Stroh zu Gold spinnen und weiß nicht, wie man es tut.“ „Was gibst du mir, wenn ich es für dich spinne?“, fragte das Männchen. „Mein Halsband“,[16] sagte das Mädchen. Das Männchen nahm das Halsband, setzte sich vor das Spinnrad, und in einer halben Stunde war die erste Spule [17] voll [18] Gold. Bald war die zweite voll, die dritte, die vierte, und so spann es bis zum Morgen, dann war alles Stroh gesponnen, und alle Spulen waren voll Gold. Als die Sonne aufging,[19] kam der König. Er war sehr erstaunt [20] und freute sich über das Gold.

Doch wer viel Gold hat, will noch mehr. Am Abend brachte der König die Müllerstochter in eine andere Kammer. Sie war größer als die erste, und es war noch mehr Stroh darin. Wieder stand da ein Spinnrad, und wieder sprach der König: „Spinne das Stroh zu Gold, wenn du dein Leben retten willst.“ Damit ließ er sie allein. Wieder fing das arme Mädchen an zu weinen, und wieder kam das Männchen und fragte: „Was wirst du mir geben, wenn ich die Arbeit für dich tue?“ „Meinen Ring“,[21] antwortete das Mädchen und nahm den Ring ab. Das Männchen nahm ihn, setzte sich vor das Spinnrad und ließ die Räder laufen, und am Morgen war alles Stroh zu glänzendem [22] Gold gesponnen. Wieder freute sich der König, aber er hatte noch nicht genug Gold und ließ die Müllerstochter in eine noch größere Kammer voll Stroh bringen. „Dies ist die dritte und letzte Nacht“, sagte er. „Kannst du all dies Stroh zu Gold spinnen, so wirst du meine

[13] (to) weep
[14] little man
[15] **hereinkommen** (to) enter
[16] necklace
[17] spool
[18] full (of)
[19] rose
[20] astonished
[21] ring
[22] shining

Gemahlin [23] werden. Wenn du es nicht kannst, mußt du sterben."

Als das Mädchen allein war, kam das Männchen wieder und fragte, was es ihm dieses Mal geben würde. Das Mädchen weinte und sagte, es hätte nichts mehr, was es ihm geben könnte. „So versprich mir", sagte das Männchen, „wenn du Königin wirst, dein erstes Kind." Was kann ich tun, dachte das verzweifelte Mädchen, und so versprach es dem Männchen ihr erstes Kind. Noch einmal spann das Männchen alles Stroh zu Gold. Und als am Morgen der König kam und alles fand, wie er es gewünscht hatte, war er sehr zufrieden und nahm sie zu seiner Gemahlin. Und so wurde die schöne Müllerstochter eine Königin.

Nach einem Jahr gebar [24] sie ein Kind, und sie dachte nicht mehr an das, was sie dem Männchen versprochen hatte. Aber dann kam es plötzlich in der Nacht in ihre Kammer und sagte: „Nun gib mir dein Kind!" Die Königin erschrak [25] und bot dem Männchen alles Gold ihres Königreichs [26] an, wenn es ihr ihr Kind lassen wollte, aber das Männchen sprach: „Nein, etwas Lebendes ist mir lieber als alles Gold der Welt." Da fing die Königin an zu weinen und war so verzweifelt, daß sie dem Männchen leid tat. „Drei Tage will ich dir Zeit lassen", sagte es, „wenn du bis dann meinen Namen weißt, so darfst du dein Kind behalten."

Nun dachte die Königin die ganze Nacht und den ganzen Tag an alle Namen, die sie je [27] gehört hatte. Und sie schickte Boten ins ganze Land und befahl ihnen, alle ungewöhnlichen [28] Namen zu sammeln [29] und ihr zu bringen. Als am Abend das Männchen kam, fing sie an mit Kaspar, Melchior, Balthasar und nannte alle Namen, die sie wußte, aber bei jedem sprach das Männchen: „Nein, so heiße ich nicht." Am zweiten Tag schickte sie ihre Diener [30] in die Stadt und ließ sie fragen, was

[23] wife
[24] gave birth to
[25] became frightened
[26] kingdom
[27] ever
[28] unusual
[29] (to) gather, collect
[30] servants

für Namen die Leute hätten, und an diesem Abend nannte sie dem Männchen die ungewöhnlichsten und seltsamsten Namen. „Heißt du vielleicht Rippenbiest oder Hammelswade oder Klumpenfuß oder Schnollegaster?“ Doch das Männchen lachte nur und sagte: „Nein, so heiße ich nicht; aber wenn du den Namen morgen nicht weißt, wirst du dein Kind verlieren.“

Der dritte Tag kam, und nun kamen die Boten, die die Königin ins Land geschickt hatte, zurück und berichteten über alle seltsamen Namen, die sie gehört hatten. Spät am Nachmittag kam der letzte Bote zurück und erzählte, er sei bis an die Grenze des Landes gekommen und habe auf einem Berg tief im Wald ein kleines Haus gesehen, vor dem Haus habe ein Feuer [31] gebrannt, und ein lächerliches,[32] kleines Männchen sei um das Feuer gesprungen und habe gesungen:

Heute back' ich, morgen brau' [33] ich,
Übermorgen [34] hol' ich der Königin Kind.
Ach, wie gut, daß niemand weiß,
Daß ich Rumpelstilzchen heiß'.

Da war die Königin sehr glücklich, und sie wartete nun ruhig auf den Abend. Als es dunkel wurde, war plötzlich das Männchen wieder da und fragte: „Nun, Königin, wie heiße ich?“ Da fragte sie zuerst: „Heißt du Tom, heißt du Dick, heißt du Harry?“ „Nein, nein, nein“, rief das Männchen und lachte laut. „Heißt du vielleicht Rumpelstilzchen?“ „Das hat dir der Teufel [35] gesagt“, schrie das Männchen. In seiner Wut [36] stieß [37] es den rechten Fuß [38] so tief in die Erde, daß es ihn nicht wieder herausziehen [39] konnte. Da packte [40] es den linken Fuß mit beiden Händen und riß sich selbst entzwei [41] und verschwand,[42] und niemand hat es wieder gesehen.

[31] fire
[32] funny
[33] I'll brew (beer)
[34] day after tomorrow
[35] devil
[36] fury, rage
[37] stamped
[38] foot
[39] (to) pull out
[40] grasped
[41] and tore himself apart
[42] disappeared

WORDS RECOMMENDED FOR ADDITION TO THE ACTIVE VOCABULARY

***arm** poor
***erschrecken (i), erschrak, ist erschrocken** (to) become frightened
***das Feuer, –** the fire
***der Fuß, ⸚e** the foot
***der Ring, –e** the ring
***sammeln** (to) gather, collect
***übermorgen** day after tomorrow
***verschwinden, verschwand, ist verschwunden** (to) disappear
***voll** full (of)
***weinen** (to) weep
***die Wut** the fury, rage

Frau Holle

Es war einmal eine Witwe,[1] die zwei Töchter hatte, von denen die eine schön und fleißig [2] war, die andere faul und häßlich.[3] Sie liebte aber die häßliche und faule mehr, weil sie ihre rechte [4] Tochter war, und die andere, ihre Stieftochter,[5] mußte alle Arbeit im Hause tun. Das arme Mädchen mußte jeden Tag bei dem Brunnen [6] sitzen und so viel spinnen,[7] daß das Blut aus den Fingern kam. Nun geschah es, daß die Spule [8] einmal blutig [9] wurde, da bückte es sich über den Brunnen, um die Spule abzuwaschen.[10] Dabei fiel die Spule in den Brunnen. Es weinte,[11] lief zur Stiefmutter [12] und erzählte, was geschehen war. Die Stiefmutter aber war unbarmherzig [13] und sagte: „Wenn du die Spule hast in den Brunnen fallen lassen, so bring sie wieder zurück." Da ging das Mädchen zum Brunnen und wußte nicht, was es tun sollte, und in seiner großen Angst sprang es in den Brunnen. Es verlor die Besinnung,[14] und als es erwachte,[15] war es auf einer schönen Wiese, wo die Sonne schien und tausend schöne Blumen standen. Es ging durch die Wiese und kam zu einem Backofen,[16] der voll [17] Brot [18] war, und das Brot rief: „Nimm mich heraus, nimm mich heraus, sonst verbrenne ich; ich bin schon gebacken." [19] Da nahm das Mädchen das Brot aus dem Backofen. Und es ging weiter und kam bald zu einem Baum, der hing voll Äpfel und rief: „Schüttele mich, schüttele mich, meine Äpfel sind alle reif." Da schüttelte es den Baum, daß

[1] widow
[2] diligent, industrious
[3] ugly
[4] real
[5] stepdaughter
[6] well
[7] (to) spin
[8] spool
[9] bloody
[10] (to) wash off, clean
[11] wept
[12] stepmother
[13] merciless
[14] consciousness
[15] woke up
[16] oven
[17] full (of)
[18] bread
[19] baked, all done

die Äpfel fielen, legte sie alle auf einen Haufen[20] und ging weiter.

Schließlich kam es zu einem Haus, vor dem eine alte Frau saß. Zuerst hatte das Mädchen Angst, doch die Alte war sehr freundlich und sagte: „Du brauchst dich nicht zu fürchten, mein Kind. Wenn du die Arbeit in meinem Hause tun willst, kannst du bei mir bleiben. Du mußt nur achtgeben,[21] daß du mein Bett gut machst und die Kissen fleißig schüttelst, so daß die Federn[22] fliegen, denn dann schneit es in der Welt. Ich bin Frau Holle." Als die Alte so freundlich zu ihm sprach, blieb das Mädchen bei ihr und ging in ihren Dienst.[23]

Es tat auch alle Arbeit so gut, daß die Frau Holle zufrieden war und schüttelte das Bett immer so gewaltig,[24] daß die Federn wie Schneeflocken[25] durch die Luft flogen. Dafür hatte es ein gutes Leben bei ihr, kein böses Wort und alle Tage gutes Essen. Nun blieb es viele Monate bei der Frau Holle, aber dann wurde es traurig und wußte zuerst nicht warum. Endlich merkte[26] es, daß es Heimweh[27] hatte. Obgleich es ihm hier so viel besser ging als zu Hause, wollte es doch wieder zu seiner Familie zurückgehen.

So sprach es zu Frau Holle: „Ich habe Heimweh, obwohl es hier so schön ist. Darf ich nun wieder zu meinen Leuten zurückgehen?" Frau Holle sagte: „Es gefällt mir, daß du wieder nach Hause willst, und weil du so treu[28] gedient[29] hast, will ich dir deine Belohnung geben." Sie nahm es bei der Hand und führte es vor ein großes Tor. Das Tor wurde geöffnet, und als das Mädchen gerade unter dem Tor stand, fiel ein großer Goldregen,[30] und alles Gold[31] blieb an ihm hängen,[32] so daß es ganz davon bedeckt[33] war. „Das Gold

[20] heap, pile
[21] (to) watch out, take care
[22] feathers
[23] service
[24] violently
[25] snowflakes
[26] realized
[27] homesickness
[28] faithfully
[29] served
[30] golden rain
[31] gold
[32] **blieb an ihm hängen** stuck fast to her
[33] covered

gehört dir, weil du so fleißig gewesen bist", sprach Frau Holle und gab ihm auch die Spule zurück, die in den Brunnen gefallen war. Dann wurde das Tor zugemacht, und plötzlich war das Mädchen wieder auf der Welt, nicht weit von dem Hause seiner Mutter. Als es in den Hof kam, saß der Hahn [34] auf dem Brunnen und rief:

Kikeriki,
Unsere goldene Jungfrau [35] ist wieder hie.[36]

Da ging es zu seiner Mutter, und weil es so mit Gold bedeckt ankam, wurde es von ihr und der Schwester gut aufgenommen.[37]

Das Mädchen erzählte alles, was geschehen war, und als die Mutter hörte, wie es zu dem großen Reichtum [38] gekommen war, wünschte sie, daß die andere, die häßliche und faule Tochter, dasselbe [39] Glück haben sollte. Sie mußte sich auch an den Brunnen setzen und spinnen; und damit die Spule blutig wurde, stach [40] sie sich selbst in die Finger. Dann warf sie die Spule in den Brunnen und sprang selbst hinein.[41]

Sie kam, wie die andere, auf die schöne Wiese und ging auf dem Weg, auf dem ihre Schwester gegangen war. Als sie zu dem Backofen kam, schrie das Brot wieder: „Nimm mich heraus, nimm mich heraus, sonst verbrenne ich; ich bin schon gebacken." Die Faule aber antwortete: „Ich habe keine Lust,[42] mich schmutzig [43] zu machen" und ging weiter. Bald kam sie zu dem Apfelbaum, der rief: „Schüttele mich, schüttele mich, meine Äpfel sind alle reif." Sie antwortete aber „O nein, es könnte mir ein Apfel auf den Kopf fallen", und ging weiter. Als sie vor der Frau Holle Haus kam, fürchtete sie sich nicht, weil sie schon von ihr gehört hatte, und ging sofort in

[34] rooster, cock
[35] young maiden, girl
[36] archaic form for **hier**
[37] received
[38] wealth
[39] the same
[40] pricked
[41] into it
[42] I do not feel like
[43] dirty

ihren Dienst. Am ersten Tage zwang [44] sie sich, war fleißig und folgte der Frau Holle, wenn sie ihr etwas sagte, denn sie dachte an das viele Gold, das sie ihr geben würde. Am zweiten Tag aber fing sie schon an, faul zu werden, am dritten noch mehr, da stand sie morgens nicht auf, sondern blieb bis Mittag im Bett. Sie machte auch nicht das Bett der Frau Holle, wie sie es wünschte, und schüttelte es nicht, daß die Federn flogen. Da hatte die Frau Holle bald genug und sagte ihr den Dienst auf.[45] Die Faule war sehr zufrieden damit und glaubte, nun würde der Goldregen kommen. Frau Holle führte sie auch zu dem Tor. Als sie aber darunter stand, wurde statt des Goldes ein großer Kessel [46] voll Pech[47] ausgeschüttet.[48] „Das ist die Belohnung für deine Dienste", sagte Frau Holle, und dann wurde das Tor schnell geschlossen.

Da kam die Faule nach Hause und war ganz mit Pech bedeckt, und der Hahn auf dem Brunnen, als er sie sah, rief laut

Kikeriki,
Unsere schmutzige Jungfrau ist wieder hie.

Das Pech aber blieb an ihr hängen, und sie konnte es, so lange wie sie lebte, nicht mehr abwaschen.

WORDS RECOMMENDED FOR ADDITION TO THE ACTIVE VOCABULARY

***aufnehmen (nimmt auf), nahm auf, aufgenommen** (to) receive
***bedecken** (to) cover
***das Brot, –e** the bread
***dienen** (*with dative*) (to) serve
***der Dienst, –e** the service
***erwachen, ist erwacht** (to) wake up
***die Feder, –n** the feather, pen
***fleißig** diligent, industrious
***schmutzig** dirty
***treu** faithful
***zwingen, zwang, gezwungen** (to) force

[44] forced
[45] **den Dienst aufsagen** (to) discharge, "fire"
[46] kettle
[47] tar, pitch
[48] poured out

LIEDER UND GEDICHTE

Volkslied

Du, du, liegst mir im Herzen,
Du, du, liegst mir im Sinn.[1]
Du, du, machst mir viel Schmerzen,[2]
Weißt nicht, wie gut ich dir bin.[3]
Ja, ja, ja, ja, weißt nicht, wie gut ich dir bin.

So, so, wie ich dich liebe,
So, so, liebe auch mich.
Die, die zärtlichsten Triebe [4]
Fühle [5] ich einzig [6] für dich.
Ja, ja, ja, ja, fühle ich einzig für dich.

Doch, doch, darf ich dir trauen,[7]
Dir, dir mit leichtem Sinn?
Du, du kannst auf mich bauen,[8]
Weißt ja, wie gut ich dir bin.
Ja, ja, ja, ja, weißt ja, wie gut ich dir bin.

Und, und wenn in der Ferne [9]
Mir, mir dein Bild erscheint,[10]
Dann, dann wünscht ich so gerne,
Daß uns die Liebe [11] vereint.[12]
Ja, ja, ja, ja, daß uns die Liebe vereint.

[1] mind
[2] pain
[3] **ich bin dir gut** I like you
[4] **die zärtlichsten Triebe** the most tender affection
[5] feel
[6] only
[7] trust
[8] rely
[9] distance
[10] appears
[11] love
[12] unites

Heidenröslein

Sah ein Knab [1] ein Röslein [2] stehen,
Röslein auf der Heiden,[3]
War so jung und morgenschön,[4]
Lief er schnell, es nah [5] zu sehn,
Sah's mit vielen Freuden.[6]
Röslein, Röslein, Röslein rot,
Röslein auf der Heiden!

Knabe sprach: Ich breche dich,
Röslein auf der Heiden.
Röslein sprach: Ich steche [7] dich,
Daß du ewig denkst an mich
Und ich will's nicht leiden.[8]
Röslein, Röslein, Röslein rot,
Röslein auf der Heiden!

Und der wilde [9] Knabe brach
's Röslein auf der Heiden;
Röslein wehrte [10] sich und stach,
Half ihm doch kein Weh [11] und Ach,[12]
Mußt' es eben leiden.
Röslein, Röslein, Röslein rot.
Röslein auf der Heiden!

Johann Wolfgang von Goethe, 1771

[1] boy
[2] little rose
[3] meadow
[4] beautiful as the morning
[5] close
[6] joy
[7] **stechen (i), stach, gestochen** (to) prick
[8] endure, suffer
[9] wild
[10] defended itself
[11] woe
[12] oh! (plaintive exclamation)

Das Zerbrochene Ringlein

In einem kühlen [1] Grunde,[2]
Da geht ein Mühlenrad; [3]
Mein' Liebste [4] ist verschwunden,[5]
Die dort gewohnet hat.

Sie hat mir Treu [6] versprochen,
Gab mir ein Ring [7] dabei.
Sie hat die Treu gebrochen,
Das Ringlein [8] sprang entzwei.[9]

Ich möcht als Spielmann [10] reisen [11]
Weit in die Welt hinaus [12]
Und singen meine Weisen [13]
Und gehn von Haus zu Haus.

Ich möcht als Reiter [14] fliegen
Wohl [15] in die blut'ge [16] Schlacht,
Um stille Feuer [17] liegen
Im Feld bei dunkler Nacht.

Hör' ich das Mühlrad gehen:
Ich weiß nicht, was ich will—
Ich möcht am liebsten sterben,
Da wär's auf einmal [18] still.

Joseph von Eichendorff, 1808

[1] cool
[2] valley
[3] mill wheel
[4] sweetheart
[5] disappeared
[6] faithfulness
[7] ring
[8] little ring
[9] in two, apart
[10] wandering musician, minstrel
[11] travel
[12] away
[13] songs
[14] horseman
[15] perhaps
[16] bloody
[17] (camp) fires
[18] all at once

Der Lindenbaum

Am Brunnen [1] vor dem Tore, da steht ein Lindenbaum,[2]
Ich träumt [3] in seinem Schatten [4] so manchen süßen [5] Traum; [6]
Ich schnitt in seine Rinde [7] so manches liebe Wort,
Es zog [8] in Freud [9] und Leide [10] zu ihm mich immer fort.

Ich mußt' auch heute wandern [11] vorbei in tiefer Nacht,
Da hab ich noch im Dunkeln die Augen [12] zugemacht.
Und seine Zweige [13] rauschten,[14] als riefen sie mir zu:
Komm her [15] zu mir, Geselle,[16] hier findst du deine Ruh.[17]

Die kalten Winde bliesen [18] mir grad [19] ins Angesicht,[20]
Der Hut flog mir vom Kopfe, ich wendete [21] mich nicht.
Nun bin ich manche Stunde entfernt [22] von jenem Ort,
Und immer hör ich's rauschen: du fändest Ruhe dort.

Wilhelm Müller, 1822

[1] fountain, well
[2] linden tree
[3] dreamed
[4] shadow, shade
[5] sweet
[6] dream
[7] bark (of a tree)
[8] **fortziehen, es zog . . fort** it drew
[9] joy
[10] sorrow
[11] **vorbeiwandern** (to) wander past
[12] eyes
[13] branches
[14] **rauschen** (to) rustle
[15] here
[16] fellow, companion
[17] rest, peace
[18] blew
[19] straight
[20] face
[21] turned around
[22] away

Die Lorelei

Ich weiß nicht, was soll es bedeuten,
Daß ich so traurig bin;
Ein Märchen [1] aus alten Zeiten,
Das kommt mir nicht aus dem Sinn.[2]

Die Luft ist kühl [3] und es dunkelt,[4]
Und ruhig fließt der Rhein;
Der Gipfel [5] des Berges funkelt [6]
Im Abendsonnenschein.[7]

Die schönste Jungfrau [8] sitzet
Dort oben wunderbar;
Ihr goldnes [9] Geschmeide [10] blitzet,[11]
Sie kämmt ihr goldenes Haar.

Sie kämmt es mit goldenem Kamme [12]
Und singt ein Lied dabei;
Das hat eine wundersame,[13]
Gewaltige [14] Melodei.[15]

Den Schiffer im kleinen Schiffe
Ergreift [16] es mit wildem [17] Weh.[18]
Er schaut [19] nicht die Felsenriffe,[20]
Er schaut nur hinauf [21] in die Höh.[22]

[1] (fairy) tale
[2] mind
[3] cool
[4] becomes dark
[5] peak
[6] is bright, sparkles
[7] evening sunshine
[8] young woman
[9] golden
[10] jewelry
[11] glistens
[12] comb
[13] strange
[14] powerful
[15] (poetic for *Melodie*), melody
[16] seizes
[17] wild
[18] woe, desire
[19] sees
[20] rocky cliffs
[21] up
[22] height

Ich glaube, die Wellen [23] verschlingen [24]
Am Ende Schiffer und Kahn; [25]
Und das hat mit ihrem Singen
Die Lorelei [26] getan.

Heinrich Heine, 1823

[23] waves
[24] swallow, devour
[25] boat
[26] Usually spelled Loreley; Heine uses this secondary form.

Weihnachtslied

Stille Nacht, heilige Nacht!
Alles schläft, einsam [1] wacht [2]
Nur das traute,[3] hoch-heilige Paar.[4]
Holder [5] Knabe im lockigen [6] Haar,
Schlaf in himmlischer [7] Ruh.[8]

Stille Nacht, heilige Nacht!
Hirten [9] erst kund gemacht! [10]
Durch der Engel [11] Halleluja
Tönt [12] es laut von fern [13] und nah: [14]
Christ, der Retter,[15] ist da.

Stille Nacht, heilige Nacht!
Gottes Sohn, o wie lacht
Lieb [16] aus deinem göttlichen [17] Mund,
Da uns schlägt die rettende Stund,
Christ in deiner Geburt.[18]

Joseph Mohr, 1818

[1] alone, lonely
[2] is awake
[3] beloved
[4] couple
[5] lovely
[6] curly
[7] heavenly
[8] rest
[9] to the shepherds
[10] made known, announced
[11] angels
[12] sounds
[13] far
[14] near
[15] savior
[16] love
[17] divine
[18] birth

WORDS RECOMMENDED FOR ADDITION TO THE ACTIVE VOCABULARY

***die Freude, –n** the joy
***fühlen** (to) feel
***kühl** cool
***das Leid, –en** the sorrow
***die Liebe** the love
***nahe** close, near by
***das Paar, –e** the couple
***der Schmerz, –en** the pain
***der Traum, ⸚e** the dream
***träumen** (to) dream
***der Zweig, –e** the twig, branch

THE ALPHABET IN ANTIQUA AND IN FRAKTUR

Roman Letters		German Letters	
a	A	𝔞	𝔄
b	B	𝔟	𝔅
c	C	𝔠	ℭ
d	D	𝔡	𝔇
e	E	𝔢	𝔈
f	F	𝔣	𝔉
g	G	𝔤	𝔊
h	H	𝔥	ℌ
i	I	𝔦	ℑ
j	J	𝔧	𝔍
k	K	𝔨	𝔎
l	L	𝔩	𝔏
m	M	𝔪	𝔐
n	N	𝔫	𝔑
o	O	𝔬	𝔒
p	P	𝔭	𝔓
q	Q	𝔮	𝔔
r	R	𝔯	ℜ
s	S	ſ, 𝔰	𝔖
t	T	𝔱	𝔗
u	U	𝔲	𝔘
v	V	𝔳	𝔙
w	W	𝔴	𝔚
x	X	𝔵	𝔛
y	Y	𝔶	𝔜
z	Z	𝔷	ℨ

STRONG AND IRREGULAR VERBS

NOTE: *Compound forms are not given if the simple form occurs; for* an-kommen, bekommen, *etc., look under* kommen.

Infinitive	*(Present 3rd Sing.)*	*Past*		*Past Participle*
backen	(bäckt)	buk		gebacken
befehlen	(befiehlt)	befahl		befohlen
beginnen	(beginnt)	begann		begonnen
begraben	(begräbt)	begrub		begraben
betrügen	(betrügt)	betrog		betrogen
bieten	(bietet)	bot		geboten
binden	(bindet)	band		gebunden
bitten	(bittet)	bat		gebeten
bleiben	(bleibt)	blieb	ist	geblieben
brechen	(bricht)	brach		gebrochen
brennen	(brennt)	brannte		gebrannt
bringen	(bringt)	brachte		gebracht
denken	(denkt)	dachte		gedacht
dürfen	(darf)	durfte		gedurft
essen	(ißt)	aß		gegessen
fahren	(fährt)	fuhr	ist	gefahren
fallen	(fällt)	fiel	ist	gefallen
fangen	(fängt)	fing		gefangen
finden	(findet)	fand		gefunden
fliegen	(fliegt)	flog	ist	geflogen
fließen	(fließt)	floß	ist	geflossen
fressen	(frißt)	fraß		gefressen
geben	(gibt)	gab		gegeben
gefallen	(gefällt)	gefiel		gefallen
gehen	(geht)	ging	ist	gegangen
geschehen	(geschieht)	geschah	ist	geschehen
gewinnen	(gewinnt)	gewann		gewonnen
gießen	(gießt)	goß		gegossen
gleichen	(gleicht)	glich		geglichen
graben	(gräbt)	grub		gegraben
haben	(hat)	hatte		gehabt
halten	(hält)	hielt		gehalten

Infinitive	*(Present 3rd Sing.)*	*Past*		*Past Participle*
hängen	(hängt)	hing		gehangen
heben	(hebt)	hob		gehoben
heißen	(heißt)	hieß		geheißen
helfen	(hilft)	half		geholfen
kennen	(kennt)	kannte		gekannt
kommen	(kommt)	kam	ist	gekommen
können	(kann)	konnte		gekonnt
laden	(ladet *or* lädt)	lud		geladen
lassen	(läßt)	ließ		gelassen
laufen	(läuft)	lief	ist	gelaufen
lesen	(liest)	las		gelesen
liegen	(liegt)	lag		gelegen
lügen	(lügt)	log		gelogen
mögen	(mag)	mochte		gemocht
müssen	(muß)	mußte		gemußt
nehmen	(nimmt)	nahm		genommen
nennen	(nennt)	nannte		genannt
rufen	(ruft)	rief		gerufen
scheinen	(scheint)	schien		geschienen
schießen	(schießt)	schoß		geschossen
schlafen	(schläft)	schlief		geschlafen
schlagen	(schlägt)	schlug		geschlagen
schließen	(schließt)	schloß		geschlossen
schmelzen	(schmilzt)	schmolz	ist	geschmolzen
schneiden	(schneidet)	schnitt		geschnitten
schreiben	(schreibt)	schrieb		geschrieben
schreien	(schreit)	schrie		geschrieen *or* geschrien
schwimmen	(schwimmt)	schwamm	ist	geschwommen
schwören	(schwört)	schwur		geschworen
sehen	(sieht)	sah		gesehen
sein	(ist)	war	ist	gewesen
singen	(singt)	sang		gesungen
sinken	(sinkt)	sank	ist	gesunken
sitzen	(sitzt)	saß		gesessen
sollen	(soll)	sollte		gesollt
sprechen	(spricht)	sprach		gesprochen
springen	(springt)	sprang	ist	gesprungen
stehen	(steht)	stand		gestanden
stehlen	(stiehlt)	stahl		gestohlen

Infinitive	*(Present 3rd Sing.)*	*Past*	*Past Participle*
steigen	(steigt)	stieg	ist gestiegen
sterben	(stirbt)	starb	ist gestorben
tragen	(trägt)	trug	getragen
treffen	(trifft)	traf	getroffen
treten	(tritt)	trat	getreten
trinken	(trinkt)	trank	getrunken
tun	(tut)	tat	getan
unterscheiden	(unterscheidet)	unterschied	unterschieden
vergessen	(vergißt)	vergaß	vergessen
verlieren	(verliert)	verlor	verloren
wachsen	(wächst)	wuchs	ist gewachsen
werden	(wird)	wurde	ist geworden
werfen	(wirft)	warf	geworfen
wissen	(weiß)	wußte	gewußt
wollen	(will)	wollte	gewollt
ziehen	(zieht)	zog	gezogen

IDIOMS AND VOCABULARY

NOTE

Plurals of nouns are listed after the singular form, e.g., **der Tag, –e.** The genitive singular is listed for those nouns which form this case by adding **–n** or **–en**—this form is given in parenthesis directly after the nominative singular, e.g., **der Junge, (–n), –n.**

The principal parts are given for all except weak verbs, e.g., **singen, sang, gesungen.** If there is a vowel change in the present tense, this is indicated in parenthesis directly after the infinitive, e.g., **geben (i), gab, gegeben.** If the auxiliary in the perfect tense is **sein,** this is indicated before the past participle, e.g., **fahren (ä), fuhr, ist gefahren.**

Separable verbs are indicated in the infinitive by a hyphen between the prefix and the verb proper.

Active vocabulary and idioms are starred (except in the English-German Vocabulary) and the lesson number is indicated after the German. For example, ***Angst haben vor (8)** (*to*) *be afraid of* shows that this idiom becomes active in Aufgabe VIII.

The following abbreviations are used:

acc.	accusative	*gen.*	genitive
adj.	adjective	*infin.*	infinitive
adv.	adverb	*plur.*	plural
conj.	conjunction	*prep.*	preposition
dat.	dative	*sing.*	singular

LIST OF IDIOMS

A

Amerika: aus Amerika from America
***Angst haben vor (8)** (to) be afraid of

B

Besuch haben (to) have visitors
***bitten um (20)** (to) ask for

D

***d.h. (12)** i.e. (*see* **heißen**)
***deutsch: auf deutsch (8)** in German

E

***englisch: auf englisch (8)** in English

F

***fahren mit (11)** (to) travel by
Fröhliche Weihnachten! Merry Christmas!

G

***geben: es gibt** (*with acc.*) **(9)** there is, there are
***gefallen: es gefällt mir (14)** I like it, it pleases me
gehen: *das geht nicht (17) that won't do
  ***wie geht es dir (14)** how are you
  ***es geht mir gut (17)** I'm fine
  ins Kino gehen (to) go to the movies
***gern** *plus verb* **(15)** (to) like to
***gestern abend (19)** last evening, yesterday evening
Glück haben (to) be lucky

H

***Halt! (16)** Stop! Halt!
***Hand: einem die Hand geben (5)** (to) shake hands with someone
***Haus: nach Hause (8)** home (*motion towards*)
  zu Hause (10) at home, home

***heißen: das heißt (12)** that is
ich heiße (17) my name is
wie heißen Sie (17) what is your name
***heute abend (15)** this evening

I

***ich auch nicht (6)** nor I either
***immer wieder (14)** again and again

J

jetzt erst only now, just now

K

***kein . . . mehr (7)** no . . . any more, no . . . any longer
klingeln: es klingelt the bell rings

L

***Land: vom Lande (4)** from the country
***leid: es tut mir leid (5)** I am sorry

M

***Mittag: zu Mittag essen (14)** (to) dine, eat dinner (*at noon*)

N

***Nachmittag: jeden Nachmittag (4)** every afternoon
***nicht nur . . . sondern auch (19)** not only . . . but also
nichts als nothing but
niemand als no one but
noch einmal again, once more
***noch nicht (5)** not yet

P

***paar: ein paar (7)** a couple of, a few

R

***recht haben (20)** (to) be right
***Reise: eine Reise machen (11)** (to) take a trip
Gute Reise! (13) Pleasant journey!

S

sehr (*when no measurable quantity is given*) very much
***so . . . wie (5)** as . . . as
***Spaziergang: einen Spaziergang machen (10)** (to) take a walk

***Stadt: in der Stadt (6)** downtown, in town, in the city
in die Stadt (6) downtown, to town, to the city
***Stunde: in einer halben Stunde (3)** in half an hour

T

Tafel: an die Tafel on(to) the blackboard

U

***Uhr: um drei Uhr (5)** at three o'clock

V

***vor vielen Jahren (12)** many years ago

W

***wahr: nicht wahr (3)** isn't it true; isn't it, doesn't he, *etc.*
***Wiedersehen: Auf Wiedersehen (13)** good-bye, au revoir

Z

***Zeit: zur Zeit (16)** at the time, at present

GERMAN-ENGLISH VOCABULARY

This vocabulary includes the words used in Sections I and VII of each lesson. The articles, unusual genitives, and plurals are given for the German nouns, and the principal parts for the German verbs, if needed. Ordinarily the English article *the* is omitted from the meanings given, as is also the sign of the English infinitive *to.* These are used on occasion where confusion might otherwise occur.

A

***der Abend, –e** (7) evening; **abends** evenings; ***gestern abend** (19) yesterday evening

***aber** (3) but, however

***ab-fahren (ä), fuhr ab, ist abgefahren** (13) leave, depart

die Abkürzung, –en abbreviation

***ab-nehmen (nimmt ab), nahm ab, abgenommen** (13) take off

***ab-schreiben, schrieb ab, abgeschrieben** copy

absolut absolute

der Absolutismus absolutism

der Abt, ⸚e abbot

***das Abteil, –e** (13) compartment

die Abteilung, –en department

***acht** (8) eight

achtzehn eighteen

achtzig eighty

der Adlige, (–n), –n nobleman

der Admiral, ⸚e admiral

die Ähnlichkeit, –en similarity

der Akzent, –e accent

der Affe, (–n), –n ape, monkey

***all** all; ***alle** (4) all; ***alles** (9) all

***allein** (13) alone

***als** (12, 16) as, like; than; when; **nichts als** nothing but; **niemand als** no one but

***alt** (1) old

***Amerika** (1) America

***der Amerikaner, –** (4) the American

***amerikanisch** (17) American

***an** (4) at, near, by, on, to, up to, onto, alongside of

***an-bieten, bot an, angeboten** (14) offer

***ander** (16) other

anders different; **anders als** different from

der Anfang, ⸚e beginning

***an-fangen (ä), fing an, angefangen** (13) begin

das Angebot, –e offer

***die Angst, ⸚e** (8) anxiety, concern, fear; ***Angst haben vor** (8) be afraid of

***an-kommen, kam an, ist angekommen** (13) arrive

die Ankunft, ⸚e arrival

an-nehmen (nimmt an), nahm an, angenommen accept

***an-rufen, rief an, angerufen** (21) call up, (tele)phone

***an-sehen (ie), sah an, angesehen** (18) look at
die Ansichtskarte, –n picture postcard
***anstatt** (*with gen.*) (14) instead of; **anstatt etwas zu tun** instead of doing something
***die Antwort, –en** (18) the answer
***antworten** (3) to answer, reply
***sich an-ziehen, zog sich an, angezogen** (17) get dressed
***der Anzug, ⸚e** (17) suit
der Apfel, ⸚ apple
der Apostel, – apostle
***der April** (18) April
***die Arbeit, –en** (3) the work
***arbeiten** (3) to work
***ärgerlich** (21) angry
ärgern annoy
***sich ärgern über** (17) be angry with, be mad at
***der Arm, –e** (7) arm
die Armbanduhr, –en wrist watch
***der Arzt, ⸚e** (14) physician, doctor
der Atlantische Ozean the Atlantic Ocean
***auch** (2) also, too; even
***auf** (3) on, upon; at; to, onto
***die Aufgabe, –n** (1) lesson
aufgeregt stirred up, excited
auf-heben, hob auf, aufgehoben remove; pick up
die Aufklärung the Enlightenment
***auf-machen** (13) open
die Aufregung, –en excitement
auf-setzen put on
***auf-stehen, stand auf, ist aufgestanden** (13) get up; stand up
auf-zählen enumerate
der Augenblick, –e moment
***der August** (18) August
***aus** (2) out of, from, of
die Ausfuhr, –en export
***außerdem** (8) besides, moreover
außerhalb (*with gen.*) outside of; **außerhalb von** outside of
die Aussicht, –en view; **Aussicht über** view of
aus-springen, sprang aus, ist ausgesprungen spring out
***aus-steigen, stieg aus, ist ausgestiegen** (13) get out, get off
ausverkauft sold out
aus-wandern emigrate
***das Auto, (–s), –s** (6) car, auto

B

der Bach, ⸚e brook, creek
backen (ä), buk, gebacken bake, roast
der Bäcker, – baker
das Bad, ⸚er bath, spa
***der Bahnhof, ⸚e** (12) railroad station
***der Bahnsteig, –e** (13) track, platform
***bald** (3) soon
der Balkon, –e balcony
die Banane, –n banana
***die Bank, ⸚e** (8) bench
der Bart, ⸚e beard
***bauen** (19) build
der Bauer, –n peasant
die Bauernfrau, –en peasant woman
***der Baum, ⸚e** (20) tree
der Bauplatz, ⸚e building lot
Bayern Bavaria
beachten observe, pay attention to, notice
bedeuten mean, signify
befehlen (ie), befahl, befohlen (*with dat.*) command, order
befreien free, liberate
das Befreiungsgesetz, –e Liberation Edict
begehen, beging, begangen commit

begeistert enthusiastic, enthused
beginnen, begann, begonnen start, begin
begraben (ä), begrub, begraben bury
behalten (behält), behielt, behalten keep
behandeln treat
*__bei__ (2) at; with; near, by; at the house of, at the place of
*__beide__ (10) both
das Beispiel, –e example; **zum Beispiel** for example
bekannt known, well known
bekehren convert
bekommen, bekam, bekommen receive, get
belebt busy, crowded
Belgien Belgium
beliebt bei popular with
bellen bark
die Belohnung, –en reward
*__der Berg, –e__ (5) mountain
*__der Bericht, –e__ (9) report
*__berichten__ (9) to report
der Berliner the Berliner, inhabitant of Berlin; of Berlin
*__berühmt__ (8) famous
die Beschränkung, –en limitation
besetzt occupied
besiegen conquer, vanquish
besonders especially
besorgt worried, apprehensive
best– best
*__bestellen__ (9) order (*e.g., to order food, etc.*)
der Besuch, –e visit; **Besuch haben** to have visitors *or* a visitor
*__besuchen__ (13) to visit
der Besucher, – visitor
*__beten__ (4) pray
*__betrügen, betrog, betrogen__ (21) cheat, deceive
*__das Bett, –en__ (1) bed; **zu Bett gehen** go to bed
bevor before
bewegt rough
die Bibel, –n Bible
das Bier, –e beer
das Bild, –er picture, portrait
billig cheap, inexpensive
*__bis__ (7) to, up to, until; **bis auf** up to
*__bitte__ (13) Please!
*__bitten, bat, gebeten__ (20) ask; *__bitten um__ (20) ask for
blaß pale
*__blau__ (15) blue
*__der Bleistift, –e__ (2) pencil
*__bleiben, blieb, ist geblieben (7)__ stay, remain; **über Nacht bleiben** stay over night
*__blond__ (8) blond
*__die Blume, –n__ (3) flower
das Blut blood
*__der Boden, ⸚__ (21) ground, floor
der Bodensee Lake Constance
Bonifatius (St.) Boniface
böse bad, evil
der Bote, (–n), –n messenger
das Brandenburger Tor the Brandenburg Gate (*in Berlin*)
*__brauchen__ (3) need, require; use
brechen (i), brach, gebrochen break
breit wide, broad
Bremen *name of a German city*
*__brennen, brannte, gebrannt__ (11) burn
*__der Brief, –e__ (2) letter
die Brieftasche, –n purse, pocketbook
die Brille glasses, spectacles
*__bringen, brachte, gebracht__ (11) bring, take
britisch British
das Brot, –e bread
die Brücke, –n bridge
*__der Bruder, ⸚__ (17) brother

*__das Buch, ⸚er__ (2) book
__das Bücherbrett, –er__ bookshelf, bookcase
__der Buchdrucker, –__ (book) printer
__die Buchdruckerkunst__ art of printing
__die Buchdruckerpresse, –n__ (book) printing press
__sich bücken__ bend down, stoop over
__die Bühne, –n__ stage
__der Bundeskanzler, –__ Federal Chancellor
__der Bundespräsident, (–en), –en__ Federal President
__die Bundesrepublik (Deutschland)__ Federal Republic (of Germany)
__der Bundesstaat, –en__ federated state
__der Bundestag__ Federal Legislature
__die Burg, –en__ (medieval) castle
__der Bürger, –__ citizen; (*plur.*) townspeople
__der Bürgermeister, –__ mayor
__der Bürgersteig, –e__ sidewalk
__das Büro, –s__ office

C

__das Café, –s__ cafe
__der Chemiker, –__ chemist
__chemisch__ chemical
__der Christbaum, ⸚e__ Christmas tree
__das Christentum__ Christianity
__christlich__ Christian
__Christus__ Christ

D

*__da__ (*adv.*) (5) there, here; then; in that case
*__da__ (*conj.*) (12) since
__das Dach, ⸚er__ roof
*__damals__ (20) then, at that time
*__die Dame, –n__ (6) lady
__damit__ by that; with that
__der Dampfer, –__ steamer, steamship
__Dänemark__ Denmark
__dankbar__ grateful
*__dann__ (4) then
__darin__ in it, in them
*__darum__ (11) therefore
*__das__ (1) that; those; *see also* __der__
*__daß__ (*conj.*) (12) that
*__dauern__ (19) last, take
*__dein__ (4) your
*__denken, dachte, gedacht__ (11) think; __denken an__ (*with acc.*) think of
__der Denker, –__ thinker
*__denn__ (1) for, because
*__der, die, das__ (1) the; this, that; who, which
*__deutsch__ (*adj. or adv.*) (1) German; *__auf deutsch__ (8) in German
*__Deutsch__ (*noun*) (1) German
*__der Deutsche__ (*adj. declension*) (4) the German
__die Deutsche Demokratische Republik__ German Democratic Republic
__das Deutsche Reich__ German Empire
*__Deutschland__ (1) Germany
*__der Dezember__ (17) December
__der Dialekt, –e__ dialect
*__d.h.__ *abbreviation for* __das heißt__ (12) i.e., that is
__dicht__ dense, close
*__der Dichter, –__ (19) poet, author
*__dick__ (21) thick; stout, fat
*__der Dienstag, –e__ (18) Tuesday
*__dieser__ (4) this; the latter
*__das Ding, –e__ (6) thing
__direkt__ direct
__diskutieren__ discuss
__die Disziplin__ discipline
__diszipliniert__ disciplined, trained

*__doch__ (11) yet, however, nevertheless, still; but; really
__der Dom, –e__ cathedral
*__der Donnerstag, –e__ (18) Thursday
__das Dorf, ⸗er__ village
*__dort__ (11) there; __dort unten__ down there
__das Drama,__ (*plur.*) __Dramen__ drama
__sich drängen__ be crowded
__draußen__ outside
*__drei__ (3) three
__dreißigjährig__ of thirty years; __der Dreißigjährige Krieg__ Thirty Years' War
__dreiviertel = drei Viertel__ three quarters, three-fourths
*__dreizehn__ (13) thirteen
__drin = darin__ in it, in them
__drinnen__ inside
__die Drucktypen__ (*plur.*) type (faces)
*__du__ (1) you
*__dumm__ (2) stupid, silly
*__dunkel__ (15) dark
*__durch__ (2) through; by
*__dürfen (darf), durfte, gedurft__ (10) may, can; be permitted, be allowed to
*__durstig__ (11) thirsty

E

__die Ebene, –n__ plain
__echt__ true, genuine
*__die Ecke, –n__ (9) corner
__Eger__ *name of a city in Bohemia*
*__ehe__ (*conj.*) (12) before
__ehren__ honor
*__ehrlich__ (21) honest
__das Ei, –er__ egg; __ein Ei legen__ lay an egg
__die Eiche, –n__ oak (tree)
__eigen__ own
*__ein, eine, ein__ (1) a, an; one
__ein-dringen, drang ein, ist eingedrungen__ penetrate
__einfach__ simple
__die Eingangshalle, –n__ entrance hall
*__einige__ (15) some, a few
__ein-laden (ladet__ *or* __lädt ein), lud ein, eingeladen__ invite
__einmal__ once, one time
__die Einrichtung, –en__ institution, arrangement
*__eins__ (1) one
*__ein-steigen, stieg ein, ist eingestiegen__ (13) get on, board
__ein-teilen__ divide
__ein-treten (tritt ein), trat ein, ist eingetreten__ enter
__der Einwohner, –__ inhabitant
__das Eisen__ iron
__die Eisenbahn, –en__ railroad
__eisern__ (of) iron
__die Elbe__ the Elbe (River)
__der Elefant, (–en), –en__ elephant
*__elf__ (11) eleven
__Elsaß-Lothringen__ Alsace Lorraine
*__die Eltern__ (*plur.*) (8) parents
*__das Ende, –n__ (9) end; __bis zum Ende__ until the end
__enden__ to end
__endlich__ finally
__eng__ narrow; close
*__englisch__ (8) English; *__auf englisch__ (8) in English
*__der Enkel, –__ (18) grandson; grandchild
__entdecken__ discover
__die Entfernung, –en__ distance
__enthaupten__ behead
__entkommen, entkam, ist entkommen__ escape
__entlassen (ä), entließ, entlassen__ remove, discharge
__die Entschuldigung, –en__ apology, excuse

entstehen, entstand, ist entstanden originate
***entweder . . . oder** (19) either . . . or
***er** (1) he; it
die Erdbeerbowle, –n strawberry punch
die Erdbeere, –n strawberry
die Erde earth
die Erfindung, –en invention
***sich erinnern an** (*with acc.*) (19) remember
erkennen, erkannte, erkannt recognize
***erklären** (10) explain; declare
ermorden murder
ernennen, ernannte, ernannt name, appoint
***ernst** (9) serious, earnest
die Eroberung, –en conquest
erschreckend startling, frightful
***erst** (*adj.*) (18) first
***erst** (*adv.*) (17) only, not until
ertrinken, ertrank, ist ertrunken drown
das Erz, –e ore
***erzählen** (9) tell, narrate
der Erzbischof, ⸚e archbishop
***es** (1) it
***essen (i), aß, gegessen** (3) eat
***das Essen, –** (4) meal
***das Eßzimmer, –** (3) dining room
***etwas** (7) some; something, anything
***euer** (4) your
***Europa** (16) Europe
europäisch European
ewig forever, eternal
existieren exist
der Expreß, (Expresses), Expresse express (train)

F

die Fabrik, –en factory
die Fahne, –n flag
die Fähre, –n ferry
***fahren (ä), fuhr, ist gefahren** (6) ride, travel, go; drive; ***fahren mit** (11) travel by
der Fährmann, ⸚er ferryman
die Fährmannsgeschichte, –n ferryman's tale
***der Fahrplan, ⸚e** (18) timetable
der Fahrpreis, –e fare
die Fahrzeit, –en travel time
der Fall, ⸚e case; fall
fallen (ä), fiel, ist gefallen fall
fällen fell, cut down
falsch false
falten fold
***die Familie, –n** (3) family
fangen (ä), fing, gefangen catch
***die Farbe, –n** (2) color
***fast** (9) almost
faul lazy
***der Februar** (18) February
feiern celebrate
der Feind, –e enemy
***das Feld, –er** (14) field
der Felsen, – rock, cliff
***das Fenster, –** (1) window
***die Ferien** (*plur.*) (11) vacation
***fertig** (7) ready, done, finished
das Fest, –e feast, festival, celebration
das Festspiel, –e festival (play)
feucht humid
die Figur, –en figure
***der Film, –e** (21) film
***finden, fand, gefunden** (21) find
der Finder, – finder
der Fisch, –e fish
der Fischer, – fisher, fisherman
***flach** (14) flat, level
***die Flasche, –n** (5) bottle
***fliegen, flog, ist geflogen** (20) fly
fließen, floß, ist geflossen flow
fließend fluent(ly)
die Flöte, –n flute
das Flötenspiel flute-playing
die Flotte, –n fleet

der Flügel, – wing
das Flugzeug, –e airplane
***der Fluß, (Flusses), Flüsse** (16) river
folgen (*with dat. and* **sein** *as auxiliary*) follow
der Förderturm, ⸚e transport tower, haul tower
***die Frage, –n** (8) the question
***fragen** (2) to question, ask
Frankfurt *name of a German city*
der Frankfurter, – inhabitant of Frankfurt
Frankreich France
französisch French
***die Frau, –en** (3) woman; wife; Mrs.
***das Fräulein, –** (8) girl; Miss
***frei** (12) free, independent
die Freiheit, –en freedom
der Freiherr, (–n), –en baron
***der Freitag, –e** (18) Friday
fressen (i), fraß, gefressen eat (*used of animals*)
***sich freuen über** (*with acc.*) (17) be glad about
***der Freund, –e** (1) friend
***die Freundin, –nen** (5) friend (*female*), girl friend
***freundlich** (16) friendly
der Friede, (–ns), –n peace
Friedrich der Große Frederick the Great
Friedrich Wilhelm I. Frederick William I
die Frömmigkeit piety
***früh** (9) early
***früher** (12) earlier, former(ly)
***der Frühling, –e** (20) spring
***führen** (19) lead, guide, conduct; **Krieg führen** conduct *or* wage war
der Führer, – leader, guide; guide-book
***fünf** (5) five
***fünfzehn** (15) fifteen
fünfzig fifty
***für** (*prep.*) (3) for
furchtbar fearful, frightful
***sich fürchten vor** (*with dat.*) (17) be afraid of
der Fürst, (–en), –en (ruling) prince
füttern feed

G

die Gabel, –n fork
***ganz** (9) whole, entire, complete
die Garde, –n guard
die Garnison, –en garrison
***der Garten, ⸚** (3) garden
***der Gast, ⸚e** (7) guest
das Gasthaus, ⸚er inn
***geben (i), gab, gegeben** (5) give; ***es gibt** (*with acc.*) (9) there is, there are
das Gebet, –e prayer
das Gebirge, – mountain range, mountain chain
***geboren** (19) born
gebrauchen use
***der Geburtstag, –e** (6) birthday
der Geburtstagstisch, –e birthday table
das Gedicht, –e poem
die Geduld patience
***die Gefahr, –en** (11) danger
***gefallen (ä), gefiel, gefallen** (14) please, be pleasing to; ***es gefällt mir** (14) I like it, it pleases me
das Gefängnis, –se prison, jail
***gegen** (3) against; toward
die Gegend, –en region
die Gegenwart present (time)
gegründet founded
***gehen, ging, ist gegangen** (3) go; ***Wie geht es Ihnen?** (14) How are you? ***Es geht mir gut.** (14) I'm fine. ***Das geht nicht.** (17) That won't do.

***gehören** (*with dat.*) (20) belong to; **gehören zu** belong to
der Geist, –er spirit
gekrönt crowned
***gelb** (6) yellow
***das Geld, –er** (5) money
gelebt lived
die Gelehrsamkeit learning
der Gelehrte, (–n), –n scholar
der General, ⁼e general
genug enough
***gerade** (13) just, just then
die Gerbergasse, –n Gerber Street, Tanner Street
die Gerechtigkeit justice
***das Gericht, –e** (21) court (of law); **vor Gericht** before the court
germanisch Germanic
***gern** (6) gladly; **Ich habe das gern.** I like that. ***Ich spiele gern Tennis.** (15) I like to play tennis.
gesamteuropäisch total European
der Gesangverein, –e choral group, singing society
das Geschäft, –e business, affairs
***geschehen (ie), geschah, ist geschehen** (9) happen
***das Geschenk, –e** (6) present, gift
***die Geschichte, –n** (8) story; history
das Gesetz, –e law
***das Gesicht, –er** (17) face
***gestern** (7) yesterday
***gesund** (17) healthy, well
die Gesundheit health
geteilt divided
getrennt separated
gewählt chosen, selected, elected
gewechselt changed
geweiht dedicated
das Gewehr, –e gun, rifle
gewinnen, gewann, gewonnen win
***gewiß** (8) certain, sure
das Gewissen, – conscience
die Gewohnheit, –en custom
***gießen, goß, gegossen** (7) pour
das Gift, –e poison
***das Glas, ⁼er** (5) glass
die Glasschüssel, –n glass dish, glass bowl
glatt smooth
***glauben** (8) believe, think, suppose
gleich same
gleichen, glich, geglichen resemble
das Glück luck, good fortune; **Glück haben** be lucky
glücklich happy, happily, fortunate
der Gott, ⁼er god
das Grab, ⁼er grave
der Graf, (–en), –en count
grau gray
grausam cruel
die Grenze, –n border, boundary
der Groschen, – groschen, penny
***groß** (2) large, big; great; tall
***die Großeltern** (*plur.*) (18) grandparents
größt– largest, greatest
der Großvater, ⁼ grandfather
das Grubenholz, ⁼er wood for the mines
***grün** (2) green
gründen found, establish
der Gründer, – founder
die Gründung, –en founding, foundation
grüßen greet
der Gulden, – guilder (*old coin*)
***gut** (1) good; well

H

***das Haar, –e** (1) hair
***haben (hat), hatte, gehabt** (1) have
der Hafen, ⁼ habor, port

der Hahn, ⸚e rooster
***halb** (18) half; ***eine halbe Stunde** (3) half an hour
halbverfault half rotten
***die Hälfte, –n** (16) the half
***Halt!** (16) Halt! Stop!
***halten (hält), hielt, gehalten** (14) hold
***die Hand, ⸚e** (4) hand; ***die Hand geben** (5) shake hands
der Handel, commerce, trade
die Handelsstadt, ⸚e commercial city
der Handelsweg, –e trade route
hangen (ä) *or* **hängen, hing, gehangen** hang
hängen hang
der Hase, (–n), –n hare, rabbit
das Hasenfell, –e rabbit pelt, rabbit fur
die Hauptstadt, ⸚e capital
***das Haus, ⸚er** (3) house; ***nach Hause gehen** (8) go home; ***zu Hause sein** (10) be (at) home
das Häuschen, – little house, hut, shack
***das Heer, –e** (19) army
***das Heft, –e** (2) notebook
der Heide, (–n), –n heathen
Heidelberg *name of a German city*
heidnisch heathen
heilen heal, cure
***heilig** (12) holy; **Heilig Abend** Christmas Eve; **das Heilige Römische Reich** Holy Roman Empire
***heimlich** (18) secret
das Heimweh homesickness
***heiß** (11) hot
***heißen, hieß, geheißen** (17) be called; ***Wie heißen Sie?** (17) What is your name? ***Ich heiße Conrad.** (17) My name is Conrad.
***helfen (i), half, geholfen** (*with dat.*) (4) help
***hell** (21) bright, light
***das Hemd, –en** (6) shirt
herab-lassen (ä), ließ herab, herabgelassen let down
herab-sehen (ie), sah herab, herabgesehen look down
heraus out
heraus-kommen, kam heraus, ist herausgekommen come out
***heraus-nehmen (nimmt heraus), nahm heraus, herausgenommen** (21) take out
***der Herbst, –e** (11) autumn, fall
***Herein!** (17) Come in!
***der Herr, (–n), –en** (19) gentleman, man; sir; Mr.; master; Lord
die Herrschaft rule, dominion
herrschen to rule
***das Herz, (–ens), –en** (15) heart (*dat. sing. form of* **Herz** *is* **Herzen**)
***herzlich** (14) hearty, cordial
der Herzog, ⸚e duke
***heute** (4) today; ***heute abend** (15) this evening
die Hexerei, –en witchcraft
***hier** (1) here
hieß was called
***der Himmel, –** (18) sky, heavens; heaven
hinaus-gehen, ging hinaus, ist hinausgegangen go out
hinaus-laufen (ä), lief hinaus, ist hinausgelaufen run out
hinein-gehen, ging hinein, ist hineingegangen go in
***hinein-tragen (ä), trug hinein, hineingetragen** (13) carry in
***hinter** (4) behind
die Hintertür, –en back door
der Historiker, – historian
***hoch** (*drops the* **c** *before* **e**) **(15)** high; tall

hochdeutsch High German
***höchst** (16) highly, very
die Hochzeit, –en marriage, wedding
der Hof, ⸚e yard, court
***hoffen (auf)** (5) hope (for)
***höflich** (9) courteous, polite
holen get, bring, fetch
***hören** (3) hear
***hübsch** (8) pretty
das Hufeisen, – horseshoe
der Hufschmied, –e blacksmith
das Huhn, ⸚er chicken
der Humor humor
der Humorist, (–en), –en humorist
der Hund, –e dog
hundert (a) hundred
Hunderte hundreds
hungrig hungry
Hurra! Hurrah!
***der Hut, ⸚e** (13) hat

I

***ich** (1) I
identifizieren identify
***ihr** (1, 4) you; her; their
***Ihr** (4) your; you (*in letters*)
***immer** (3) always; ***immer wieder** (14) again and again; **immer schneller** faster and faster
***in** (1) in, into
das Individuum, (*plur.*) **Individuen** individual
die Industrie, –n industry
das Industriegebiet, –e industrial region
die Industriestadt, ⸚e industrial city
inner inner, internal
die Insel, –n island
der Intellektuelle, (–n), –n intellectual
***interessant** (14) interesting
***das Interesse, –n** (7) interest
sich interessieren für be interested in
international international
Italien Italy
italienisch Italian

J

***ja** (1) yes; indeed
die Jagd, –en chase, hunt
der Jäger, – hunter
***das Jahr, –e** (7) year; **im Jahre** in (the year); ***vor vielen Jahren** (12) many years ago; **viele Jahre** for many years
***das Jahrhundert, –e** (14) century; **seit Jahrhunderten** for centuries
***der Januar** (18) January
***jeder** (4) each, every
***jemand** (21) someone
jener that; the former
jenseits (*with gen.*) the other side of
***jetzt** (2) now; **jetzt erst** only now
***der Juli** (18) July
***jung** (8) young
***der Junge , (–n), –n** (10) boy
der Jünger, – apostle, disciple
***der Juni** (18) June

K

die Kadettenanstalt, –en military college
***der Kaffee** (9) coffee
der Käfig, –e cage
der Kaiser, – emperor
***kalt** (9) cold
kämmen comb
kämpfen fight, struggle
der Kanal, ⸚e canal
die Kanone, –n cannon
die Kanonenkugel, –n cannonball
der Kanonier, –e gunner
der Kanton, –e canton (*Swiss political subdivision, corre-*

sponding to a state in the U.S.)

das Kapitel, – chapter

kaputt broken, smashed, ruined, done for, "all shot"

Karl der Große Charles the Great, Charlemagne

die Karte, –n map

***die Kartoffel, –n** (4) potato

die Kaste, –n caste

die Katze, –n cat

***kaufen** (6) buy

***kaum** (15) hardly, scarcely

***kein** (*adj.*) (4) no, not any; **keiner** none, neither; ***kein . . . mehr** (7) no . . . any more, no . . . any longer

***kennen, kannte, gekannt** (11) know, be acquainted with

die Kerze, –n candle

***das Kind, –er** (7) child

der Kindergarten, –̈ kindergarten

***das Kino, –s** (21) movie; **ins Kino gehen** go to the movies

***die Kirche, –n** (6) church

die Kirsche, –n cherry

das Kissen, – pillow, cushion

***klar** (18) clear

das Klavier, –e piano

***das Kleid, –er** (6) dress; (*plur.*) clothes

***klein** (16) small, little

das Klima climate

klingeln ring; **es klingelt** the bell is ringing

***klopfen** (17) knock; **an die Tür klopfen** knock on the door

das Kloster, –̈ cloister, monastery

die Klosterkultur cloister *or* monastic culture

***klug** (20) clever

Koblenz *name of a German city*

der Koffer, – trunk; suitcase, valise

die Kohle, –n coal

der Kohlenberg, –e pile of coal

die Kohleproduktion production of coal

Köln Cologne (*a German city*)

***kommen, kam, ist gekommen** (2) come

der Komponist, (–en), –en composer

der König, –e king

***können (kann), konnte, gekonnt** (10) can, be able to; know (*of languages*)

der Kontinent, –e continent

das Konzertprogramm, –e concert program

***der Kopf, –̈e** (4) head

der Korb, –̈e basket

***kosten** (6) cost

das Kostüm, –e costume

der Kragen, – collar

***krank** (1) sick, ill

das Krankenhaus, –̈er hospital

die Krawatte, –n (neck)tie

***die Kreide** (2) chalk

das Kreuz, –e cross

kreuzen to cross; **sich kreuzen** cross

der Kreuzweg, –e crossroad

der Krieg, –e war; **Krieg führen** conduct *or* wage war

krönen crown

***die Küche, –n** (3) kitchen

***der Kuchen, –** (9) cake; (*plur.*) cookies

die Kugel, –n ball, bullet

die Kuh, –̈e cow

die Kultur, –en culture

kulturell cultural

das Kulturzentrum, (*plur.*) **–zentren** cultural center

der Künstler, – artist

der Kurfürst, (–en), –en elector

kurz short

kürzen shorten

der Kuß, (Kusses), Küsse kiss

L

***lächeln** (3) smile
***lachen** (2) laugh
***die Lampe, –n** (6) lamp
der Lampenschirm, –e lamp shade
***das Land, ¨–er** (4) land; country; **auf dem Lande** in the country; **auf das Land** to the country; ***vom Lande** (4) from the country
landen to land
***die Landschaft, –en** (11) landscape, scenery
der Landvogt, ¨–e governor
***lang** (16) long; **eine Stunde lang** for an hour
lange a long time, for a long time
langsam slow
der Lärm noise
lassen (ä), ließ, gelassen let, allow; **ich lasse mir einen neuen Anzug machen** I'm having a new suit made (for myself)
der Lauf, ¨–e course
***laufen (äu), lief, ist gelaufen** (13) run
***laut** (10) loud, noisy; aloud
***leben** (5) live
***das Leben** (9) life, living
***leer** (20) empty, vacant
***legen** (18) lay, place, put; set out
die Legende, –n legend
***lehren** (1) teach
***der Lehrer, –** (1) teacher
***leicht** (21) easy; **leicht nehmen** take easy
***leid tun** (5) be sorry; ***es tut mir leid** (5) I am sorry
***leider** (13) unfortunately
***leise** (7) soft, gentle; low; quiet
***lernen** (8) learn; study
***lesen (ie), las, gelesen** (3) read
das Lesestück, –e reading exercise
***letzt** (15) last
***die Leute** (*plur.*) (6) people
***lieb** (14) dear
***lieben** (19) love, like
***das Lied, –er** (15) song
***liegen, lag, gelegen** (4) lie, be situated
die Limonade lemonade
link– left
links left, to the left
die Literatur, –en literature
locken lure
der Löffel, – spoon
der Löwe, (–n), –n lion
das Löwenmaul, ¨–er snapdragon
der Löwenzahn, ¨–e dandelion
***die Luft, ¨–e** (2) air
***lügen, log, gelogen** (19) lie, tell a lie
der Lügner, – liar
***lustig** (7) merry, gay

M

***machen** (3) make, do
***mächtig** (19) mighty, powerful
***das Mädchen, –** (5) girl
***der Mai** (18) May
der Main the Main (River)
Mainz *name of a German city*
Mainzer Mainz, of Mainz
***das Mal, –e** (18) time; **zweimal, zehnmal,** *etc.* twice, ten times. *etc.*
der Maler, – painter
***man** (*indefinite pronoun*) (9) one, people, they
***mancher** (4) many a; some
***manchmal** (15) sometimes
***der Mann, ¨–er** (5) man; husband
das Märchen, – fairy tale
***die Mark** (5) mark (*German coin worth 23.8¢*)
der Markt, ¨–e market; fair; market place; **der innere Markt**

internal trade, local consumption
der Marktplatz, ⸚e market place
der Martinitag St. Martin's (Day)
***der März** (18) March
die Maschine, –n machine
der Mast, –e mast
der Matrose, (–n), –n sailor
die Medizin, –en medicine
der Mediziner, – medical man; medical student
***mehr** (13) more; **mehr als** more than; **nicht mehr** no longer
***mehrere** (15) several
die Meile, –n mile
***mein** (2) my
***meinen** (8) think, believe; mean; say
meist– most
meistens mostly, usually, for the most part
der Meistersinger, – meistersinger
die Melodie, –n melody, tune
die Menge, –n crowd, throng
der Mensch, (–en), –en man, human being; (*plur.*) people
die Menschlichkeit humaneness
das Messer, – knife
die Million, –en million
die Millionenstadt, ⸚ city with a million inhabitants
der Ministerpräsident, (–en), –en prime minister
***die Minute, –n** (18) minute
***mit** (2) with; along
***mit-kommen, kam mit, ist mitgekommen** (17) come along, come too
mit-nehmen (nimmt mit), nahm mit, mitgenommen take along
der Mittag, –e noon, midday; ***zu Mittag essen** (14) eat dinner (*at noon*)
***die Mitte, –n** (7) middle
das Mittelalter Middle Ages
mittelgroß medium-sized
der Mittelpunkt, –e center
mitten in in the middle of
die Mitternacht, ⸚e midnight
***der Mittwoch** (18) Wednesday
die Möbel (*plur.*) furniture
modern modern
***mögen (mag), mochte, gemocht** (10) like, like to; may; **möchte (gern)** would like to
***möglich** (21) possible
***der Monat, –e** (10) month
der Mönch, –e monk
***der Montag, –e** (18) Monday
***morgen** (1) tomorrow
***der Morgen, –** (18) morning
morgens mornings, in the morning
die Mosel the Mosel *or* Moselle (River)
die Möwe, –n seagull
***müde** (17) tired, weary
München Munich (*a German city*)
der Mund, ⸚er mouth
das Münster, – minster, cathedral
das Museum, (*plur.*) **Museen** museum
die Musik music
musikalisch musical
der Musiker, – musician
***müssen (muß), mußte, gemußt** (10) must, have to; can't help
***der Mut** (20) courage
***die Mutter, ⸚** (10) mother
die Mütze, –n cap
die Mythologie, –n mythology

N

***nach** (2) to, toward; after; according to
der Nachbar, (–s *or* **–n), –n** neighbor
***nachdem** (*conj.*) (12) after

*__der Nachmittag, –e__ (4) afternoon
*__nachmittags__ (9) afternoons, in the afternoon
__nach-sehen (ie), sah nach, nachgesehen__ look up, look and see
*__nächst–__ (17) next, nearest
*__die Nacht, ⸚e__ (7) night
__nachts__ nights, at night
__nähen__ sew
__naiv__ naive
__der Name, (–ns), –n__ name (*dat. and acc. sing.* __Namen)__
__die Nase, –n__ nose
*__natürlich__ (11) naturally, of course; natural
__die Naturwissenschaften__ (*plur.*) natural sciences
*__neben__ (4) beside, next to, alongside of
__der Nebenfluß, (–flusses), –flüsse__ tributary
__der Nebensatz, ⸚e__ dependent clause
__der Neckar__ the Neckar (River)
__der Neffe, (–n), –n__ nephew
*__nehmen (nimmt), nahm, genommen__ (5) take
*__nein__ (1) no
*__nennen, nannte, genannt__ (11) name, call
__nett__ nice
__das Netz, –e__ network
*__neu__ (12) new, recent
*__neugierig__ (20) curious, inquisitive
__Neujahr__ New Year's (Day)
*__neun__ (9) nine
__neutral__ neutral
__das Neutrum__ neuter (gender)
*__nicht__ (1) not; __nicht mehr__ no longer; *__nicht nur . . . sondern auch__ (19) not only . . . but also
*__nichts__ (8) nothing; __nichts als__ nothing but
*__nie__ (9) never; *__noch nie__ (9) never (yet)
__die Niederlande__ Netherlands = Holland
*__niemand__ (17) nobody, no one; __niemand als__ no one but
__der Nikolaus__ St. Nicholas
__der Nikolaustag__ St. Nicholas' Day
*__noch__ (16) still, yet, in addition; __noch einmal__ again, once more; *__noch nicht__ (5) not yet; *__noch nie__ (9) never (yet)
__norddeutsch__ North-German
__der Norden__ north
__nördlich__ northern; to the north
__die Nordsee__ North Sea
__die Nord-Süd-Verbindung__ north-south connection
*__der November__ (18) November
*__null__ (18) zero
*__die Nummer, –n__ (6) number
*__nun__ (3) now; __nun__ *comma in German means* well *comma in English*
*__nur__ (9) only
__die Nuß,__ (*plur.*) __Nüsse__ nut
__nutzlos__ useless

O

*__ob__ (12) whether, if
*__oben__ (17) above, upstairs
*__obgleich__ (12) although
*__obwohl__ (12) although
*__oder__ (12) or
__die Oder__ the Oder (River)
*__offen__ (*adj. or adv.*) (2) open
__öffentlich__ public
__der Offizier, –e__ officer
*__öffnen__ (18) to open
*__oft__ (16) often
*__ohne__ (3) without; __ohne etwas zu tun__ without doing something
*__der Oktober__ (18) October
__die Oper, –n__ opera

der Opernkomponist, (–en), –en composer of operas
die Organisation, –en organization
der Osten east
die Ostsee Baltic Sea
der Ostsektor, –en East Sector
***Österreich** (17) Austria
der Österreicher, – the Austrian
österreichisch (*adj.*) Austrian
der Ozean, –e ocean

P

***ein paar** (7) a couple of, a few
der Papa, –s papa
der Papst, ⸚e pope
***der Park, –e** *or* **–s** (6) park
das Parlament, –e parliament
die Pause, –n pause, intermission, recess
der Pelzhandel, ⸚ fur trade
der Pelzhändler, – fur trader, furrier
Petrus (St.) Peter
das Pfand, ⸚er security, pledge
die Pfeife, –n pipe
der Pfeil, –e arrow
***der Pfennig, –e** (5) pfennig (*German coin worth 1/100 of a mark*); **das kostet zwanzig Pfennig** that costs twenty pfennigs
pflanzen plant
das Pfund, –e pound; **geben Sie mir zwei Pfund Butter** give me two pounds of butter
der Philologe, (–n), –n philologist (*in the broad sense of a student of language and literature*)
die Philologie philology, language and literature
der Philosoph, (–en), –en philosopher
die Philosophie, –n philosophy
die Physik physics
der Physiker, – physicist
der Platz, ⸚e place, seat; square, plaza
***plötzlich** (5) sudden(ly)
poetisch poetic
Polen Poland
die Politik politics; policy
der Polizist, (–en), –en policeman
die Post mail; **mit der Post** by mail
der Präsident, (–en), –en president
predigen preach
die Predigt, –en sermon
Preußen Prussia
preußisch Prussian
privat private
die Probe, –n trial; rehearsal
das Problem, –e problem
problematisch problematical
das Produkt, –e product
produzieren produce
der Professor, –en professor
das Programm, –e program
***Prost!** *or* **Prosit!** (11) Here's to you! Here's how! *i.e., a toast before drinking*
protestieren protest
das Prozent, –e percent
***die Prüfung, –en** (8) text, examination
psychologisch psychological
das Pulver, – powder
der Pumpernickel pumpernickel (*a type of dark bread*)

Q

die Quadratmeile, –n square mile
die Qualität, –en quality
die Quantität, –en quantity
die Quelle, –n spring; source

R

***das Rad, ⸚er** (11) wheel, bicycle
das Radio, –s radio
die Radtour, –en bicycle trip

der Rat, ⸚e advice; council; councillor, alderman; **Rat wissen** know what to do
***das Rathaus, ⸚er** (12) city hall
der Ratskeller, – rathskeller (*basement tavern in a city hall, or even elsewhere at times*)
die Ratte, –n rat
der Rattenfänger, – rat catcher
der Rauch, (*plur. rare*) **–e** smoke
***rauchen** (8) to smoke
die Rebe, –n grape
das Recht, –e right; **mit Recht** rightly
recht right; ***recht haben** (20) be right
rechts right, to the right
die Reform, –en reform
***regieren** (12) reign, govern, rule
die Regierung, –en government
***regnen** (12) rain
das Reh, –e stag, deer, roebuck
das Reich, –e empire
***reich** (20) rich
die Reichsstadt, ⸚e imperial city (*responsible only to the imperial central government*); **Freie Reichsstadt** independent imperial city
das Reichstagsgebäude parliament building
reif ripe, mature
reifen ripen
die Reihe, –n row, series
rein pure, clean
***die Reise, –n** (11) trip; ***eine Reise machen** (11) take a trip; ***Gute Reise!** (13) Pleasant journey!
die Religion, –en religion
reparieren repair, fix
repräsentieren represent
republikanisch republican
die Residenz, –en residence, seat
***das Restaurant, –s** (11) restaurant
***retten** (19) save
***der Rhein** (11) the Rhine (River); **am Rhein** on the Rhine, *i.e., on the banks of the Rhine*
***das Rheinland** (11) the Rhineland
***der Richter, –** (21) judge
richtig correct
der Ring des Nibelungen Ring of the Nibelung
das Rohmaterial, (*plur.*) **Rohmaterialien** raw material
der Römer, – Roman; the "Römer" (*old city hall of Frankfurt*)
römisch (*adj.*) Roman
die Röntgenstrahlen (*plur.*) X-rays, Roentgen rays
***rot** (2) red
***der Rücken, –** (18) back
Rüdesheim *name of a German city*
***rufen, rief, gerufen** (4) call (*in the sense of* shout *or* call out)
***ruhig** (21) calm, quiet
ruhmreich glorious
die Ruhr the Ruhr (River)
das Ruhrgebiet Ruhr region
die Rundfahrt, –en trip around, sightseeing trip
russisch Russian
Rußland Russia

S

das Saargebiet the Saar District
das Saarland the Saarland (*after 1920 the so-called Saar District; became the tenth German State in 1957*)
Sachsen Saxony
der Sack, ⸚e sack, bag
***sagen** (1) say, tell
die Sage, –n saying, legend

*__der Samstag, –e__ (18) Saturday
Sankt Saint
*__der Satz, ¨–e__ (2) sentence
das Sauerkraut sauerkraut
die Schachtel, –n box
der Schaffner, – conductor
*__sich schämen über__ (*with acc.*) (17) be ashamed of
der Schauspieler, – actor
*__scheinen, schien, geschienen__ (18) shine; seem, appear
schicken send
schießen, schoß, geschossen shoot
*__das Schiff, –e__ (14) boat, ship
der Schiffer, – boatman
die Schlacht, –en battle
*__schlafen (ä), schlief, geschlafen__ (4) sleep
schläfrig sleepy
schlagen (ä), schlug, geschlagen strike, hit, beat; defeat
die Schlagsahne whipped cream
*__schlecht__ (19) bad
*__schließen, schloß, geschlossen__ (18) close, shut; lock; end
*__schließlich__ (19) finally
das Schloß, (Schlosses), Schlösser castle
*__schmecken__ (7) taste; taste good
schmelzen (i), schmolz, ist geschmolzen melt
schmücken adorn, decorate
*__der Schnee__ (18) snow
*__schneiden, schnitt, geschnitten__ (7) cut
der Schneider, – tailor
*__schneien__ (18) to snow
*__schnell__ (6) fast, quick, swift
die Schokolade chocolate
*__schon__ (17) already
*__schön__ (7) beautiful; nice
der Schornstein, –e chimney
der Schoß, ¨–e lap
*__schreiben, schrieb, geschrieben__ (1) write
der Schreibtisch, –e writing table, desk
die Schreibtischlampe, –n desk lamp
*__schreien, schrie, geschrieen__ (10) cry, shout
*__der Schuh, –e__ (2) shoe
das Schulbuch, ¨–er schoolbook
*__die Schule, –n__ (1) school
der Schuljunge, (–n), –n schoolboy
der Schuß, (Schusses), Schüsse shot
die Schüssel, –n (serving) dish, bowl, platter
schütteln shake
der Schütze, (–n), –n marksman, shot
*__schwarz__ (2) black
der Schwarzwald Black Forest
die Schwarzwaldberge (*plur.*) Black Forest mountains
der Schwede, (–n), –n Swede
Schweden Sweden
das Schweigen silence
der Schweinebraten, – roast pork
*__die Schweiz__ (13) Switzerland
Schweizer (*adj.*) Swiss, of Switzerland
der Schweizer, – the Swiss
*__schwer__ (1) heavy; hard, difficult
das Schwert, –er sword
*__die Schwester, –n__ (18) sister
schwierig difficult
*__schwimmen, schwamm, ist geschwommen__ (10) swim
schwören, schwur, geschworen take an oath, swear
Schwyzerdütsch *Swiss word for* Swiss-German
*__sechs__ (6) six
sechshundert six hundred
*__sechzehn__ (16) sixteen
sechzig sixty
die See, –n sea
segnen bless, give a blessing to

***sehen (ie), sah, gesehen** (3) see
***sehr** (1) very; very much
die Seidenindustrie silk industry
***sein** (4) his; its
***sein (ist), war, ist gewesen** (1) be
***seit** (*prep.*) (2) since; for
***seitdem** (*conj.*) (18) since
***die Seite, –n** (20) side, page
selber self, *e.g.*, myself, yourself, himself, herself, itself, ourselves, yourselves, themselves
***selbst** (12) self (*as for* **selber**); even
selbständig independent
die Selbstverwaltung, –en self-government
seltsam strange
***der September** (18) September
***der Sessel, –** (1) easy chair, armchair
setzen set, place, put; ***sich setzen** (17) sit down, be seated
***sich** (*reflexive*) (17) himself, herself, itself, themselves, yourself, yourselves; each other
sicher safe, secure
***sie** (1) she; they; it
***Sie** (1) you (*polite form, sing. or plur.*)
***sieben** (7) seven
***siebzehn** (17) seventeen
sieh! see!; **sieh da** lo and behold
***singen, sang, gesungen** (7) sing
der Sitz, –e seat
***sitzen, saß, gesessen** (1) sit
die Sitzung, –en session, meeting
skeptisch sceptical
***so** (1) so, thus, (in) this way; ***so . . . wie** (5) as . . . as
das Sofa, –s sofa
***sofort** (1) at once, immediately
sog. *abbreviation for* **sogenannt**
***sogar** (13) even
sogenannt so-called
***der Sohn, ¨e** (10) son
***solcher** (4) such (a)
***der Soldat, (–en), –en** (19) soldier
der Soldatenkönig, –e soldier-king
***sollen (soll), sollte, gesollt** (10) shall, be to; be said to; should, ought to
***der Sommer, –** (9) summer; **im Sommer** in the summer
die Sonate, –n sonata
***sondern** (7) but
***der Sonnabend, –e** (18) Saturday
***die Sonne, –n** (11) sun
sonnig sunny
***der Sonntag, –e** (12) Sunday
***sonst** (16) otherwise
die Sorge, –n care, worry, concern
sozial social
die Sparsamkeit thrift, economy
der Spaß, ¨e fun; joke
***spät** (3) late
***später** (11) later
***der Spaziergang, ¨e** (10) walk; ***einen Spaziergang machen** (10) take a walk
***spielen** (17) play
die Spitze, –n point, head, top; **an der Spitze** at the head
***die Sprache, –n** (8) language, speech
***sprechen (i), sprach, gesprochen** (3) speak
das Sprichwort, ¨er proverb
springen, sprang, ist gesprungen spring, jump
St. *abbreviation for* **Sankt** Saint
***der Staat, –en** (16) state
der Staatsdienst, –e state service
die Staatsform, –en form of government
***die Stadt, ¨e** (6) city; ***in der Stadt** (6) in the city, down-

town; ***in die Stadt** (6) to the city, downtown
die Städteordnung Municipal Autonomy Statute
das Stadtparlament, –e city council
der Stadtstaat, –en city-state
der Stahl steel
der Stamm, ⸚e tribe
die Stange, –n pole
***stark** (16) strong
die Statue, –n statue
staubig dusty
der Staubsauger, – vacuum cleaner
stecken put
***stehen, stand, gestanden** (4) stand; be
***stehlen (ie), stahl, gestohlen** (21) steal
***der Stein, –e** (10) stone
die Steinkohle, –n hard coal
***stellen** (7) place, put
die Stellung, –en position, situation
***sterben (i), starb, ist gestorben** (12) die
die Steuer, –n tax
***still** (6) still, silent, calm, quiet
***die Stimme, –n** (13) voice
der Stock, ⸚e stick, cane (*see also next entry*)
der Stock, (*plur.*) **Stockwerke** floor, story
***stolz (auf)** (16) proud (of)
die Strafe, –n punishment, penalty, fine
strafen punish
***die Straße, –n** (6) street
***die Straßenbahn, –en** (6) trolley (car), street car
sich strecken extend
der Streich, –e trick, prank
der Streit, –e dispute, quarrel
streng strict, severe
das Stück, –e piece, bit
***der Student, (–en), –en** (1) (university) student
***studieren** (12) study
***der Stuhl, ⸚e** (1) chair
***die Stunde, –n** (3) hour
der Sturm, ⸚e storm
suchen seek, look for
der Süden south
südwestlich (von) southwest (of)
der Superlativ, –e superlative
die Suppe, –n soup
die Süßigkeiten (*plur.*) sweets, candies
das Symbol, –e symbol
die Symphonie, –n symphony
das Synonym, –e synonym

T

***die Tafel, –n** (1) blackboard
***der Tag, –e** (8) day; **eines Tages** one day; **in einem Tage** in a day
***das Tal, ⸚er** (20) valley
***die Tasche, –n** (5) pocket
***die Tat, –en** (16) deed
tausend (a) thousand
Tausende thousands
das Taxi, –s taxi
der Teich, –e pond
der Teil, –e part
teilen divide
***der Teller, –** (4) plate
der Tennisplatz, ⸚e tennis court
der Teufel, – devil
der Text, –e text, libretto
das Theater, – theater
***tief** (17) deep
***das Tier, –e** (10) animal
der Tiger, – tiger
***der Tisch, –e** (1) table
***die Tochter, ⸚** (17) daughter
der Tod, (*plur. rare*) **–e** death; **zum Tode verurteilt** condemned to death
die Tomate, –n tomato

der Tomatensalat, –e tomato salad
die Tonne, –n ton
das Tor, –e gate
töten kill
die Touristenklasse, –n tourist class
***tragen (ä), trug, getragen** (3) carry, bear; wear
transportieren transport, ship
die Traube, –n grape
***traurig** (8) sad
***treffen (i), traf, getroffen** (5) meet; hit
die Trennung, –en separation
treten (i), trat, getreten kick, step
***trinken, trank, getrunken** (5) drink
das Trinkgeld, –er tip
trocken dry
trotz (*with gen.*) in spite of
***trotzdem** (18) in spite of it, nevertheless
die Tschechoslowakei Czechoslovakia
die Tulpe, –n tulip
***tun, tat, getan** (10) do
***die Tür, –en** (17) door
der Tyrann, (–en), –en tyrant

U

***üben** (2) exercise, practice, drill
***über** (4, 8) over, above; concerning, about
überall everywhere
übernehmen (übernimmt), übernahm, übernommen take over, assume
überreif over-ripe
die Überreste (*plur.*) remains, ruins
***übersetzen, übersetzte, übersetzt** (14) translate
***die Übersetzung, –en** (8) translation
das Ufer, – bank
***die Uhr, –en** (18) clock, watch; o'clock
***um** (3) around, about; at (*with hours of the day*); ***um . . . zu** (*with infinitive*) (12) in order to (*with infinitive*), *e.g.*, **um etwas zu tun** in order to do something
umgeben (i), umgab, umgeben surround
um-steigen, stieg um, ist umgestiegen transfer, change trains
***und** (1) and; **und so weiter** (*abbreviation* **usw.**) and so on, etc.
ungefähr about, approximately
der Ungehorsam disobedience
das Ungetüm, –e monster
unhöflich discourteous, impolite
die Universität, –en university
die Universitätsstadt, ⸚e university city
das Unrecht injustice; **mit Unrecht** unjustly, wrongly
unruhig unquiet, restless
***unser** (4) our
***unten** (14) below, downstairs; **dort unten** down there
***unter** (4, 15) under, below; among
Unter den Linden *name of a street in Berlin; it means* "Under the Lindens."
***unterbrechen (i), unterbrach, unterbrochen** (8) interrupt
unterdrücken oppress
unterhaltsam entertaining
die Unterordnung subordination
sich unterscheiden, unterschied, unterschieden (von) be different (from)
der Unterschied, –e difference
der Untertan, –en subject
***das Urteil, –e** (21) judgment, verdict

usw. *abbreviation for* **und so weiter** and so on, etc.

V

***der Vater, ⸚** (12) father
die Verabredung, –en appointment, date
die Verantwortung responsibility
das Verb, –en verb
verbinden, verband, verbunden connect
die Verbindung, –en connection, combination, union
der Verbraucher, – consumer
verbrennen, verbrannte, verbrannt burn
verbringen, verbrachte, verbracht spend, pass (*time*)
verbunden connected
das Verderben destruction, ruin
verehren honor, respect, venerate
***die Vereinigten Staaten** (5) United States
die Verfassung, –en constitution
die Vergangenheit past
***vergessen (i), vergaß, vergessen** (13) forget
das Vergißmeinnicht, –e forget-me-not
verheiratet married
***verkaufen** (5) sell
***der Verkäufer, –** (6) salesman, seller, vendor
***die Verkäuferin, –nen** (6) saleslady, seller, vendor
der Verkehr traffic, communication
der Verkehrsunfall, ⸚e traffic accident
verkünden announce; render
verlassen (ä), verließ, verlassen leave
***verlieren, verlor, verloren** (20) lose
vermissen miss
der Vers, –e verse
versammeln call together, assemble
die Versammlung, –en meeting
verschieden different
die Verschiedenheit, –en difference
***versprechen (i), versprach, versprochen** (21) promise
verstecken hide, conceal
versteckt concealed, hidden
***verstehen, verstand, verstanden** (14) understand
versuchen try, attempt
der Vertreter, – representative
verurteilen sentence; **zum Tode verurteilt** condemned to death
verzweifelt desperate, in despair
***viel** (1) much, a lot (of)
***viele** (4) many
***vielleicht** (10) perhaps
***vier** (4) four
***das Viertel, –** (18) quarter, fourth
der Vierwaldstättersee Lake Lucerne
***vierzehn** (14) fourteen
vierzig forty
vivat! *Latin term, meaning* "Long may he live!"
das Vöglein, – little bird
***das Volk, ⸚er** (12) folk, people
das Volkslied, –er folksong
der Volkswagen, – *name of a German automobile*
***von** (2, 19) of, from; by
***vor** (4) before, in front of; ago, *e.g.,* ***vor vielen Jahren** (12) many years ago
voran-gehen, ging voran, ist vorangegangen go ahead
***der Vorhang, ⸚e** (19) curtain
***vormittags** (12) mornings, forenoons, in the morning, in the forenoon

die Vorstellung, –en performance
***der Vortrag, ⸚e** (21) lecture

W

***wachsen (ä), wuchs, ist gewachsen** (3) grow
die Wahl, –en choice, selection, election
wählen choose, select, elect
***wahr** (21) true; ***nicht wahr** (3) is it not true
***die Wahrheit, –en** (21) truth
***während** (*conj.*) (19) while
***während** (*with gen.*) (14) during
***wahrscheinlich** (21) probable, likely
***der Wald, ⸚er** (5) woods, forest
das Walroß, (–rosses), Walrosse walrus
***die Wand, ⸚e** (2) wall
***wann** (*for questions only*) (1) when
das Warenhaus, ⸚er department store
***warm** (3) warm
***warten auf** (*with acc.*) (4) wait for
***warum** (2) why
***was** (1) what
***das Wasser, –** (10) water
die Wasserleitung plumbing
die Wasserverbindung, –en water connection
wechseln change
wecken awaken
***weder . . . noch** (10) neither . . . nor
***weg** (6) away, off, gone
der Weg, –e road, way
***wegen** (*with gen.*) (14) on account of, because of
die Weichsel the Vistula (River)
***Weihnachten** (*plur.*) (17) Christmas; **Fröhliche Weihnachten** Merry Christmas
der Weihnachtsengel, – Christmas angel
das Weihnachtsgebäck Christmas cookies *or* pastry
die Weihnachtsgeschichte, –n Christmas story
das Weihnachtslied, –er Christmas carol
***weil** (12) because
***der Wein, –e** (7) wine
der Weinberg, –e vineyard
das Weinland, ⸚er wine country
***weiß** (1) white
weit far, distant
weiter-führen carry on
weiter-gehen, ging weiter, ist weitergegangen go on
***welcher** (4) which, what
***die Welt, –en** (14) world
der Weltkrieg, –e World War
***wenig** (15) little
***wenige** (15) few
weniger less
***wenn** (12) if; when(ever)
***wer** (8) who; whoever, he who
***werden (wird), wurde, ist geworden** (3) get, become; *with infinitive* = shall, will; *with past participle* = be
***werfen (i), warf, geworfen** (8) throw
***das Werk, –e** (19) work, work of art, creative work
***wertvoll** (20) valuable
die Weser the Weser (River)
Westdeutschland West Germany
der Westen west
der Westsektor, –en West Sector
das Wetter, – weather
der Wetterbericht, –e weather report
***wichtig** (11) important
widersprechen (i), widersprach, widersprochen contradict

*__wie__ (1) how, as, like
*__wieder__ (4) again
*__wiederholen__ (20) repeat
__wieder-sehen (ie), sah wieder, wiedergesehen__ see again; *__Auf Wiedersehen__ *or* __Auf Wiedersehn__ (13) good-bye, au revoir
__Wien__ Vienna
*__die Wiese, –n__ (14) meadow
__wieviel__ how much
__Wilhelm__ William
*__der Wind, –e__ (16) wind
__winken__ wave
*__der Winter, –__ (9) winter; __im Winter__ in the winter
*__wir__ (1) we
*__wirklich__ (21) real, actual
__das Wirtshaus, ⸚er__ inn, tavern
*__wissen (weiß), wußte, gewußt__ (11) know (*facts*)
__der Witz__ wit, joke
*__wo__ (1) where
*__die Woche, –n__ (11) week
__der Wochentag, –e__ day of the week, weekday
*__wohin__ (6) where (to), to what place
*__wohnen__ (1) live, dwell, reside
*__das Wohnzimmer, –__ (3) living room
*__wollen (will), wollte, gewollt__ (10) want to, wish to
*__das Wort, –e__ *or* __⸚er__ (15) word
__das Wörterbuch, ⸚er__ dictionary
__das Wörterverzeichnis, –se__ vocabulary
__wörtlich__ literal
__wunderbar__ wonderful
*__wünschen__ (21) wish
__würde__ would
__Württemberg__ Wurttemberg (*name of a former German state which, together with Baden, composes one of the present German political subdivisions known as Länder*)

Z

__die Zahl, –en__ number
*__zahlen__ (5) pay
*__zählen__ (18) count; __zählen zu__ count among
__der Zahn, ⸚e__ tooth
__die Zauberflöte__ (Mozart's opera) "The Magic Flute"
__z.B.__ *abbreviation for* __zum Beispiel__ e.g., for example
*__zehn__ (10) ten
__das Zeichen, –__ sign; sign-post
*__zeigen__ (2) show, point (out)
*__die Zeit, –en__ (10) time; *__zur Zeit__ (16) at the time
*__die Zeitung, –en__ (3) (news) paper
__das Zentrum,__ (*plur.*) __Zentren__ center
__zerbrochen__ broken
__zerstören__ destroy
__ziehen, zog, gezogen__ pull
__die Ziffer, –n__ figure, number, cipher
*__die Zigarette, –n__ (8) cigaret
*__die Zigarre, –n__ (7) cigar
*__das Zimmer, –__ (1) room
__der Zoo, –s__ zoo, zoological garden
__zoologisch__ zoological
*__zu__ (2) to, toward; too; closed, shut
__der Zucker__ sugar
*__zuerst__ (11) first, at first
*__zufrieden__ (12) content, contented, satisfied
*__der Zug, ⸚e__ (13) train
__zu-geben (i), gab zu, zugegeben__ admit
__zu-hören__ listen
__der Zuhörer, –__ listener; (*plur.*) audience
*__zu-machen__ (13) shut, close

***zurück** (5) back, behind
zurück-bleiben, blieb zurück, ist zurückgeblieben remain behind
***zurück-bringen, brachte zurück, zurückgebracht** (21) bring back
***zurück-geben (i), gab zurück, zurückgegeben** (21) give back, return
zurück-gehen, ging zurück, ist zurückgegangen go back, return
***zurück-kommen, kam zurück, ist zurückgekommen** (13) come back, return
zurück-rufen, rief zurück, zurückgerufen call back
***zusammen** (15) together
zusammen-kommen, kam zusammen, ist zusammengekommen meet, come together
zuvor before
***zwanzig** (6) twenty
***zwei** (2) two
zweit– second
***zwischen** (4) between
***zwölf** (12) twelve

ENGLISH-GERMAN VOCABULARY

A

a ein, eine, ein
able to = can können (kann), konnte, gekonnt
about = concerning über (*with acc.*); **= around** um
account: on account of wegen (*with gen.*)
afraid: to be afraid of Angst haben vor (*with dat.*); sich fürchten vor (*with dat.*)
after (*conj.*) nachdem; (*prep.*) nach
afternoon der Nachmittag, –e
afternoons nachmittags, am Nachmittag
again wieder; **again and again** immer wieder
ago vor, *e.g.*, **many years ago** vor vielen Jahren
air die Luft
all all, alles
almost fast
already schon
also auch
although obgleich, obwohl
always immer
am to sollen (soll), sollte, gesollt
America Amerika
an ein, eine, ein
and und
angry ärgerlich; **be angry with** sich ärgern über (*with acc.*)
animal das Tier, –e
answer die Antwort, –en
answer antworten
arm der Arm, –e
around um
arrive an-kommen, kam an, ist angekommen
as wie; **as . . . as** so . . . wie
ask (*a question*) fragen; (*a favor*) bitten, bat, gebeten; **ask for** bitten um
at auf, bei, an, gegen, nach; (*with hours of the day*) um
author der Dichter, –
auto das Auto, –s
autumn der Herbst, –e
away weg

B

back zurück
be sein (ist), war, ist gewesen; **How are you?** Wie geht es dir?
beautiful schön
because weil
bed das Bett, –en
before (*conj.*) ehe; (*prep.*) vor
begin an-fangen (ä), fing an, angefangen
behind hinter
believe meinen, glauben
bench die Bank, ⸚e
best best–
better besser
between zwischen
bicycle das Rad, ⸚er
big groß
birthday der Geburtstag, –e
black schwarz
blackboard die Tafel, –n
boatman der Schiffer, –
book das Buch, ⸚er
bottle die Flasche, –n
boy der Junge, (–n), –n
bring bringen, brachte, gebracht

burn brennen, brannte, gebrannt
but aber; (*preceded by a negative and meaning "on the contrary"*) sondern
buy kaufen
by an, bei; (*by train, trolley, bus, car, bicycle, etc.*) mit; (*with the passive*) von

C

call = to call out rufen, rief, gerufen; **= to name** nennen, nannte, genannt
call up = telephone an-rufen, rief an, angerufen
can können (kann), konnte, gekonnt
can't help müssen (muß), mußte, gemußt, *e.g.,* **He couldn't help laughing** Er mußte lachen
car das Auto, –s
carry tragen (ä), trug, getragen
carry into hinein-tragen (ä), trug hinein, hineingetragen
century das Jahrhundert, –e
chair der Stuhl, ⸚e
cheat betrügen, betrog, betrogen
child das Kind, –er
Christmas Weihnachten; **at Christmas** zu Weihnachten, an Weihnachten
church die Kirche, –n; **go to church** in die Kirche *or* zur Kirche gehen
cigar die Zigarre, –n
cigaret die Zigarette, –n
city die Stadt, ⸚e
city hall das Rathaus, ⸚er
clever klug
clock die Uhr, –en
close zu-machen
clothes die Kleider (*plur.*)
cold kalt
color die Farbe, –n
come kommen, kam, ist gekommen
come back zurück-kommen, kam zurück, ist zurückgekommen
compartment das Abteil, –e
cost kosten
count zählen
couple: a couple of ein paar
court (*of law*) das Gericht, –e

D

danger die Gefahr, –en
dark dunkel
day der Tag, –e
dear lieb
December der Dezember
department store das Warenhaus, ⸚er
desk der Schreibtisch, –e
didn't you *see* **is it not true**
dining room das Eßzimmer, –
dinner das Mittagessen, –; **eat dinner** zu Mittag essen
do machen; tun, tat, getan
doctor = physician der Arzt, ⸚e
don't you *see* **is it not true**
door die Tür, –en
downtown (*motion toward*) in die Stadt; (*place where*) in der Stadt
drink trinken, trank, getrunken
drive fahren (ä), fuhr, ist gefahren
during während (*with gen.*)

E

earlier früher
early früh
easy chair der Sessel, –
eat essen (i), aß, gegessen
eight acht
eleven elf
English (*as a noun*) Englisch; (*as an adjective or adverb*) englisch; **in English** auf englisch
entire(ly) ganz
even selbst, auch, sogar
evening der Abend, –e

every jeder
everything alles
exercise die Aufgabe, –n
explain erklären

F

fall = autumn der Herbst, –e
family die Familie, –n
famous berühmt
fast schnell
fat dick
father der Vater, ¨–
few = a few ein paar
field das Feld, –er
fifty-second zweiundfünfzigst
finally schließlich
first erst–
five fünf
flower die Blume, –n
for (*prep.*) für; (*conj.*) denn
forest der Wald, ¨–er
forget vergessen (i), vergaß, vergessen
four vier
friend der Freund, –e; **female** *or* **girl friend** die Freundin, –nen
from von, aus
front: in front of vor

G

garden der Garten, ¨–
gay lustig
German (*as a noun*) Deutsch; (*as an adj. or adv.*) deutsch; **in German** auf deutsch
Germany Deutschland
get = become werden (wird), wurde, ist geworden
get = fetch holen
get off (*e.g., a train*) aus-steigen, stieg aus, ist ausgestiegen
get on (*a train*) ein-steigen, stieg ein, ist eingestiegen, *e.g.,* **he gets on a train** er steigt in den Zug ein
get up auf-stehen, stand auf, ist aufgestanden
girl das Mädchen, –
give geben (i), gab, gegeben
glad: be glad about sich freuen über (*with acc.*)
glass das Glas, ¨–er
go gehen, ging, ist gegangen
go to *e.g.,* **I am going to read a book** (= *future tense*) Ich werde ein Buch lesen
good gut
good-bye Auf Wiedersehen
grandchild der Enkel, –
grandparents die Großeltern
green grün
grow wachsen (ä), wuchs, ist gewachsen
guest der Gast, ¨–e

H

hair das Haar, –e
half halb; **half an hour** eine halbe Stunde; **in half an hour** in einer halben Stunde; **half past,** *e.g.,* **half past six** halb sieben
happen geschehen (ie), geschah, ist geschehen
hard schwer
hardly kaum
hat der Hut, ¨–e
have haben (hat), hatte, gehabt
have to = must müssen (muß), mußte, gemußt
he er
head der Kopf, ¨–e
hear hören
help helfen (i), half, geholfen (*with dat.*); *cf.* **He helps me with my work** Er hilft mir bei der Arbeit
her ihr
here hier
high hoch (*drops the* c *before* e)
higher höher
highly höchst

himself selbst; (*reflexive*) sich
his sein
history die Geschichte, –n
home (*motion toward*) nach Hause; (*place where*) = **at home** zu Hause
honest ehrlich
hot heiß
hour die Stunde, –n
house das Haus, ⸚er
how wie
how long wie lange, seit wann
how many wie viele
hungry hungrig
husband der Mann, ⸚er

I

I ich
if wenn; *meaning* **whether** ob
in in
in front of vor
instead of anstatt, statt (*with gen.*); *cf.* **instead of doing something** anstatt etwas zu tun
interesting interessant
interrupt unterbrechen (i), unterbrach, unterbrochen
into in
is it not true nicht wahr
isn't he *see* **is it not true**
it es; (*to agree with a masculine noun*) er; (*to agree with a feminine noun*) sie
its sein

J

January der Januar
just gerade
judge der Richter, –

K

kitchen die Küche, –n
know = **be acquainted with** kennen, kannte, gekannt; = **know facts** wissen (weiß), wußte, gewußt

L

lady die Dame, –n
lamp die Lampe, –n
large groß
last letzt–; = **yesterday** gestern, *e.g.*, **last evening** gestern nachmittag, gestern abend
late spät
later später
laugh lachen
leave = **depart** ab-fahren (ä), fuhr ab, ist abgefahren
lecture der Vortrag, ⸚e
lemonade die Limonade
lesson die Aufgabe, –n
letter der Brief, –e
lie liegen, lag, gelegen
like mögen (mag), mochte, gemocht. *Cf. the following:* **I don't like that** Das mag ich nicht; **I like that** Das gefällt mir; **I like him very much** Ich habe ihn sehr gern; **I like to play tennis** Ich spiele gern Tennis; **I like these flowers best of all** Ich habe diese Blumen am liebsten; **I like to play tennis best of all** Ich spiele am liebsten Tennis.
little (*in size*) klein; = **not much** wenig
live = **dwell** wohnen
living room das Wohnzimmer, –
long lang
lose verlieren, verlor, verloren
loud(ly) laut

M

make machen
man der Mann, ⸚er
many viele; **how many** wie viele
mark = *German coin* die Mark
market place der Marktplatz, ⸚e
meadow die Wiese, –n

meet treffen (i), traf, getroffen
middle die Mitte
minute die Minute, –n
mister der Herr, (–n), –en
money das Geld, –er
more mehr; *cf.* **more and more thirsty** immer durstiger
morning der Morgen, –
most meist–
mother die Mutter, ⸚
mountain der Berg, –e
movie das Kino, –s; **go to the movies** ins Kino gehen
Mr. *see* **mister**
Mrs. Frau
much viel
must müssen (muß), mußte, gemußt; **must not** nicht dürfen
my mein
myself selbst; (*reflexive*) mir, mich

N

naturally natürlich
need brauchen
neither . . . nor weder . . . noch
never nie
new neu
New Year's das Neujahr
newspaper die Zeitung, –en
next nächst–
night die Nacht, ⸚e
nights nachts
nine neun
no (*adj.*) kein
no one but niemand als
noon der Mittag, –e
noon dinner *see* **dinner**
not nicht
not a kein
not any kein
not any more kein . . . mehr
notebook das Heft, –e
nothing nichts
nothing but nichts als
now jetzt; **up to now, up till now** bis jetzt

O

o'clock Uhr
of von
often oft
old alt
on auf; = **alongside of** an; (*with the word* **day,** *days of the week, and dates*) am; **travel on the train** mit dem Zug fahren
once einmal; **at once** sofort
one ein; eins; (*indefinite pronoun*) man
only nur; = **not until** erst
open auf-machen
or oder
order (*e.g., from a waiter*) bestellen; **in order to** um . . . zu
other ander–
otherwise sonst
ought to sollte; **ought to have** hätte . . . sollen (*plus infin.*), *e.g.,* **He ought to have come** Er hätte kommen sollen
our unser
ourselves selbst; (*reflexive*) uns

P

paper = **newspaper** die Zeitung, –en
parents die Eltern
park der Park, –e
pencil der Bleistift, –e
people die Leute
perhaps vielleicht
permit = **be permitted to** dürfen (darf), durfte, gedurft
pfennig der Pfennig, –e; *cf.* **That costs fifty pfennigs** Das kostet fünfzig Pfennig
place setzen, stellen
plate der Teller, –
platform der Bahnsteig, –e
play spielen

please! bitte! **to please** *see next entry*
please gefallen (ä), gefiel, gefallen, *e.g.,* **It pleases me** *or* **I like it** Es gefällt mir
pocket die Tasche, –n
possible möglich
pour gießen, goß, gegossen
practice üben
present das Geschenk, –e
pretty hübsch
put setzen, stellen

Q

quarter das Viertel, –
question die Frage, –n
quick(ly) schnell
quiet(ly) ruhig
quiz die Prüfung, –en

R

rain regnen
read lesen (ie), las, gelesen
really doch, wirklich
red rot
remain bleiben, blieb, ist geblieben
repeat wiederholen (*inseparable*)
report berichten
restaurant das Restaurant, –s
Rhine der Rhein
Rhineland das Rheinland
river der Fluß, (Flusses), Flüsse
room das Zimmer, –

S

sad traurig
saleslady die Verkäuferin, –nen
salesman der Verkäufer, –
Santa Claus der Nikolaus
say sagen
scenery die Landschaft, –en
school die Schule, –n
second zweit–
see sehen (ie), sah, gesehen
sell verkaufen
sentence der Satz, ⸚e
serious ernst
seven sieben
shake hands (with one) (einem) die Hand geben
she sie
shirt das Hemd, –en
shoe der Schuh, –e
should = **ought to** sollte
shout = **yell** schreien, schrie, geschrieen
show zeigen
shut zu-machen
sick krank
since (*conj.*) da; (*prep.*) seit
sing singen, sang, gesungen
sister die Schwester, –n
sit sitzen, saß, gesessen
sit down sich setzen
situated = **be situated** liegen, lag, gelegen
sixtieth sechzigst–
sleep schlafen (ä), schlief, geschlafen
smile lächeln
smoke rauchen
snow der Schnee
snow schneien
so so
soft(ly) leise
some (*sing.*) etwas, *e.g.,* etwas Wein; (*plur.*) einige, manche, *e.g.,* einige Leute, manche Männer
someone man, jemand
something etwas
song das Lied, –er
soon bald
sorry: be sorry leid tun, *e.g.,* **I am sorry** Es tut mir leid
speak sprechen (i), sprach, gesprochen
spring der Frühling, –e
stand stehen, stand, gestanden
stand up auf-stehen, stand auf, ist aufgestanden
state der Staat, –en

station der Bahnhof, ⸚e
stay bleiben, blieb, ist geblieben
steal stehlen (ie), stahl, gestohlen
stick der Stock, ⸚e
still noch
stone der Stein, –e
story die Geschichte, –n
strawberry punch die Erdbeerbowle, –n
street car die Straßenbahn, –en
strong stark
student der Student, (–en), –en
study lernen, studieren
such (a) solcher
suit der Anzug, ⸚e
suitcase der Koffer, –
summer der Sommer, –
sun die Sonne
Sunday der Sonntag, –e

T

table der Tisch, –e
take nehmen (nimmt), nahm, genommen; **take a trip** eine Reise machen; **take a walk** einen Spaziergang machen
take off ab-nehmen (nimmt ab), nahm ab, abgenommen
talk sprechen (i), sprach, gesprochen
teacher der Lehrer, –
tell sagen; = **narrate** erzählen
ten zehn
tennis das Tennis
tennis court der Tennisplatz, ⸚e
test die Prüfung, –en
than als
that das; *accented* der, die, das *as adjective*
that (*conj.*) daß
that is das heißt
the der, die, das
their ihr
then dann; *after a* wenn *clause* so
there da, dort
there is, there are es ist, es sind; es gibt (*with acc.*)
therefore darum
these diese, dies, das
they sie
thing das Ding, –e
think denken, dachte, gedacht; **think of** denken an (*with acc.*)
thirsty durstig
this dieser, diese, dieses, dies; = *today* heute, *e.g.*, **this morning** heute morgen
those diese, dies, das
three drei
through durch
throw werfen (i), warf, geworfen
time die Zeit, –en; = **occurrence** das Mal, –e
to zu, nach; = **until** bis; *cf.* **ten minutes to two** zehn Minuten vor zwei
today heute
tomorrow morgen
too zu; = **also** auch
train der Zug, ⸚e
travel fahren (ä), fuhr, ist gefahren; **travel by** *or* **on** *or* **with** fahren mit
tree der Baum, ⸚e
trip die Reise, –n **take a trip** eine Reise machen
trolley (car) die Straßenbahn, –en
true wahr
truth die Wahrheit, –en
Tuesday der Dienstag, –e
twenty zwanzig
twenty-fifth fünfundzwanzigst–
twenty-four vierundzwanzig
two zwei; **the two** = **both the** die beiden

U

under unter
unfortunately leider
until bis
up to now bis jetzt

V

vacation die Ferien (*plural*)
valley das Tal, ⸚er
very sehr
visit besuchen
voice die Stimme, –n

W

wait warten; **wait for** warten auf (*with acc.*)
walk der Spaziergang, ⸚e; **take a walk** einen Spaziergang machen
wall die Wand, ⸚e
want to wollen (will), wollte, gewollt
warm warm
wasn't it *see* **is it not true**
water das Wasser, –
we wir
week die Woche, –n
well gut; *introductory, followed by comma* nun,
what was; (*adj.*) welcher
when = whenever wenn; *for questions, direct or indirect* wann; *otherwise use* als
where wo; **where to** wohin
whether ob
which (*pronoun*) was; (*adj.*) welcher; (*relative*) der
white weiß
who wer; (*as relative with antecedent*) der
why warum
wife die Frau, –en
will (*for future*) werden *plus infin.*
wind der Wind, –e
window das Fenster, –
wine der Wein, –e
winter der Winter, –
with mit; *cf.* **live with the family, help with the work** bei der Familie wohnen, bei der Arbeit helfen
without ohne; *cf.* **without doing something** ohne etwas zu tun
woman die Frau, –en
word das Wort, –e *or* ⸚er
work die Arbeit, –en
work arbeiten
write schreiben, schrieb, geschrieben; **write a letter to** einen Brief schreiben an (*with acc.*)

Y

year das Jahr, –e
yesterday gestern
yet noch; **not yet** noch nicht
you du (*2nd person sing. familiar*); ihr (*2nd person plur. familiar*); Sie (*polite form, sing. or plur.*)
young jung
young boy der Junge, (–n), –n
your dein, euer, Ihr

Z

zero null

INDEX

0 50 100 Meilen
0 100 200 Km.
Nordsee
DÄNEMARK
Kiel
I
Lübeck
Bremerhaven
Hamburg
II
III
Bremen
IV
Elbe
NIEDERLANDE
BUNDESREPUBLIK
Rotterdam
Weser
Hannover
Hameln
Rhein
Dortmund
V
Göttingen
DEMOKRATIS
Duisburg
Ruhr
Düsseldorf
Köln
Aachen
BELGIEN
Bonn
Marburg
VI
Weimar
REPUBLIK
Fulda
Wiesbaden
Frankfurt
LUXEMBURG
Mosel
Mainz
VII
DEUTSCHLAND
Main
Bayreuth
Eger
Saarbrücken
VIII
Speyer
Heidelberg
Nürnberg
Neckar
Stuttgart
X
FRANKREICH
Straßburg
SCHWARZWALD
IX
Donau
München
Bodensee
ALPEN
Basel
St. Gallen
Bern
Innsbruck
Vierwaldstättersee
SCHWEIZ
ITALIEN